Yo odio el sistema colonial porque ese sistema es la muerte del espíritu, es la degradación del hombre por el hombre.

I detest the colonial system because that system embodies the death of the spirit, it is the degradation of man by man.

Román Baldorioty de Castro (1822–1889)

Educator, political activist, and founder of Puerto Rico's Autonomist movement

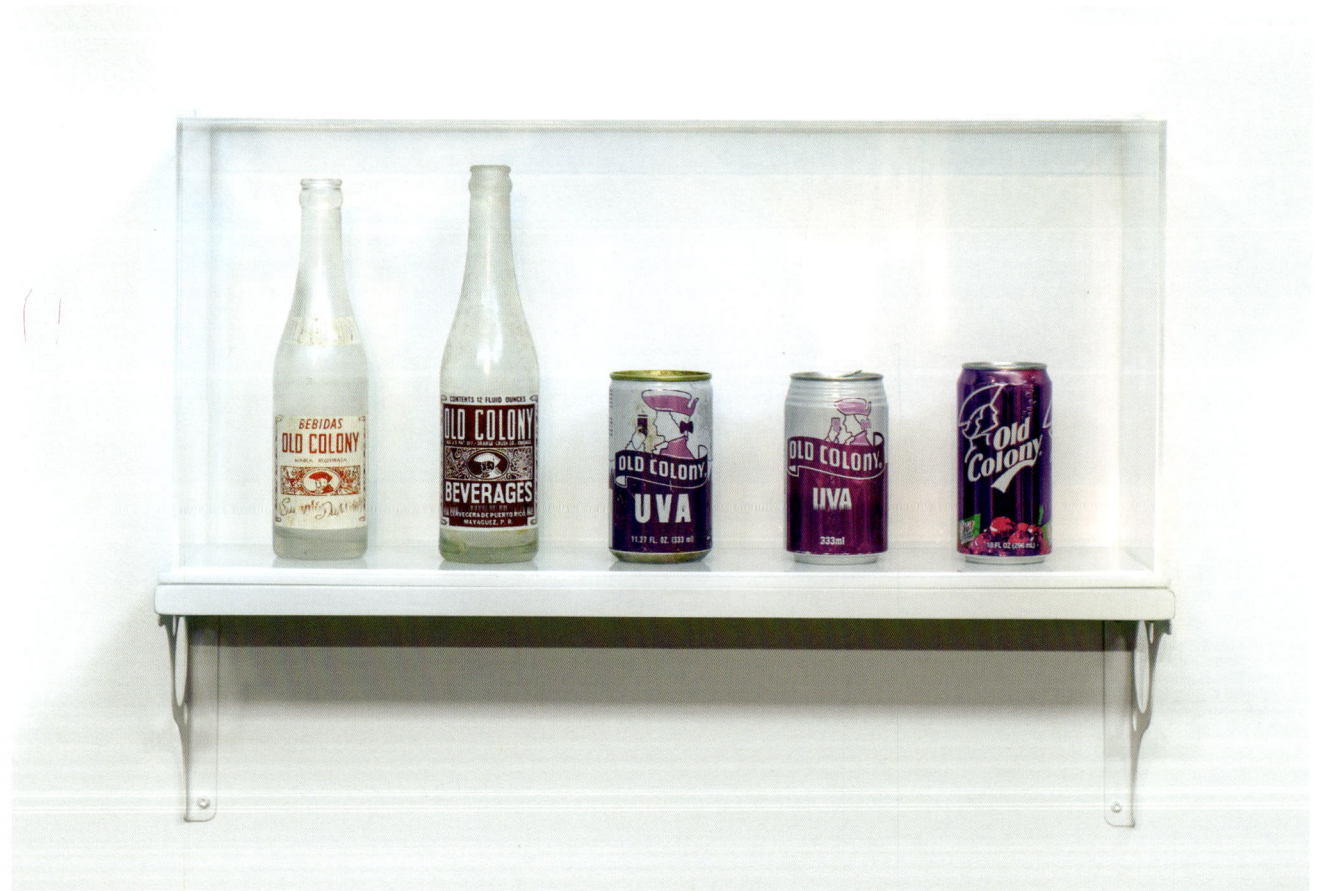

THE MUSEUM OF THE OLD COLONY

AN ART INSTALLATION BY PABLO DELANO

EDITED BY LAURA KATZMAN

Duke Hall Gallery of Fine Art
James Madison University
University of Virginia Press

ISBN 978-1-63944-287-4

Duke Hall Gallery of Fine Art
820 S. Main Street, MSC 7101
Harrisonburg, Virginia 22807
jmu.edu/dukehallgallery

University of Virginia Press
P.O. Box 400318
Charlottesville, Virginia 22904
upress.virginia.edu

This publication accompanies an exhibition held at the Duke Hall Gallery of Fine Art, James Madison University, February 1 to March 26, 2022. Funding was provided by the JMU College of Visual and Performing Arts' Cultural Connections Artist-in-Residence Program and the School of Art, Design, and Art History Dorothy Liskey Wampler Distinguished Professorship Art Series. Sponsors include the JMU Office of Civic Engagement and the College of Arts and Letters' Latin American, Latinx, and Caribbean Studies Program and the School of Media Arts and Design. Additional catalogue funding was provided by Michael D. Abrams and Sandra L. Stewart, Washington, D.C.; the JMU Art History Area; the Office of Faculty Access and Inclusion; and the General Education Program. The Office of the Dean of Faculty, Trinity College, Hartford, Connecticut, contributed a Project Completion Grant.

Guest Curator and Editor: Laura Katzman
Gallery Director: Beth Hinderliter
Designer: Carissa Henriques
Assistant Editor: Nicholas Acker
Printer: Progress Printing Plus, Lynchburg, Virginia
Installation photographs by Pablo Delano
Distributed by University of Virginia Press

Quote (page 1): From one of Román Baldorioty's speeches made in the Spanish Parliament, circa 1871. Quoted by Francisco Oller y Cestero in his 1871 portrait of Baldorioty in the *Museo de Historia, Antropología y Arte, Universidad de Puerto Rico*, Río Piedras. Special thanks to María de los Ángeles Castro, Gervasio García, and Arcadio Díaz Quiñones for their research on this topic.

Quote (page 7): Edited from Ivette Romero, "Pablo Delano: A Brief Interview with *Repeating Islands*," *Repeating Islands*, February 9, 2017, https://repeatingislands.com/2017/02/09/pablo-delano-a-brief-interview-with-repeating-islands/.

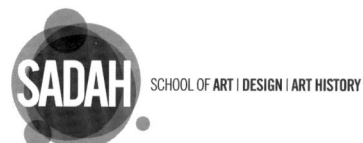

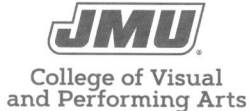

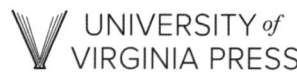

Contents

THE MUSEUM OF THE OLD COLONY

AN ART INSTALLATION BY PABLO DELANO

The Museum of the Old Colony is an ongoing, site-specific, conceptual art installation by Pablo Delano, which he has titled, with irony and a hint of nostalgia, after the sugary *Old Colony* soft drink sold in Puerto Rico to this day. The installation addresses the most vexing issues that Puerto Rico has faced since the Spanish-American War of 1898, when the American military invaded the archipelago, seizing it from Spain to ▓▓▓▓▓▓ ▓ ▓▓▓▓▓▓▓▓▓▓ ▓▓▓▓ ▓▓▓▓ ▓▓▓▓▓▓▓.

Appropriating archival photographs, film footage, and popular artifacts that Delano collects and "curates" for his performative museum, the installation provocatively critiques the stereotypes and entrenched misperceptions of Puerto Rico disseminated in mainstream media. The work thus speaks to the relationship between U.S. imperial power and the island nation, and to the lasting and devastating legacies of colonial rule. With dry wit and sardonic humor, the installation equally illuminates the power of images to inculcate cultural values, and the authority of museums to confer meaning on the objects that such trusted institutions acquire and display.

An art of activist intervention, *The Museum of the Old Colony* offers alternative narratives of the modern history of Puerto Rico, compelling viewers to decode meanings and check their own relationship to and/or complicity in traditional narratives. *The Museum of the Old Colony* also casts a critical eye on the legacy of U.S.-backed modernization efforts in the second half of the 20th century—their fragility thrown into sharp relief by the current debt crisis, the infrastructure collapse, and the humanitarian catastrophe resulting from Hurricanes Irma and Maria. Ultimately, the installation is Delano's personal and heartfelt response to the troubling and complex history of the land where he was born, raised, and educated.

Laura Katzman
Guest Curator and Professor of Art History
James Madison University

Pablo Delano is a Hartford-based visual artist, who trained in painting and drawing at Tyler School of Art and Yale University, before turning to photography in the early 1980s. His ▓▓▓▓▓▓▓▓▓▓ ▓▓▓▓▓▓▓▓ ▓▓▓▓▓▓▓▓ ▓▓▓▓▓▓▓▓ and Latino/a communities in the continental U.S. as well as in Trinidad, Honduras, and his native Puerto Rico.

The Museum of the Old Colony resides in the permanent collection of the Museum of Contemporary Art of Puerto Rico / Museo de Arte Contemporáneo de Puerto Rico.

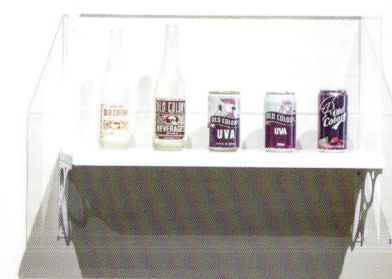

The emotions evoked by the title *The Museum of the Old Colony* are contradictory. The title has difficult and painful associations, but it is also playful. The Old Colony brand is long gone in the U.S., just as around the world—most everywhere except Puerto Rico—colonial rule is generally a thing of the past. Puerto Rico is often referred to as the world's oldest colony. We all know that sugary-sweet drinks are bad for us and often leave a bitter aftertaste; yet our thirst for these drinks seems unquenchable. Old Colony is artificially flavored, kind of like the benefits U.S. occupation was supposed to bring to Puerto Rico. All these metaphors seemed irresistible to me, not to mention the irony. On the other hand, Caribbean people—and I think all people who have suffered a colonial regime—have found ways to cope, and one of them is humor, sometimes self-deprecating humor. So, in addition to being quite serious, there is also something carnivalesque and performative about *The Museum of the Old Colony* title. The Caribbean is full of contradictions!

—Pablo Delano

Foreword
Marianne Ramírez Aponte

In December 2017, just two months after Hurricane Maria devastated Puerto Rico, Dominica, and Saint Croix, the *Museo de Arte Contemporáneo de Puerto Rico* (MACPR), the museum in which I serve as director and chief curator, opened the exhibition *Entredichos* [*In Question*] as an emergency project. It revealed the social and political conditions of a particular moment in Puerto Rican history and proposed an approach to our culture with regard to its tensions, contradictions, and complexities and to our shared history with other non-sovereign nations in the Caribbean. The exhibit was our response to a time of grave collective danger we face in Puerto Rico today, a situation that has exacerbated the need for community organization and for building greater political and social power for Puerto Ricans. We also felt the urgency to respond in our own voices to the broad interest generated internationally by Hurricane Maria's destruction and our socioeconomic situation, as well as to the many visions held about our history and the complex relationship between Puerto Rico and the United States—a relationship that affects virtually every aspect of Puerto Ricans' lives.

In addressing the social and political struggles in Puerto Rico and the United States, and our constant negotiation with history, *Entredichos* brought together artists such as Daniel Lind Ramos, Elsa María Meléndez, Garvin Sierra, Rafael Vargas Bernard, Viveca Vázquez, and Máximo Colón, among others. The physical center of the exhibition was occupied by Pablo Delano's installation, *The Museum of the Old Colony* (2015–2017), which is part of the permanent collection of MACPR and which is an earlier version of the artwork. This work of conceptual art is named after a brand of soft drink that has been consumed in Puerto Rico since the 1940s, as a reminder that the island, an "unincorporated territory" of the U.S., is considered the world's oldest colony.

Delano's "museum" comprises reproductions of archival photographs of Puerto Rico made mostly by North American photographers (news, military, or government) and intended for mainland and worldwide audiences. The images served as a kind of propaganda, at first to document the new U.S. "possessions" and later to portray an idealized vision of Puerto Rico's progress under American rule. To facilitate the viewer's interpretation of the images, Delano strategically mutes his voice as an artist, allowing the viewer to face and share the critical space with the colonizer, with no intermediation. The visual and discursive imagery of the photographs and accompanying captions disclose a colonial form of representation that is embedded with arrogant, racist, sexist, misogynistic, and paternalistic attitudes. The installation upends the notion of photography's faithful representation of reality, revealing instead the complexity of photographic narratives and the importance of context in analyzing images and texts.

The placement of *The Museum of the Old Colony* in a separate gallery within *Entredichos* reinforced the concept of a museum of history or anthropology within a museum of art, and Delano's questioning of the role, or complicity, of museums in the process of imperial domination. Following this idea, our curatorial vision involved presenting the project in salon-style, hanging works from floor to ceiling to evoke grand European museums—spaces of artistic validation in the history of Western art. This display of Delano's installation is a deliberate commentary on the privileged authority that has historically been shared by nations that comprise the so-called "First World"—an authority from which colonized nations deemed "Third World," such as Puerto Rico, have traditionally been excluded.

Delano's installation at MACPR enveloped the gallery with the images hung closely together and in several rows spanning much of the height of the walls. Our intention was to create an immersive and overpowering experience for viewers, who could not escape the discomfort in recognizing the moral misery that looking at these images produces. We aimed to show how Delano's work compels viewers to confront the ways Puerto Rico's colonial history in relation to U.S. history has been greatly silenced. His critical work, in conjunction with the work of museums like MACPR, committed to promoting visual literacy and critical thinking skills that, we believe, are essential for creating awareness of centuries of colonization—the dire consequences of which need to be reckoned with and repaired.

In February 2022, I was delighted to accept the invitation to participate in public programs around Delano's latest version of *The Museum of the Old Colony*, mounted in the Duke Gallery of Fine Art at James Madison University. It was fascinating to see how the artist has expanded his vision to include objects, tableaus, videos, and music, and to see how he has adapted the installation to the context of a southern U.S. city with its own particular relationship to the racism referenced in his appropriated photographs and objects. This experience strengthened my commitment to feature Delano's conceptual project again at MACPR, this time in the current exhibition, *(Re)conocer el futuro* [*(Re)knowing the Future*]. The show includes Puerto Rican, Caribbean, and Latin American artists of different generations and promotes dialogue around the most pressing issues of our time: environmental destruction; social justice in labor, health, education, housing, and land ownership; the ethical implications of science and technology; and political polarization. It deals with the effectiveness of models of political governance and economic development (critical for Puerto Ricans today living under a U.S.-imposed fiscal control board). The exhibition recognizes the past as a vast source of energy. The reflection proposed by the art not only reveals the mistakes of our history, but also reiterates our social capital and our capacity, guided by experience, to determine the society we want to inhabit in the future. As before, I placed Delano's installation at the heart of this group exhibition because of the powerful ways in which his work insists that viewers face a troubling past in order to envision more promising futures.[1]

1 Part of this text is adapted from Marianne Ramírez-Aponte, "The Importance of Politically Engaged Artistic and Curatorial Practices in the Aftermath of Hurricane María," in *Aftershocks of Disaster: Puerto Rico Before and After the Storm*, ed. Yarimar Bonilla and Marisol LeBrón (Chicago: Haymarket Books, 2019), 170–173.

Curator's Preface and Acknowledgments
Laura Katzman

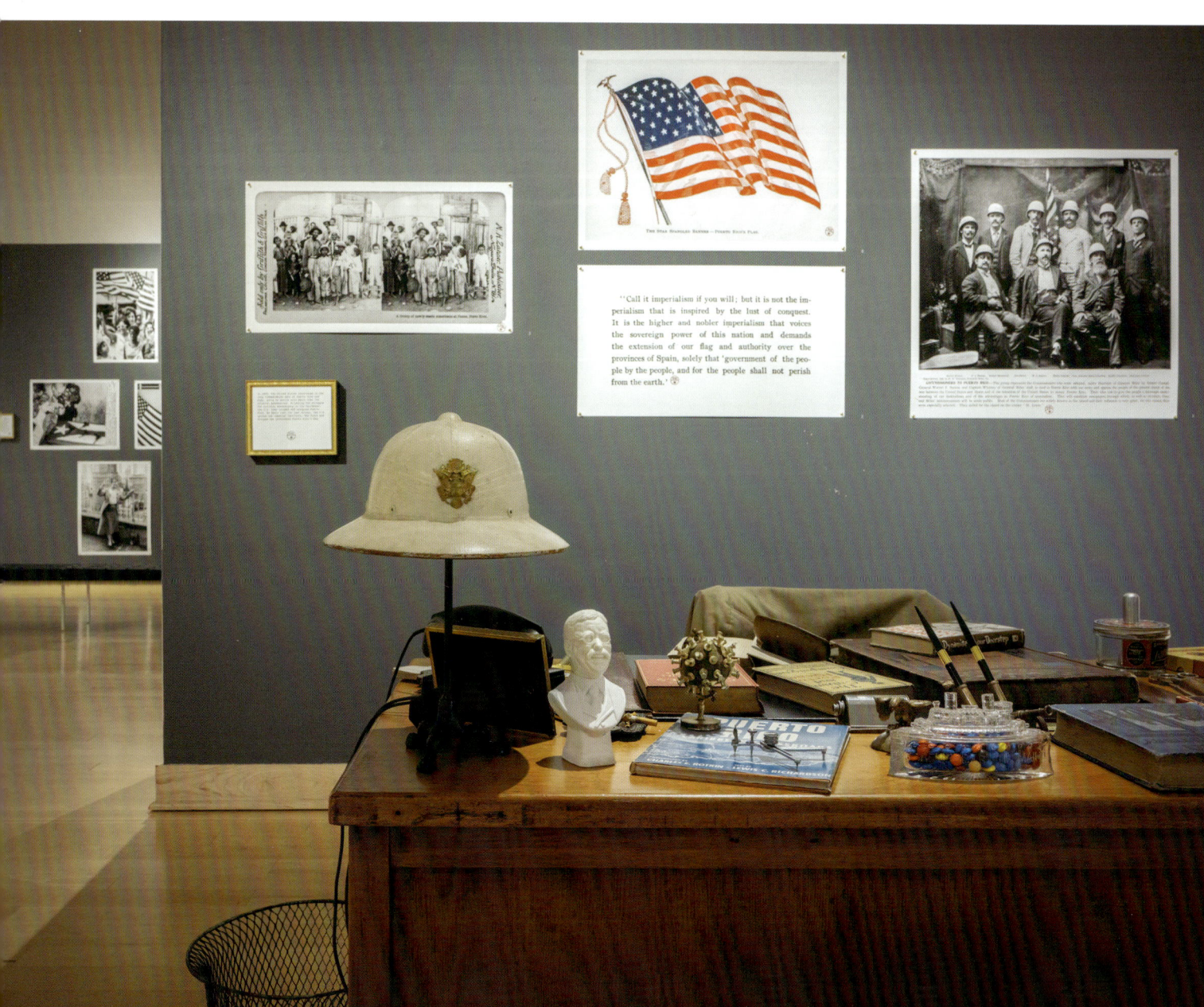

Plate 3. Installation view. *The Museum Desk* and
U.S. empire-related photographs and captions. *The
Museum of the Old Colony*, Duke Hall Gallery of Fine
Art, 2022. Checklist Nos. 4, 5–8.

It has been a privilege to have organized *The Museum of the Old Colony: An Art Installation by Pablo Delano* for the Duke Gallery of Fine Art, School of Art, Design, and Art History (SADAH), James Madison University (JMU), the most extensive presentation of the artist's provocative site-specific work to date. This multimedia exhibition, which examines the ways in which the artist's native Puerto Rico has been represented in mainstream U.S. and Puerto Rican visual culture since 1898, had been in the works for several years. I first saw *The Museum of the Old Colony* in summer 2018 at the *Museo de Arte Contemporáneo de Puerto Rico* in Santurce, as part of the exhibition *Entredichos*, the realization of which was a remarkable feat given that Hurricane Maria had devastated Puerto Rico just two months before the show opened in December 2017. Another unexpected crisis, the global Covid-19 pandemic, forced us to delay the installation at JMU three times. More tragically, Covid-19 fatally struck several cherished colleagues in our field, including Dr. Maurice Berger, the distinguished cultural historian and curator, with whom we had hoped to collaborate on public programs. Berger died on March 22, 2020, eight days after his curated iteration of *The Museum of the Old Colony* closed at the Center for Art, Design and Visual Culture at the University of Maryland, Baltimore County. Berger recognized the power and urgent relevance of Delano's project, for which he became a staunch advocate. Many in the art world have mourned the loss of this courageous scholar, who left a legacy of brilliant writing and path-breaking exhibitions that navigate the most uncomfortable truths about race and civil rights in the United States.

During the Covid-19 lockdown, Delano acquired new artifacts and images for his "museum" and further developed his plans for the JMU venue. At the same time, Duke Gallery Director Beth Hinderliter and I arranged for the construction of a new wall for the Duke Gallery (at the artist's request) to expand its hanging wall space of 3,000 square feet. We gathered an expert installation team with third year MFA student Haden King '22 and freelance exhibition preparator Chelsea Rowe at the helm, who carried out Delano's vision for the show, which he meticulously planned in a three-dimensional scale model (figure 12). Fellow MFA students Hannah Patteson '23, Mia Greenwald '23, and Yulin Yuan '24, as well as a dedicated group of undergraduate interns, assisted in the multilayered installation. Eric Morris, woodshop technician, and Karen Gerard, assistant to the SADAH director, lent their invaluable skills.

Colleagues from various disciplines contributed to the project in innumerable ways. Elizabeth Wisler, assistant professor of theatre and costume design, found dynamic solutions for presenting the clothing in the exhibition, and generously donated "real" objects to Delano's fictive museum from her family collection. These include a pair of scissors and a letter opener that belonged to her great-grandfather, who was an admiral in the U.S. Navy during World War I. Later, they were passed on to Wisler's grandfather, who served in the Navy in World War II. The objects, she believes, traveled from Puerto Rico to Panama to the Solomon Islands. Carissa Henriques, associate professor of graphic design, designed the striking signage for the show, as well as this handsome publication. Nefin Dinç, filmmaker and assistant professor of video production, supervised media studies major Jolie Snavely '23, who created a thoughtful video of the installation. This video, along with one made by Cooper Schwartz '22, a theatre major, have given permanent documentation to a temporary installation. Ángel A. Garcia, Jr., assistant professor of geology and environmental science, has created a 3D visualization of the exhibition, the first stages of which we present here. As a fruitful art and science collaboration, this visualization promises to archive the exhibition in novel ways, making the installation accessible for future study and immersive engagement. Hannah Sions, assistant professor of art education, worked with her students to create an educational brochure for middle school students on the more challenging content in the installation. Jolie Shank, public relations and visual resources assistant, disseminated press materials for media outlets. Lydia Davis '20, my research assistant, created the exhibition poster and announcement, and culled a bibliography for the catalogue, thanks to a College of Visual and Performing Arts (CVPA) Faculty Development Grant, which we were awarded for spring/summer 2021.

Funding for the exhibition was awarded through competitive university grants from the CVPA Cultural Connections Artist-in-Residence Program and the SADAH Dorothy Liskey Wampler Distinguished Professorship Art Series. Additional funding was provided by our enthusiastic sponsors: Latin American, Latinx, and Caribbean Studies Program and the School of Media Arts and Design (both in the College of Arts and Letters or CAL), as well as the Office of Civic Engagement. Other funders include the Office of Faculty Access and Inclusion; the General Education Program; the Honors Program; University Studies; Foreign Languages, Literatures, and Cultures; the Institute for Creative Inquiry; and the SADAH Graduate Program and Art History Area. Michael D. Abrams and Sandra L. Stewart, Washington, D.C. art philanthropists, generously offered a subvention for the catalogue, which was matched by a Project Completion Grant, awarded by the Office of the Dean of Faculty at Trinity College, Hartford, Connecticut. We extend deep gratitude to these supportive partners.

The JMU grants funded a series of public programs, including the opening on February 1, 2022, which featured Pablo Delano's fascinating talk, *The Decolonial Paintbox: Three Projects, 1997-2022*. Along with Meg Mulroney, senior associate vice provost for academic programs and equity, and Martha Hemingway, her administrative assistant, Beth Hinderliter and I hosted in the installation a celebration for General Education faculty on February 17, 2022. We arranged with Julia Merkel, preservation officer at Carrier Library, a special tour on March 25, 2022 for attendees of the Mid-Atlantic Archives Regional Conference. On February 23, 2022 we led a panel discussion on the lauded art documentary by Cecilia Aldarondo, *Landfall* (2020), about the aftermath of Hurricane Maria in Puerto Rico. Heartfelt thanks go to the panelists, who offered impassioned insights and perspectives: Taína Caragol, curator of painting and sculpture and Latinx art and history,

Smithsonian National Portrait Gallery; Nefin Dinç; Ángel A. García, Jr.; Amanda J. Guzmán, assistant professor of anthropology, Trinity College; and Marianne Ramírez Aponte, director, *Museo de Arte Contemporáneo de Puerto Rico*, who traveled from San Juan. Ramírez also led a workshop in the installation for K-12 teachers in Rockingham County, sponsored by *Cultura y Comunidad* (CyC). Karina Kline-Gabel, assistant dean for diversity, equity, and inclusion, CAL, expertly led the CyC program for 2022 with her welcoming and inclusive approach. We greatly appreciate the generous funding she secured from the CAL Dean's Office and the College of Education.

The response to *The Museum of the Old Colony* at the Duke Gallery has been moving. Many Puerto Rican and non-Puerto Rican visitors traveled to see the exhibition from the Washington, D.C. region, across the state of Virginia, and even from Puerto Rico. Scores of students who visited the installation noted how little they knew about Puerto Rico or its relationship to the U.S., many wondering why these topics constitute such a big gap in their education. They grappled with the experience of viewing a conceptual art installation that compelled them to actively engage not only with the content but also with the presentation of an exhibition. It was uncomfortable for many U.S. students to consider their own relationship to the history of their nation, especially to its more troubling aspects and its inconvenient truths. Some students expressed their appreciation for how Delano does not "sugar-coat" the historical record and rose to the challenge of unpacking the layers of complexity he presents.

The revelatory moments were many. One JMU student from a small town in Appalachian Virginia was struck by the demeaning nature of the pictures of Puerto Ricans disseminated in mainstream U.S. media after 1898. He saw parallels between such reductive images and the stereotypes to which residents of his region have been subjected. Numerous JMU students from Puerto Rico were enlightened by the exhibition; one who was forced to leave Ponce with his family in the wake of the 2008 economic crisis was so grateful to learn more about his beloved childhood home, which looms large in his imagination, and to meet Delano. He was impressed that JMU would "shine a light" on Puerto Rico—a place that is unfamiliar, even invisible, to so many beyond its shores. Another student with roots in Manatí and Arecibo, who grew up in the Puerto Rican diaspora, was equally surprised and excited. Both students volunteered to promote the exhibition and its public programs on and off campus by doing outreach in local Spanish-speaking Caribbean communities and specifically in Harrisonburg's small Puerto Rican community, which has grown in recent years, due in part to the mass displacement of islanders spawned by Hurricane Maria in 2017 and by the economic recession of a decade earlier.[1]

The Museum of the Old Colony attracted numerous writers and scholars of contemporary U.S., Puerto Rican, and Caribbean art, culture, and politics. We offer sincere thanks to José A. Delgado, Washington, D.C. correspondent for *El Nuevo Día*, Puerto Rico's leading newspaper; Paul Ryan, artist and contributing editor, *Art Papers* magazine; Jim Sconyers, professor of art, Mary Baldwin College; Ivette Romero, professor of Spanish, Marist College and co-founder of *Repeating Islands*, the digital site for news and commentary on Caribbean culture; Charlotte Rogers, associate professor of Spanish, University of Virginia (UVA); Elizabeth Mirabal, writer and doctoral candidate at UVA; and Nicole Delgado, noted poet and book artist who made a special visit to the exhibition when she was awarded the Frank Riccio Artist Residency from the Virginia Center for the Book. JMU colleagues Joanne V. Gabbin and Lauren Alleyne, director and assistant director of the Furious Flower Poetry Center, respectively, graciously assisted in hosting Delgado and Rogers in the exhibition on March 22, 2022.

For the intellectual content of this publication, immense thanks go to Pablo Delano and the essayists; we shared much stimulating exchange in Zoom meetings, with virtual walkthroughs of the exhibition arranged by Delano. The essayists' input, from art historical, anthropological, curatorial, museological, literary, political, and historical perspectives, helped shape the catalogue's scholarly framework. They include Amanda J. Guzmán, Beth Hinderliter, Marianne Ramírez Aponte, Laura Roulet, independent curator of contemporary Latinx and Latin American art, and César A. Salgado, associate professor of Spanish and Portuguese languages, University of Texas, Austin. In addition, we thank Jason Coleman, marketing and sales director, University of Virginia Press, and Maureen Shanahan and David Ehrenpreis, SADAH art history professors, who initially forged Duke Gallery's relationship to UVA Press. The artist, the editor, and the essayists thank Sofía Gallisá Muriente and Antonio Martorell for granting permissions to reproduce their artworks and Nicholas Acker for his meticulous editing of this volume. We are indebted to attorney José Roberto Martínez, former director of the *Fundación Luis Muñoz Marín*; anthropologist Jorge Duany, director of the Cuban Research Institute, Florida International University; archivist emeritus Pedro Juan Hernández, Center for Puerto Rican Studies, Hunter College; and one of the world's foremost scholars of Hispanic-Caribbean culture, Arcadio Díaz Quiñones, professor emeritus, Princeton University, for sharing their deep knowledge of Puerto Rico.

Administrative leaders at JMU strongly supported the project and believed in its potential to further the university's goals of diversity, equity, and inclusion. We thank especially CVPA Dean Rubén Graciani, Associate Dean Wren Stevens, and Assistant Dean Susan Zurbrigg; former SADAH Director Kathy Schwartz; Provost for Diversity and Executive Director of Faculty Access and Inclusion David Owusu-Ansah; Meg Mulroney; Director of the School of Media Arts and Design Gwyneth Mellinger; Karina Kline-Gabel; CAL Dean Robert Aguirre; Director of the Office of Civic Engagement Abe Goldberg; SADAH Graduate Director of Studio Art Corinne Diop; and the SADAH Galleries Committee. JMU President Jon Alger and his senior staff took great interest in how the installation "created these extraordinary learning opportunities for our students and community." I must single out

Beth Hinderliter, who in her triple role as Duke Gallery director, associate professor of art history, and noted scholar of contemporary art, boosted our efforts to realize Delano's ambitious vision for the show. With her tireless behind-the-scenes work, she has been an extraordinary collaborator and cherished colleague throughout this whole endeavor.

Pablo Delano, Beth Hinderliter, and I wish to thank additional friends and colleagues who deserve special mention for the loyal support they provided to the project and its contributors. These include Joanne Berger-Sweeney, Christina Bleyer, Sarah Brooks, Sonia Cardenas, Christopher Cozier, Flavio Cumpiano, Federico de Jesús Febles, Laura Delano Duncan, Dymph de Wild, Ana Dopico, Darío Euraque, Dolores Flamiano, Jeannie Gallowitz, Eric Galm, Symmes Gardner, David Gonzalez, Amy Halliday, Rafael Hernández Mayoral, Guillermo B. Irizarry, David Jones, Anne Lambright, Nicholas Laughlin, Sean Leonard, Greacely C. Negron-Lozada, Evelyn Nieves, Julio Pantoja, Mitch Polin, Veerle Poupeye, Milla Riggio, Nelson Rivera, Teresa Tió, Wilson Valentin, and Bill White. Delano also wishes to acknowledge the long-standing support of the Center for Caribbean Studies and the Office of the Dean of Faculty at Trinity College.

Finally, on behalf of our colleagues, Beth Hinderliter and I extend our greatest thanks to Pablo Delano himself, the Charles A. Dana Professor of Fine Art, Trinity College, who served as JMU's Wampler Distinguished Professor and Cultural Connections Artist-in-Residence during the 2021-2022 academic year. Delano made a site visit to the Duke Gallery in September 2021 to meet with the installers and assess the space. When he returned in January 2022 to oversee the hanging of the show, he generously mentored our MFA students in installation design, devoting several weeks to the multifaceted process. He graciously led graduate and undergraduate classes and workshops in the gallery. This was especially critical for my museum studies seminar, since we used the installation as a "laboratory" during the 2022 spring semester. (Delano donated to SADAH his scale model of the Duke Gallery to aid future exhibition planning.) He offered studio critiques to the MFA students, several of whom had worked on his installation. Delano helped conceive of the film program, offered critical input into the catalogue, granted interviews to the essayists, and advised students in the crafting of installation videos. As a prominent photographer, he created superb installation views, which enrich this publication and stand as an enduring record of this site-responsive conceptual exhibition.

On a personal note, it has been enormously rewarding to have hosted Delano at JMU. I have admired his work over the past two decades and have long been moved by his commitment to Puerto Rico and its daily presence in his life—which is particularly poignant given that he has lived away from San Juan for more than 50 years. We first met through my own ongoing research project—a cultural analysis of a post-World War II photography archive of Puerto Rico amassed by New Deal-era artists, including his parents, Jack and Irene Delano. As cultural icons, they pioneered national art forms in the island's so-called "golden age." I often seek Delano's advice on all matters Puerto Rican and appreciate his keen eye, perfectionism, honesty, generosity, sharp wit, irreverent sense of humor, and infectious love of cooking and appreciation of good food. He has opened my eyes to hidden gems in Harrisonburg, especially new Latin American and Caribbean markets and restaurants—which has, in turn, inspired me to see this city, and its fast-changing demographics, with fresh eyes. For this, for his decades of aesthetically rigorous and socially engaged projects, and for bringing *The Museum of the Old Colony* to our campus, I am forever grateful.

---

1 People of Central/Latin American and Spanish-speaking Caribbean descent make up a total of 20% of Harrisonburg's population (according to the 2020 U.S. Census), while only 7% of JMU's student body consists of self-identified Hispanics. Most of the city's Latino/a/x residents are of Mexican, Salvadoran, or Honduran descent.

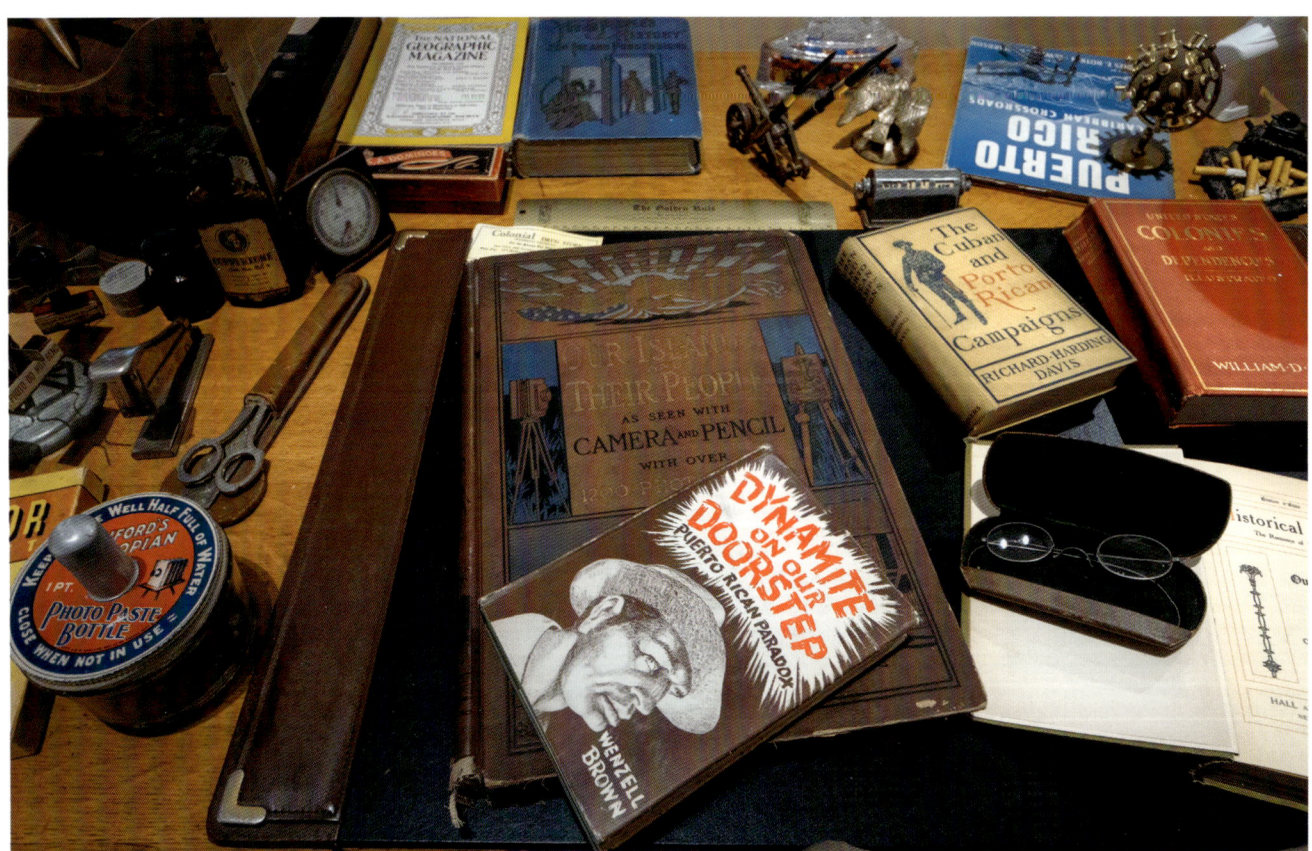

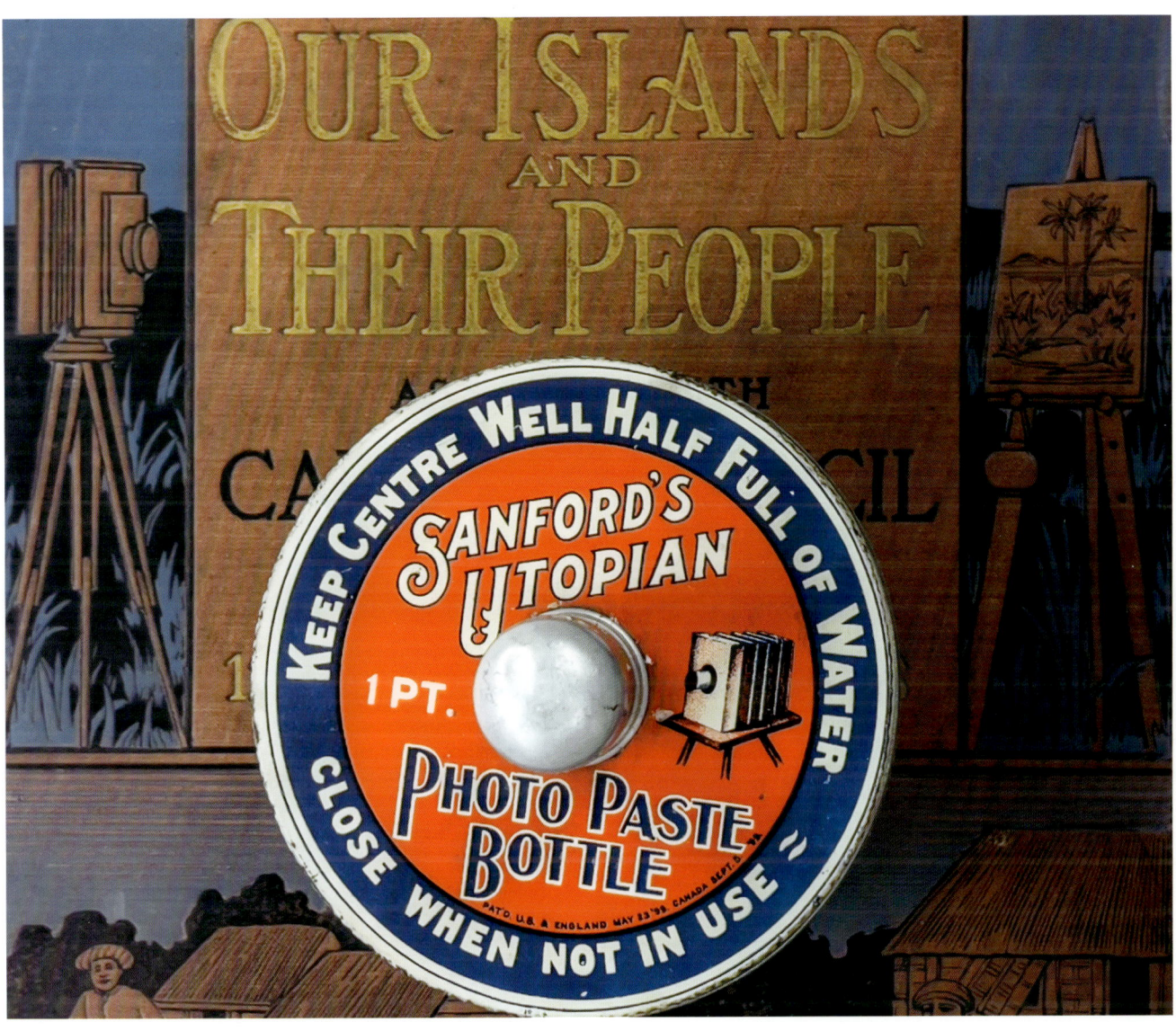

Plate 6. *"Be it ever so humble, there's no place like Home"—Cayey, Porto Rico.* Strohmeyer & Wyman, 1899 | 2021. *The Museum of the Old Colony*, Duke Hall Gallery of Fine Art, 2022. Checklist No. 40.

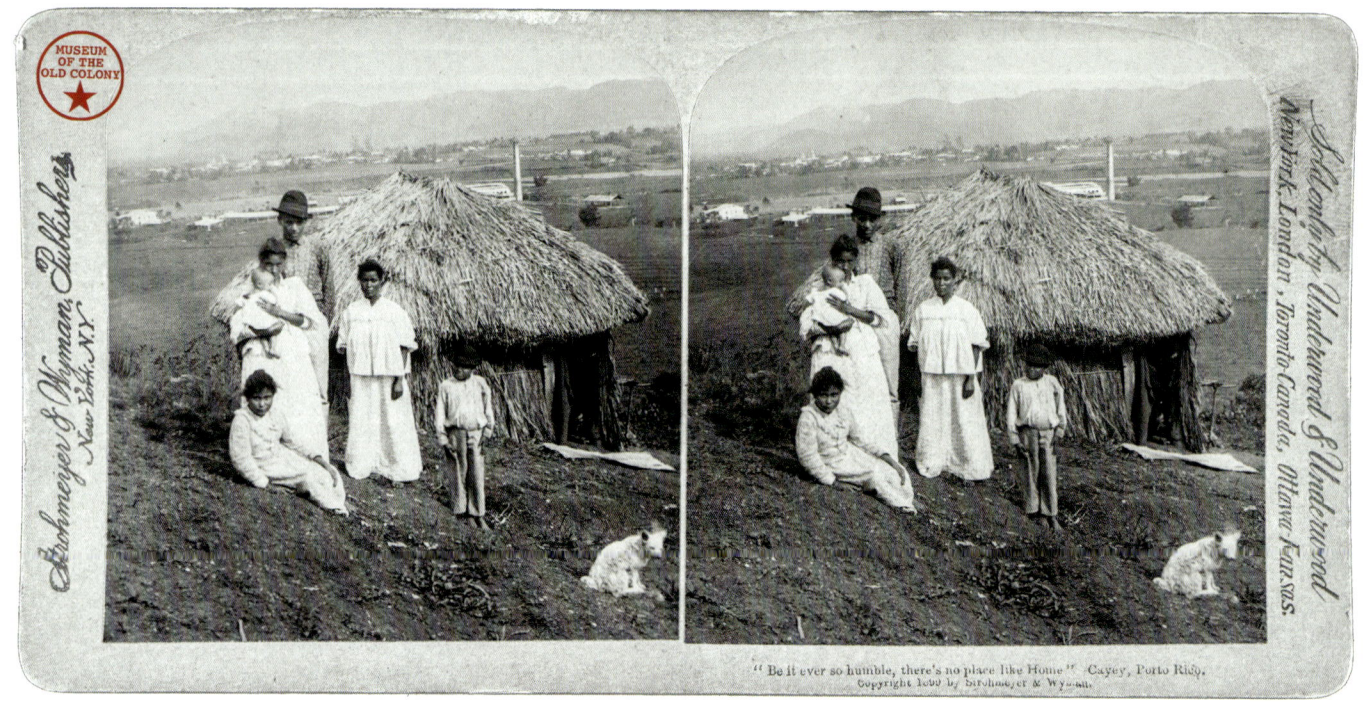

Plate 7. *A Group of newly made Americans at Ponce, Porto Rico.* M. H. Zahner, 1898 | 2019. *The Museum of the Old Colony*, Duke Hall Gallery of Fine Art, 2022. Checklist No. 5.

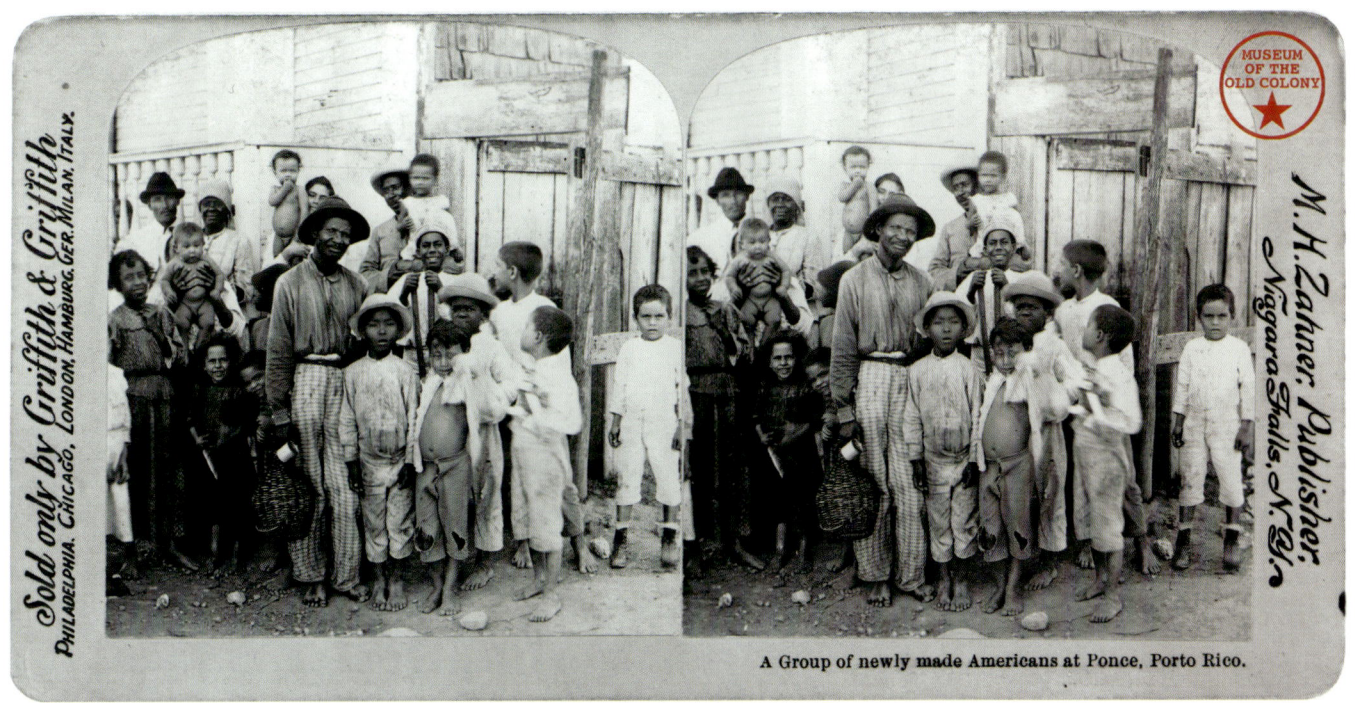

A Group of newly made Americans at Ponce, Porto Rico.

Note to the Reader:
A Brief Sketch of Puerto Rico

Laura Katzman

The island of Puerto Rico resides in the West Indies, as the smallest and most eastern of the Greater Antilles chain. Puerto Rico is actually an archipelago—a group of islands situated between the Caribbean Sea and the North Atlantic Ocean. It lies east of the Dominican Republic, west of the Virgin Islands and north of Venezuela, and is 1,000 miles southeast of the U.S. state of Florida. The main island extends east to west approximately 110 miles and from north to south about 40 miles. Puerto Rico boasts a tropical marine climate, extraordinary geographic biodiversity, with breathtaking beaches, mountains, caves, waterfalls, and a rain forest; hence its popular name, *la Isla del Encanto*.

Since circa 1000 CE, Puerto Rico (and other parts of the Caribbean) were inhabited by *Taínos*, who called their land *Boriquén* (*Borinquén* or *Boriken*). This subgroup of the Arawak Indians were the first Indigenous peoples of the Americas to encounter Europeans; in 1493 Christopher Columbus and his large expedition claimed Puerto Rico for the Spanish crown. The Spanish Conquest led to the near decimation of the native population of the Greater Antilles, which succumbed to forced labor, starvation, violence, and European diseases. Interaction and intermarriage with Spaniards and Africans (whom the former enslaved beginning in the 16th century) further contributed to the dilution of *Taíno* culture (although genetic studies have shown a high percentage of Puerto Ricans today have substantial Indigenous ancestry).

Four hundred years of largely monarchical and hierarchal Spanish colonial rule had profound impact on Puerto Rican language, religion, agriculture, architecture, and cultural traditions. The Spanish-American War (or the War of 1898)[1] served as the final blow to the Spanish Empire and catalyzed the rise of United States imperialism, when the U.S. military invaded Puerto Rico, seizing it, along with Guam, as a "possession." (The U.S. "purchased" the Philippines from Spain and occupied Cuba until 1902.) While many Puerto Ricans initially saw the annexation by the U.S. as promising a more modern and democratic future than was possible under an authoritarian Spain, this view was short-lived. The fight for self-determination and sovereignty in various forms gained strength in the decades after 1898.

Puerto Rico, in legal terms, is an "unincorporated territory" of the United States whose people have held U.S citizenship since the Jones-Shafroth Act of 1917. Since 1952, with the ratification of its own constitution, Puerto Rico was officially deemed a Commonwealth—a status that brought a degree of self-government. It has the largest population of the 16 current U.S. territories, with close to 3.3 million people. A population decline began early in the economic recession around 2006, with more dramatic losses seen in recent years in the wake of Hurricanes Irma and Maria. (Large migration waves started earlier with the "Great Migration" of the 1950s and 1960s, which greatly increased diaspora populations.)

Today, roughly 5.8 million Puerto Ricans live on the U.S. mainland. But with the long tradition of back-and-forth migration, Puerto Rico has been called "transnational" by prominent anthropologist Jorge Duany—a "nation on the move," with a strong national

Figure 1. Map of Puerto Rico. Associated Press, circa 1940 | circa May 2017. *The Museum of the Old Colony.*

21

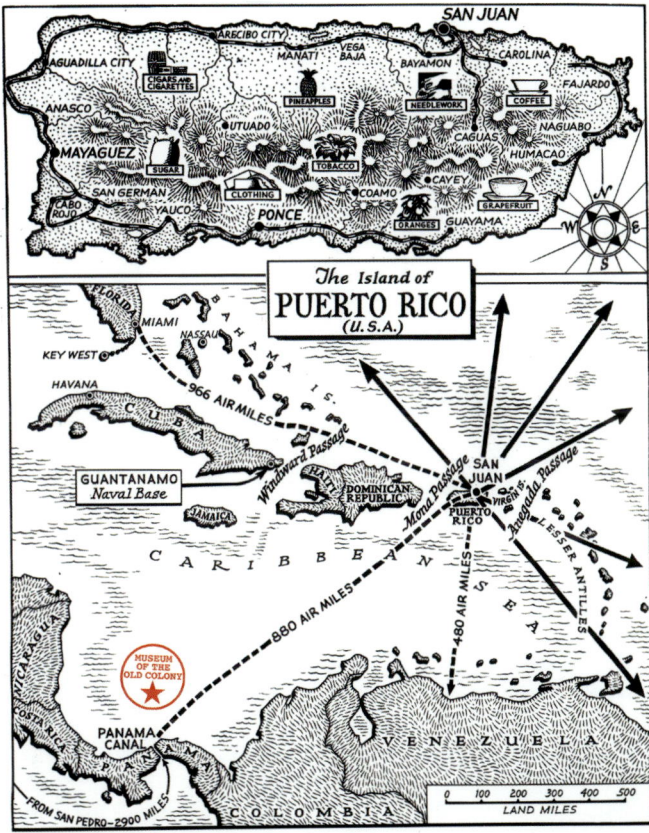

culture that transcends geographic boundaries. He has termed it a "postcolonial colony" in the sense of a people with a persistent national identity but little desire for a nation-state, living in a territory that legally "belongs to but is not part of the United States." According to Duany: "At the beginning of the twenty-first century, Puerto Rico presents the apparent paradox of a stateless nation that has not assimilated into mainstream U.S. culture." Despite nearly 125 years of U.S. influence and control with regard to economic, legal, educational, and governmental customs, "the Island remains a Spanish-speaking, Afro-Hispanic-Caribbean nation."[2]

1 For some time, scholars have offered alternative names for the conflict to reflect the multiple parties involved. These include Spanish-Cuban-American War and Spanish-American-Cuban-Filipino War. In this volume, the essayists use the most widely recognized term, Spanish-American War, or a term that is gaining currency, War of 1898. See, for example, the pioneering exhibition and book, Taina Caragol, Kate Clarke Lemay, and Carolina Maestre, *1898: Visual Culture and U.S. Imperialism in the Caribbean and the Pacific* (Princeton: Princeton University Press for the National Portrait Gallery, Smithsonian Institution, 2023).

2 Jorge Duany, *Puerto Rico: What Everyone Needs to Know* (New York: Oxford University Press, 2017), 4, 2. See also Duany, *Puerto Rican Nation on the Move: Identities on the Island and in the United States* (Chapel Hill: University of North Carolina Press, 2002). According to the Supreme Court's Insular Cases, "the island of Porto Rico is a territory appurtenant and belonging to the United States, but not a part of the United States within the revenue clauses of the Constitution." See Downes v. Bidwell, 182 U.S. 244 (1901). For broad histories of Puerto Rico, see the authoritative texts of Fernando Picó and Francisco Scarano, as well as those of Silvia Álvarez Curbelo, César J. Ayala and Rafael Bernabe, Loida Figueroa, Olga Jiménez de Wagenheim, Arturo Morales Carrión, and Blanca G. Silvestrini, among others.

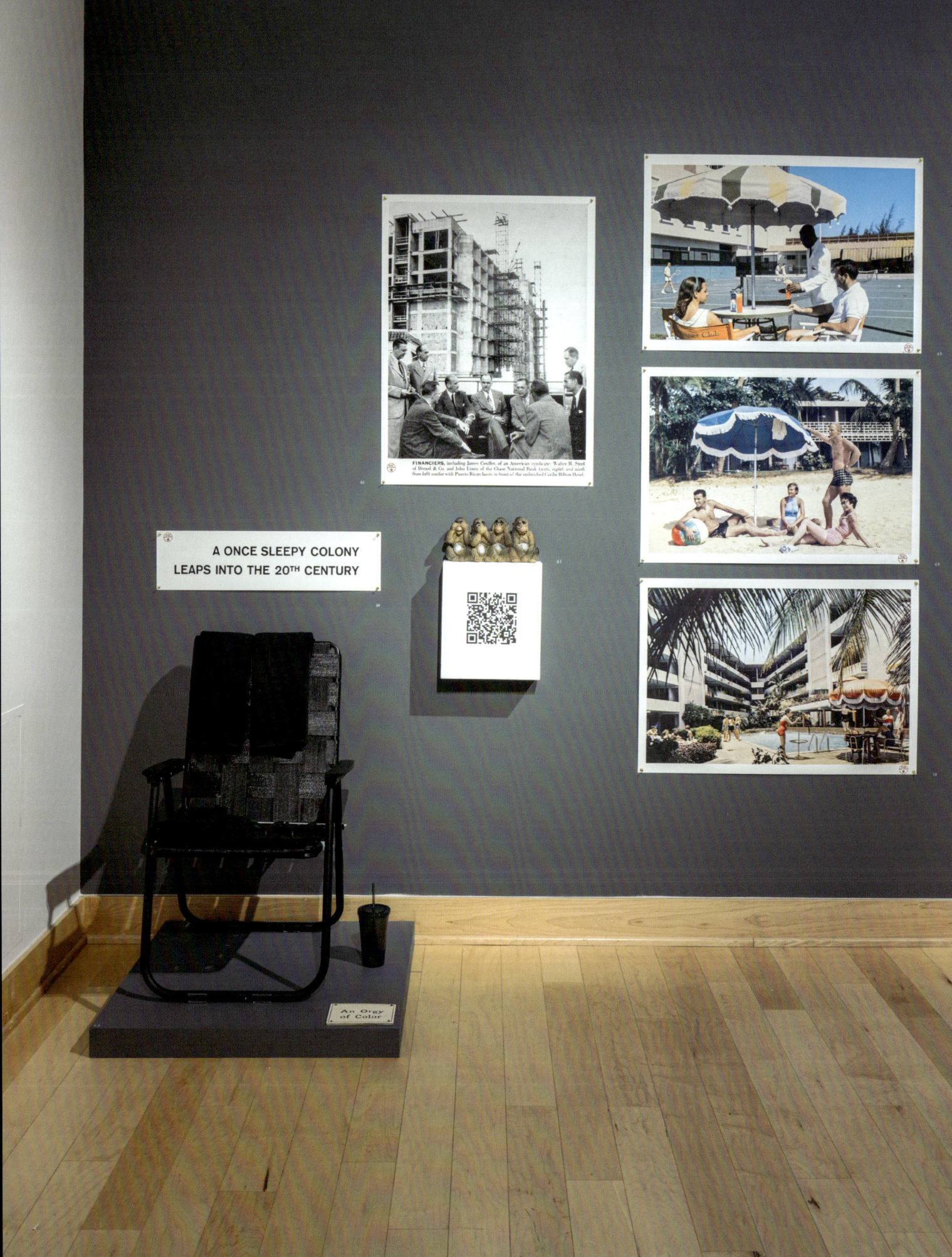

FINANCIERS, including James Coulter, of an American syndicate; Walter H. Steel of Drexel & Co. and John Linen of the Chase National Bank (sixth, eighth and ninth from left confer with Puerto Rican hosts in front of the unfinished Caribe Hilton Hotel.

A ONCE SLEEPY COLONY
LEAPS INTO THE 20TH CENTURY

An Orgy
of Color

Essays

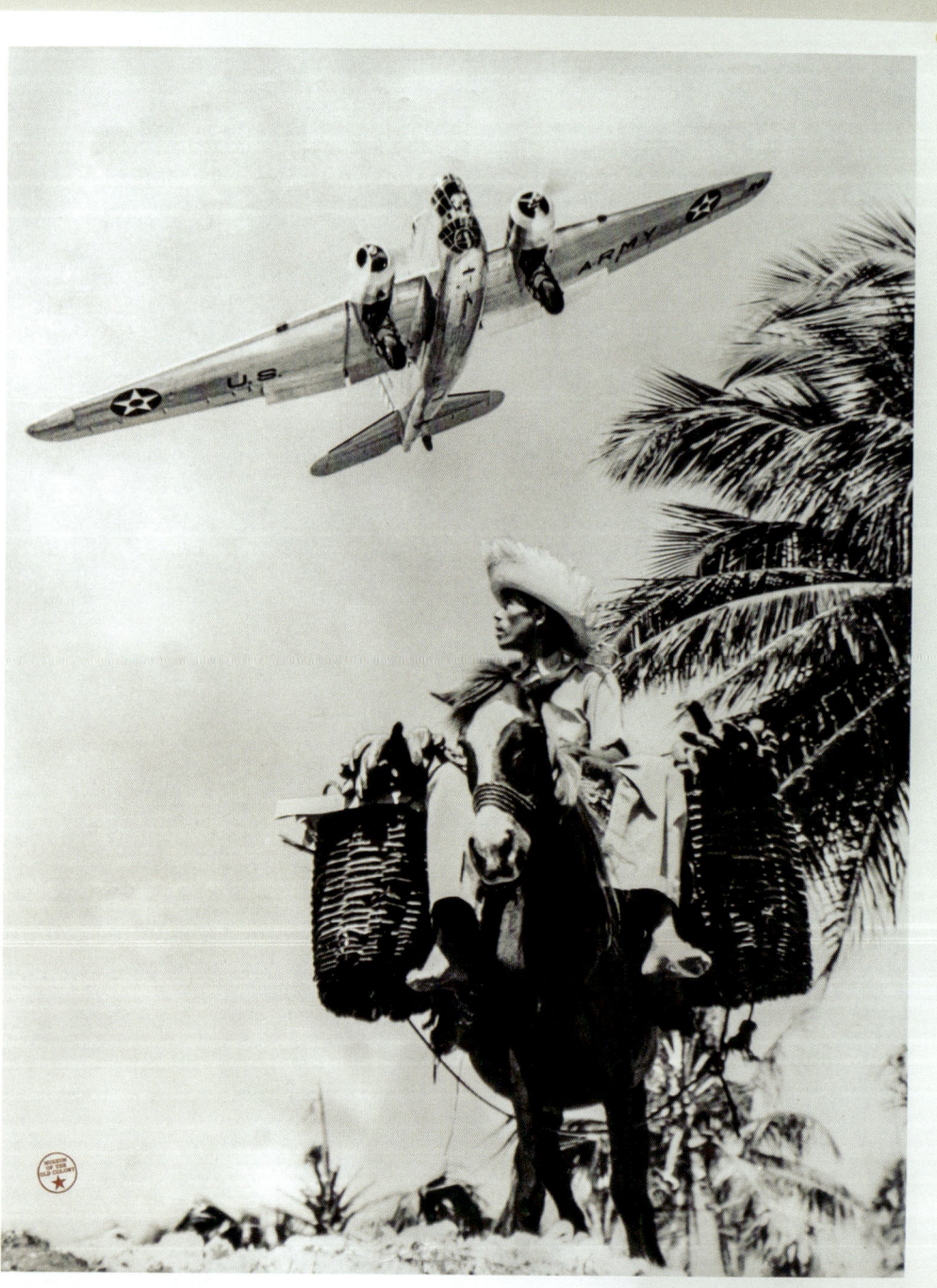

"Puerto Rico in the American Century": Reflections on Pablo Delano's *The Museum of the Old Colony*[1]

Laura Katzman

The Museum of the Old Colony is as much an exploration of history as it is an intensely personal exercise by its creator to understand and come to terms with the present-day realities where he was born and raised.[2]

Pablo Delano, the acclaimed, Hartford-based visual artist, has for over four decades focused his practice on the histories, struggles, and traditions of Latin American and Caribbean peoples in their homelands and in the diaspora. After earning art degrees from Temple University's Tyler School of Art and Yale University, both in painting, he moved from New Haven to New York City in 1979. He gravitated to documentary photography, as it offered him a "satisfying, interactive, and visceral connection to the world."[3] Documenting the vibrancy of life in often-marginalized neighborhoods, with sensitivity, humor, and wit, Delano developed a unique vision within the pervasive social documentary tradition—one he knew well from his father, the eminent New Deal photographer Jack Delano. His photographs of Dominican and African American cultural traditions counter negative perceptions of New York's Washington Heights in the 1990s, while his earlier images of Puerto Rican neighborhoods on the Lower East Side reveal the humanity and tenacity of residents amid deteriorating buildings, when heroin was running rampant and gentrification was just taking off.[4] A professorship, begun in 1996, at Trinity College in Hartford, Connecticut, which Delano calls "a very Caribbean city," gave him the opportunity to photograph in the Republic of Trinidad and Tobago, which began a long fascination that culminated in his book, *In Trinidad* (2008). Witnessing the public rituals and nation-building processes of this young, post-colonial country profoundly impacted Delano's understanding of the persistent colonial condition in his native Puerto Rico and the latter's ambiguous political status as an "unincorporated territory" of the United States.[5]

In recent years, Delano has documented the dynamic urban art scene centered in Santurce, Puerto Rico, which intensified with the 2008 economic recession and the rising number of abandoned buildings—a powerful phenomenon of painted walls that he states "may serve as conduits to examine…territoriality, commodification, urban renewal, gentrification and displacement."[6] He has also illuminated the built environment of Hartford, revealing the changing physical character of a city affected by global migrations—aspects of which have long been "unseen" by outsiders in this capital city.[7] Concurrent with these projects, yet decidedly distinct, is *The Museum of the Old Colony*, which marks a shift in Delano's work from a documentary to a conceptual approach. This is suggested by his naming of the installation, with irony and a hint of nostalgia, after the sugary soft drink, Old Colony, which is still sold today in Puerto Rico. This site-specific, multimedia, and ever-evolving project was inaugurated in 2016 at Alice Yard, the experimental art collective in Port of Spain, Trinidad, and has since been adapted in various galleries and alternative spaces in Kingston, Jamaica; Tucumán, Argentina; Manhattan and Brooklyn, New York; San Juan, Puerto Rico; Amherst, Massachusetts; Baltimore, Maryland; and Hartford. The exhibition at the Duke Gallery of Fine Art, James Madison University, in Harrisonburg, Virginia, represents the largest and most extensive version of the installation to date.

The Museum of the Old Colony addresses the most vexing issues that Puerto Rico has faced since the Spanish-American War (or the War of 1898), when the U.S. military, under President William McKinley, invaded the archipelago, seizing it from Spain and annexing it as a "possession" of the United States. Under the Treaty of Paris, Spain ceded its colonies of Guam and Puerto Rico to the U.S., ending roughly 300 and 400 years of Spanish colonial rule, respectively. (The U.S. also "purchased" the Philippines from Spain and occupied Cuba until 1902, when it became an independent republic.) Historical accounts indicate that many Puerto Ricans welcomed the new power, believing they could benefit from greater freedoms under the American flag. U.S. assurances of self-government looked more promising than the autonomy that the Spanish constitutional monarchy finally conceded to give Puerto Rico in 1897. But these hopes were soon dashed, for while the U.S. military government (1898-1900) "built sanitation networks, highways, and other public works," the "administrative arrangement allowed for little input by Puerto Ricans." The Foraker Act of 1900, which laid out the legal structure for a civil government, afforded local political leaders little of the autonomy they rightfully demanded.[8]

Although health and sanitary conditions improved with U.S. involvement, most Puerto Ricans' standard of living did not improve on a large scale until after World War II. An Act of Congress in 1917 (the Jones-Shaforth Act, commonly called the Jones Act) granted U.S. citizenship to Puerto Ricans. However, Puerto Ricans living on the island could not (and still cannot) exercise full constitutional rights, such as voting for the U.S. president and having voting representation in the U.S. Congress. U.S. rule attempted, but failed, to impose the English language in public instruction and tried to Americanize many facets of Puerto Rican life. Powerful U.S. companies, with the complicity of wealthy Puerto Rican sugar barons, exploited the sugar crop for financial gain at the expense of cultivating a diversity of other more nutritious crops. The U.S. government long recognized Puerto Rico for its strategic military location, and by World War II this "Gibraltar of the Caribbean" was "transformed into a major military enclave." By 1947, the U.S. Navy controlled roughly two-thirds of the island-municipality of Vieques, which by then was serving as a weapons depot and as a site for bombing practice. Such hazardous activities continued until mass civil protests forced the Navy to finally withdraw in 2003.[9]

The 1898 invasion, in essence, launched a new chapter in U.S. empire-building, as the country flexed its military might to become a world power, and exercised its economic and geopolitical ambition to "acquire" territories that would not necessarily be "incorporated" into the United States.[10] Simultaneously, the U.S. occupation catalyzed a new chapter in the Puerto Rican struggle (*la brega*) for self-determination, the development of a fervent nationalism, and the affirmation of distinct cultural identities.[11] Drawing on three predominant identities—Taíno, African, and Spanish—Puerto Rican artists, through murals, prints, literature, music, and other artforms, have expressed a dynamic and diverse sense of *puertorriqueñidad* (Puerto Rican-ness).[12]

Puerto Rico in the twentieth century also saw the development of a rich and complex political culture, with the formation of numerous political parties, each with its own approach towards the island's status. The most influential of these today are the *Partido Popular Democrático* (PPD) and the *Partido Nuevo Progresista* (PNP). The former, founded in 1938, established the Commonwealth status with a measure of self-government that exists to this day. The latter, founded in 1967 as heir to the *Partido Estadista Republicano* (PER), supports a pro-statehood platform. The alternating of power between the PPD and PNP for more than 50 years, along with multiple contested status referendums, reflects the deep divisions and seemingly irreconcilable convictions within the Puerto Rican electorate on the status question. The smaller yet enduring *Partido Independentista Puertorriqueño* (PIP), established in 1946, has never controlled the legislature or the governorship. The *Partido Nacionalista de Puerto Rico* (PNPR) was formed in 1922 and is dormant today. Even though it did not attract a large following, it still holds symbolic significance and many of its ideas remain strong through such groups as the *Movimiento Independentista Nacional Hostosiano* (MINH). Under the fiery leadership of Pedro Albizu Campos, the armed struggles of the *nacionalistas* gained a heroic, even mythic status for many Puerto Ricans, while they were rejected by others. Indeed, images of a determined and striking Lolita Lebrón and her Nationalist compatriots occupy a prominent wall in *The Museum of the Old Colony* installation.[13]

It is the second colonial era of Puerto Rico's history (from 1898), and its visual representation in mainstream U.S. and Puerto Rican media, that *The Museum of the Old Colony* weighs in on. Delano, the artist, assumes the performative role of collector, archivist, photographer, and curator, acquiring items for his fictive museum through eBay and other online sites. He began *The Museum of the Old Colony* not by deploying photographs he himself took, but rather by using archival/historical photographs and captions created by others (plate 9). He soon expanded the project to include film footage, vintage cartoons, books, music, and tableaus comprised of popular artifacts. Appropriating such material culture, Delano scans or rephotographs the original photographs and their captions or the half-tone reproductions in vintage books. He enlarges them so that viewers can really see them (without cropping or altering content) and juxtaposes them in provocative ways. He then amplifies their meanings with video pieces sourced from news and film clips and with assemblages of objects he displays in vitrines, on tables, and on walls (plates 45, 56). While many of the objects he presents were made for U.S. tourist consumption, some were made by and for Puerto Ricans and are still made, sold, and/or used today, such as Old Colony soda, the *jíbaro* costumes, and the *Mamá Inés-Yaucono* coffeepot. The nostalgia some Puerto Rican viewers may have towards these objects, which Delano acknowledges, speaks to the complex ways in which colonized peoples may co-opt, transform, or come to "own" the cultural artifacts imposed by imperial powers.[14]

Using the framework of a conceptual installation—a common form in contemporary art indebted to the subversive Dada movement, whereby artists seek to transform the perception of traditional gallery space—Delano presents his project in a loosely chronological but also thematic fashion. The installation covers topics such as rural labor, religion, the military, the economy, tourism, politics, the flag, transportation, reproductive issues, the beauty industry, industrialized food, popular culture, education, and race and ethnicity. The racial dimension of the installation is pronounced in the Duke Gallery venue, as Delano includes numerous turn-of-the-20th-century stereographs, for example, that speak to an invidious preoccupation with race: U.S. photographers, reporters, editors, ethnographers, public officials, and stereo card manufacturers, in documenting these Caribbean, Spanish-speaking, "newly made Americans," denigrated them as "foreign." With captions like "Plantation Joe," a racialized language resonant of the Jim Crow South was imposed onto images of America's "new possessions." Stereographs of destitute, often naked children were described as "Waiting for Uncle Sam," conveying the perceived need for U.S. tutelage from the White Anglo-Saxon Protestant savior to "civilize" so-called "inferior" races. Deprived, dark-skinned children (dubbed "pickaninnies" in the popular press) emerged as metaphors for Puerto Rico, whose people were seen as incapable of self-rule (plates 34–35).[15]

The amplification of race issues in the Duke Gallery iteration of *The Museum of the Old Colony* is not accidental. Delano is well aware of Virginia's prominence in Civil War and Jim Crow-era history and its centrality to the contemporary Confederate monument controversies—as well as James Madison's legacy as a slaveholder. (He is also keenly attuned to the complexity of race in Puerto Rico, the prevailing ideology of color blindness, and the persisting but increasingly contested view that little overt racial discrimination exists on the island, as compared to the United States.)[16] By contrast, a topic that is less pronounced in the installation than one might expect is the influx of factories onto the island spawned by *Manos a la Obra* (Operation Bootstrap), that is, the ambitious modernization project launched by the PPD government that industrialized Puerto Rico in the post-World War II period, which secured financial investment from largely U.S. manufacturing companies in exchange for generous tax incentives. While the second part of the installation includes a few pictures of hotels and one lingerie factory—and many of the products resulting from the Bootstrap project—we do not see the massive number of factories (or factory workers) that were fast-emerging on the Puerto Rican landscape as the most overt symbols of "progress" and employment, changing forever the rural way of life and accelerating the process of internal migration and urbanization. These factories, and the changes they brought, were well documented by Puerto Rican government photographers like Jack Delano and widely celebrated in the popular U.S. and Puerto Rican press in the early Cold War years; the Caribbean territory was touted as "a showcase of democracy," a market-oriented success story—strategically set in opposition to communist Cuba.[17]

Providing a comprehensive coverage of the history of 20th-century Puerto Rico, however, is not what Delano aims to do. He states that *The Museum of the Old Colony* "is a work of art, not a reference work or a historical text or a sociological analysis…It's not meant to be authoritative in any sense."[18] (The artist clearly cares about history and respects the documentary tradition; he retains the integrity of original images and captions, provides his own history-informed texts, and crafts checklists of objects that are painstakingly sourced.) *The Museum of the Old Colony* instead aims for metacommentary, using provocative juxtapositions of photographs—and photographs and objects—to critique the enduring stereotypes and entrenched misperceptions of Puerto Rico that have been disseminated by U.S. media and government agencies for well over a century. For instance, a promotional image (circa 1970s) of a barefoot *coquero* atop a palm tree cutting coconuts for tourists at a luxury hotel in Dorado assumes more disturbing implications when seen close to an eerily similar photograph of a naked young man of color engaged in the same activity from an 1899 U.S. War Department Annual Report. The identical photograph appeared in another book from the era, with a caption stating that the "native lad" had just climbed up a coconut palm to "cut down as many as the *'Americanos'* wanted" (plate 13).[19]

Such visual strategies compel viewers to draw connections between past and present, to see the continuation of offensive tropes molded in the wake of 1898, and to consider the power dynamics between the "colonizer" and the "colonized." While many images are demeaning, others capture the subjects' humanity, even resistance, as if the documented individuals are defying or pushing against the power of the stereotype.[20] An image of a self-possessed laundress from circa 1898, paired with a reproduction of an ancient Greek sculpture, and referred to as "half-breed" or "colored," peers out at the viewer with an unwelcoming stare (plate 39).[21] Likewise, Lolita Lebrón looks defiantly at the camera—with a hauntingly piercing expression—as she is arrested in 1954 after she and fellow Nationalists fired pistols in the U.S. Capitol to bring attention to the cause of Puerto Rican independence (plate 57). (She fired at the ceiling in a spectator's gallery while her co-assailants fired onto the House floor.) *The Museum of the Old Colony* thus speaks to the complex relationship between U.S. imperial power and the island-nation and underscores the lasting legacies of colonial rule.

With dry wit and sardonic humor, *The Museum of the Old Colony* also comments on photography and on museums. Delano plays with the power of photographic images and their repetition of visual tropes to inculcate cultural values. Indeed, in addition to displaying a group of original stereograph cards, a stereoscopic viewer, and vintage booklets like "Better Photography Made Easy" on what appears to be a U.S. colonial officer's desk, Delano devotes an entire display case entitled "Tools of the Trade" to early-to-mid-20th century cameras (new to the Duke Gallery venue). These include a Graflex 3A, a Stereo Kodak Model 1, and a Speed Graphic—the most famous press camera in the U.S. until the

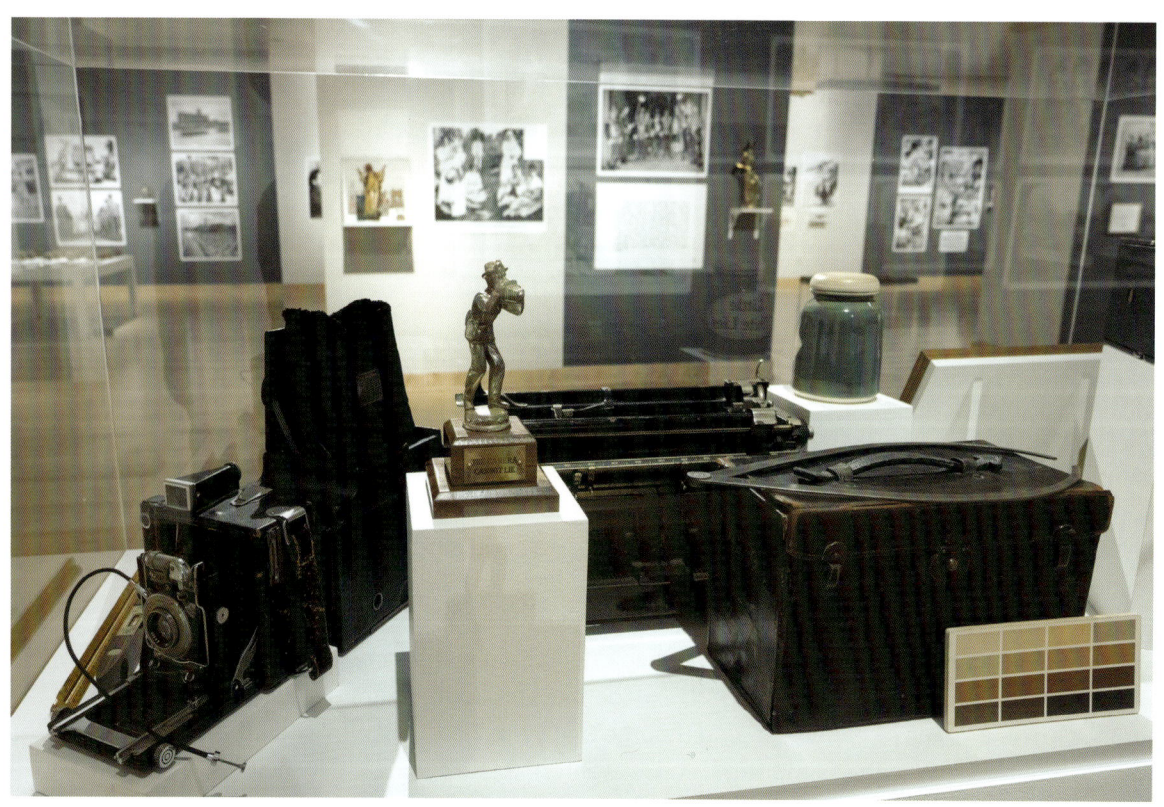

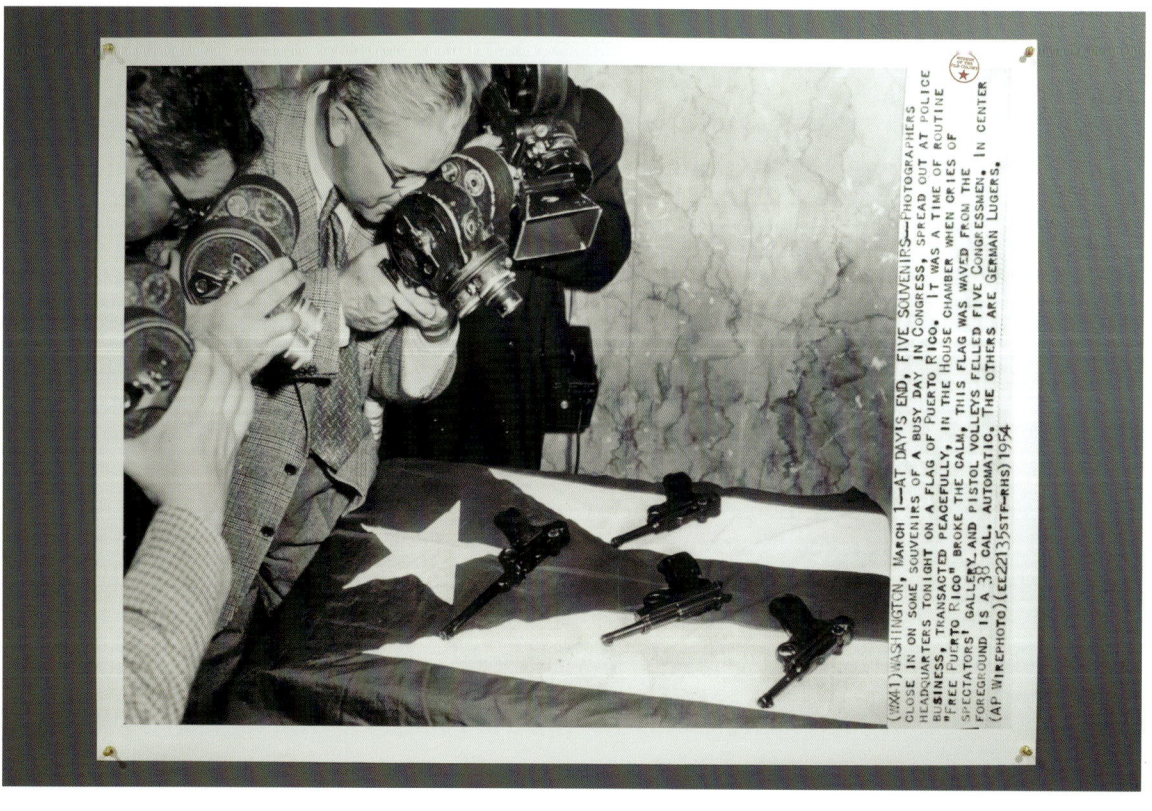

Plate 10. *Tools of the Trade*. Assemblage of found and fabricated objects | 2021. *The Museum of the Old Colony, Duke Hall Gallery of Fine Art*, 2022. Checklist No. 22.

Plate 11. *Photographers close in on some souvenirs of a busy day in Congress*. Associated Press Wirephoto, March 1, 1954 | 2021. *The Museum of the Old Colony*, Duke Hall Gallery of Fine Art, 2022. Checklist No. 95.

31

mid-1960s. The cameras flank an old-fashioned Underwood typewriter and a large set of calipers reminiscent of devices used to measure human skulls, as well as a skin color chart, both calling up the racist theories endemic to the long-discredited pseudoscience of phrenology. This display case also holds a little statue of a photo reporter with a camera whose base reads "The Camera Cannot Lie" (fittingly, one of the few objects Delano has altered) and a cookie jar inscribed with the words "Little White Lies" (plates 10, 36–37, 73).

From Delano's perspective, these are "the tools of the colonizer" and reinforce the notion that these works were consciously made, written, and circulated by individuals who used the technologies available to them, operating within the cultural values of their time. Such extensive photographic documentation would have been difficult to develop in the era of Spanish rule, for while the official invention of photography dates to 1839, the practice only became more accessible towards the latter part of the 19th century with the availability of portable cameras and faster lenses. The first photographs in newspapers in the U.S. (thanks to halftone reproduction processes) did not appear until the 1880s. This partly explains the plethora of photographs of Puerto Rico that proliferated under U.S. rule compared to the limited photographic coverage under the Spanish empire.[22]

The Museum of the Old Colony might be read as a critique, even indictment, of social documentary photography—the very art form that Delano has practiced for decades and with which his father achieved renown as the premier artist-documentarian of Puerto Rico for the U.S. Farm Security Administration and the Puerto Rican Office of Information (OIPR) in the 1940s. And yet Jack Delano's work (and that of his close colleagues Edwin and Louise Rosskam, and others) is not in the installation.[23] Are these photographers protected from this critique because they are exceptions to the rule? Indeed, as left-leaning New Deal liberals working for the OIPR, they were part of a generation of photographers who sought to counter the overtly racist and reductive images of Puerto Rico from earlier decades, as well as the simplistic, picturesque images of the island as a tourist paradise. Their complex documentations of social and economic conditions recognized the dignity of the people they photographed; but as reform-minded activists, they also engaged in nuanced social critique. Pablo Delano explained in an extensive interview that this was not a conscious omission, and that he has even contemplated using a well-known image by Jack Delano, "Pledging allegiance to the flag, in a school in Corozal" (1946), a poignant picture reproduced in his celebrated book *Puerto Rico mío* (1990). The work not only sensitively captures the humanity of the protagonist but it also raises uncomfortable questions about the U.S. presence in Puerto Rico (figure 5).[24]

Yet within the logic of *The Museum of the Old Colony*, such classic works by famous photographers could distract viewers from engaging with the artist's performative space, which is not primarily concerned with the authorship of photographs, promoting the art of photography, or privileging one type of documentary practice over another. Rather, the focus is on the photographs' content, dissemination, and circulation in mass culture and their effects on viewer perception. Delano's concern is also the conceptual use of photography, which then invites comparison to the work of self-described "*Nuyorican*" photographer-provocateur Adál Maldonado. While their work differs visually—Delano's "muting" of himself contrasts with ADÁL's intense engagement with his own body—they share an activist approach to employing photographs for satirical play and subversive political commentary related to the self-determination of Puerto Rico and to the physical damage and psychic pain wrought by the colonial condition. Both compel viewers to imagine new futures for Puerto Rico.[25] Delano's engagement with conceptual art strategies further emerges in the picture of cameramen zooming in on the pistols laid on the Puerto Rican flag of the Nationalists who had just shot on the U.S. Congress—a clever metacommentary on the role news photographers play in not only "getting the great shot" to inform the public of dramatic events, but also in sensationalizing, simplifying, and/or reinforcing popular perceptions about such events (plate 11). Indeed, Delano expresses that at this point in his artistic trajectory, Marcel Duchamp's philosophy of *art as idea* and Dada humor, which revel in irony and conscious contradictions, are stronger guiding lights for him than the formalist innovations of European modernists, whose art Duchamp famously rejected as too "retinal."[26]

Relatedly, the installation does not include photographs of two of the most iconic political figures of 20th-century Puerto Rico—Pedro Albizu Campos (long-time president of the Nationalist Party) and Luis Muñoz Marín (the first democratically elected governor, founder of the PPD, and architect of the island's modernization). Each advocated for Puerto Rican self-determination in very different ways: Albizu fought for complete independence from the U.S. even if that meant resorting to armed struggle; Muñoz (after an earlier period as an independence supporter) fought for more self-government with an incremental approach that retained a relationship with the United States.[27] Reflecting on this point, Delano contends that their inclusion would have run the risk of rendering *The Museum of the Old Colony* overly literal, reducing his multilayered project to a didactic debate about these two dichotomous visions, or leading viewers to read the installation as a straightforward display of historical pictures. It could also have induced viewers to ask which iconic figure Delano himself might sympathize with, shifting attention to the artist's own political views, which are not his focus here.[28] Delano prefers to keep the focus on his open-ended artwork, which foregrounds the long and troubling history of the visualization of the colonial plight in Puerto Rico in what influential publisher Henry Luce called "the American Century."

As to museums, *The Museum of the Old Colony* comments on the authority of these trusted institutions to confer meaning on the images and objects that they acquire and display. Delano's fascination with museums (especially with how Western anthropological

Figure 2. *Otra sala del Museo de Historia Natural*/Another
room of Natural History Museum. Antonio M. Monteagudo and
Antonio M. Escámez, eds., *Álbum de oro de Puerto Rico*/Golden
Album of Puerto Rico, Artes gráficas, La Habana, 1939.

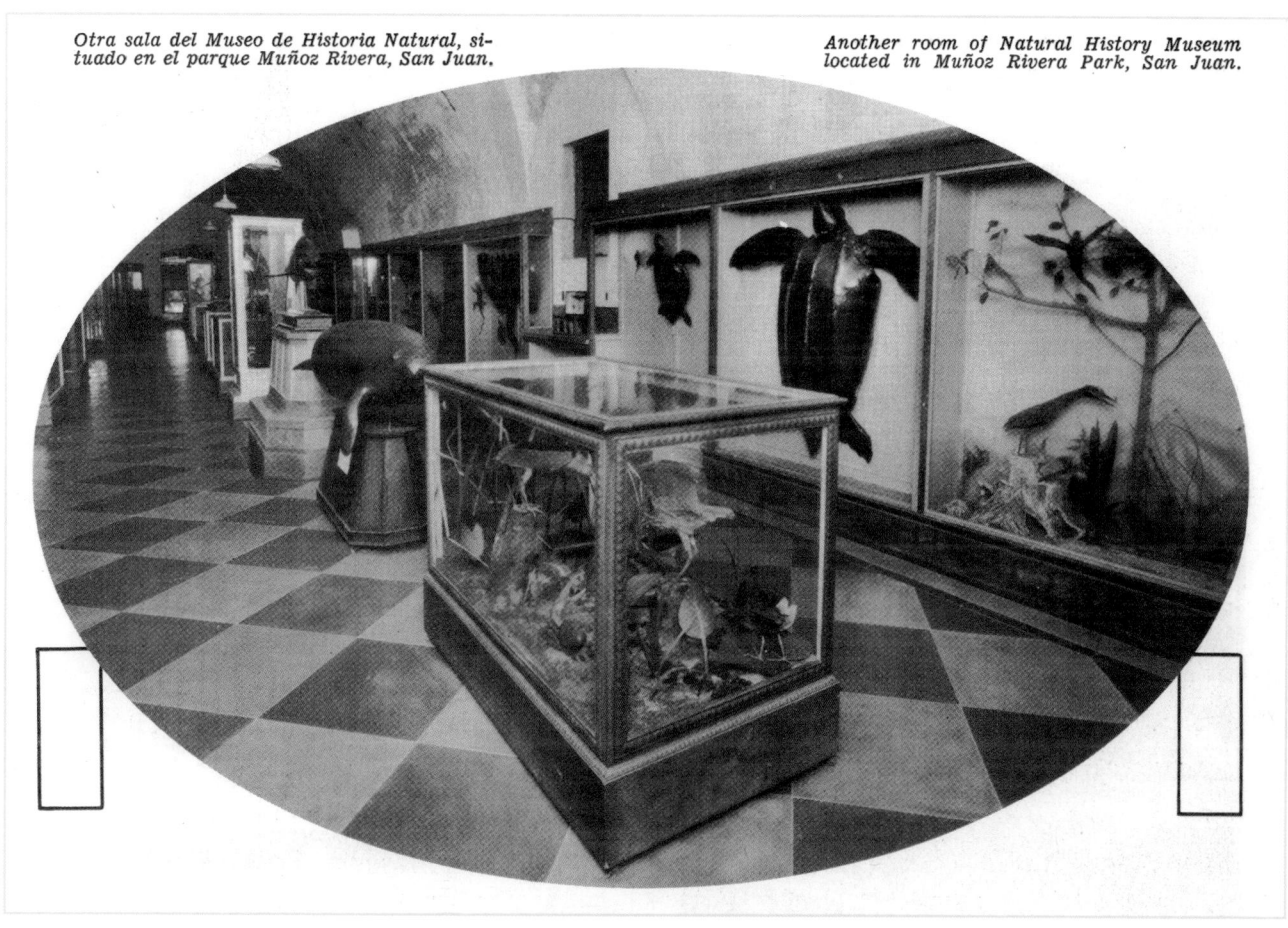

*Otra sala del Museo de Historia Natural, si-
tuado en el parque Muñoz Rivera, San Juan.*

*Another room of Natural History Museum
located in Muñoz Rivera Park, San Juan.*

and ethnographic museums have historically objectified non-Western peoples and cultures) dates to his childhood, when his father took him to the old *Museo de Historia Natural* in Puerta de Tierra, San Juan (figure 2).[29] He uses the physical, visual, and textual language of museums and installation techniques to lure viewers into his fictive museum only to undercut the authority of such spaces. The artist plays with museum "framing," choosing not to frame the photographs, as one would expect in a museum setting, but rather to place his own narrative texts that run through the installation in cheap, gold-painted frames. Installing the photographs unmatted and unframed and securing them with gold-colored push pins challenge any perceptions of them as precious, vintage collectibles, rendering the entire ensemble a work-in-progress. This, in turn, suggests larger metaphors for viewers to contemplate on the installation's content.

In addition, Delano carefully designs museum-like vitrines to house ordinary consumer items, such as Old Colony soda bottles, five of which he lines up chronologically, using the museum strategy of a "timeline," which suggests the evolution of something important (plate 1). The encasing of throw-away products asks viewers to examine the iconography of those products more closely than they would in their original commercial contexts, and to realize that even the most commonplace objects are embedded with values. Given that this soft drink has been manufactured in Mayagüez since the 1940s, how can we read the continued use of the Old Colony moniker and the U.S. Revolutionary War-era patriot on its can? If the image of the colonist in his 18th-century tricorn hat was used to promote a feeling of "Americanism" in Puerto Ricans, the "American" values it features, ironically and/or deliberately, signify the American colonist's rebellion against British colonial rule. The moniker could also be an omnipresent reminder to consumers that Puerto Rico is often considered the world's oldest colony.

In all these ways, *The Museum of the Old Colony* intersects with the phenomenon of institutional critique whereby contemporary artists have exposed the subjectivities and biases of museums, challenging their reputed neutrality. By questioning the power structures of empire, the installation also connects to the very topical "decolonization" movement, which has pushed museums and other influential cultural institutions to become more transparent and accountable to the diverse publics they serve and represent, to interrogate with closer scrutiny the provenance and funding of their collections and exhibitions, and to work towards greater inclusion and equity in their practices.[30] Like Fred Wilson's now-classic *Mining the Museum* (1992), Delano's installation is an art of activist intervention. Wilson used works "hidden" in storage at the Maryland Historical Society and powerful juxtapositions to curate alternative histories of Maryland—histories of marginalized Black and Native American populations whose narratives were long suppressed by the dominant White leadership of the institution. Delano, for his part, uses mainstream images and objects made largely by and for U.S. culture, also in provocative pairings, to subvert their original usages aimed at justifying U.S. control in Puerto Rico, creating alternative narratives of the modern history of the island-nation.

This asks viewers to decode meanings and check their own relationship to the traditional narratives, challenging them, according to Maurice Berger, "to question their passivity about or complicity with the ongoing disenfranchisement of their fellow citizens."[31] Berger assumes a non-Puerto Rican audience here, but how might Puerto Rican audiences (in all their diversity) relate to Delano's installation and decode his coded language? What viewers take away from the installation depends on what they bring to it. The two miniature U.S. and Puerto Rican flags sitting side by side atop the Libby's Corned Beef can, for example, might be read by viewers with little knowledge of Puerto Rico as a symbol of equality between two nations. But many Puerto Ricans would recognize this as an overt symbol of the Commonwealth, acutely aware of the fraught history of two flags being flown together on official buildings in Puerto Rico since 1952.[32] Similarly, uninitiated mainland viewers might read the plastic decor palm tree as an innocuous symbol of a tropical

Figure 3. Delano family house, near Trujillo Alto, Puerto Rico. Gelatin silver print, early 1960s. Pictured: Pablo Delano (in car) and his paternal grandmother, Sonia Ovcharov. Jack and Irene Delano Estate. Courtesy of Pablo Delano and Laura Delano Duncan.

Figure 4. *El Morro* Golf Course. Hole #5 (of nine) of the first golf course in Puerto Rico. Gelatin silver print, circa 1960. Source: San Juan National Historic Site Facebook page, February 4, 2015.

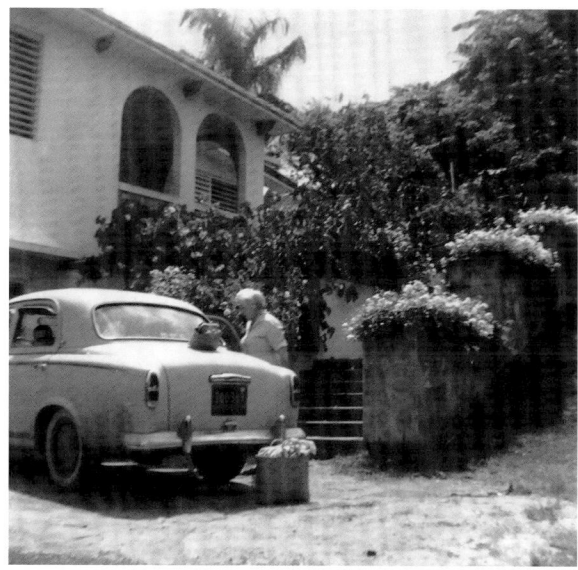

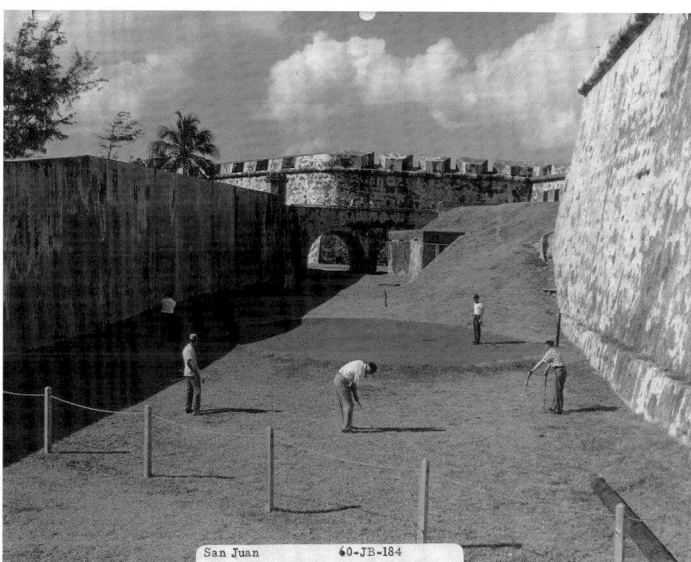

island, while many Puerto Ricans would see it immediately as the icon of the PNP, the pro-statehood party currently in power on the island. Delano thus suggests that one's "insider" knowledge of his coded language might elicit an empowering experience for viewers who are clued into the doubling of meanings with which the artist plays (plates 38, 58).

Ultimately, as Delano has often articulated, *The Museum of the Old Colony* is the artist's personal response to the land where he was born, raised, and educated. And although Puerto Rico has not been his daily home for five decades, the island remains the place to which he feels he most belongs. Delano holds fond and vivid memories of growing up on a hill near Trujillo Alto outside San Juan, where he made lifelong friends, and where his cultural tastes, interests, and humor were partly shaped by a Caribbean sensibility (figure 3). He speaks with affection and respect about his *nortemericano* parents, Jack Delano and graphic artist Irene Delano, and when asked, reflects eloquently on their lives and work. Hailing from Eastern European, Jewish backgrounds (Jack was an immigrant from Russian-controlled Ukraine), the Delanos fully embraced Puerto Rican culture. As "adopted" Puerto Ricans, they were pioneers in the creation of a cultural nationalism through photography, graphic design, scenography, music, and film in the post-World War II (early *muñocista*) era (figures 5–6).[33] Pablo Delano also recalls from his youth the pervasive U.S. military presence on the island. He remembers *El Morro* fortress being used as a golf course for military personnel (figure 4); military parades on July 4th and 25th broadcast on WIPR-television, when his father ran the station; and U.S. sailors walking in and out of brothels in broad daylight. He remembers the often "obnoxious" behavior of some "entitled" U.S. tourists, whose presence increased with the rapid growth of the tourism industry in the 1950s and 1960s.[34] Indeed, his upbringing coincided with the aforementioned U.S.-backed modernization project led by Muñoz and his *populares*—the stunning transformation of the island from a poor, agricultural economy to a middle-class, industrial one, which helped many escape poverty. He witnessed the early years of the Commonwealth, or *Estado Libre Asociado*, whereby Puerto Rico would be neither a sovereign nation nor a U.S. state, in the wake of the ratification of Puerto Rico's own constitution in 1952, which brought a measure of political autonomy. This happened at a time when decolonization movements were emerging full force around the globe.[35]

Delano's installation casts a critical eye on the legacy of the whole experiment with "in-between" status that is the Commonwealth. The fragility of this status has been thrown into sharp relief by the U.S. Congress' passage in 2016 of the Puerto Rico Oversight, Management, and Economic Stability Act (PROMESA), and its creation of an external fiscal control board ("*La Junta*" in local parlance) to manage the island's troubled finances. Many have argued that this control board, with its imposition of austerity measures to restructure debt, holds more economic power than any elected official in Puerto Rico.[36] This has been a humiliating challenge to self-rule and a painful reminder that Puerto Ricans on the island have diminished rights vis-à-vis the U.S. compared with their fellow Puerto Ricans on the mainland. Such humiliation was only amplified by the disastrously slow recovery efforts under the Federal Emergency Management Agency (FEMA) in the Trump administration following the devastation caused by hurricanes Irma and María in 2017, and by the exposure of the scandalous political corruption of the island's pro-statehood government in 2019. Delano's incisive critique has gained urgency from these events and is invigorated by a new generation of impassioned, grass roots activism on the island. This energy is seen everywhere: in the civil protests of the *Verano del 19* that forced the resignation of disgraced PNP Governor Ricardo Rosselló; in the food sovereignty movement supporting community agriculture; in Casa Pueblo's solar power projects; and in artist-run cultural organizations like *Beta-Local*.[37]

The Museum of the Old Colony, therefore, in the words of Nelson Rivera, "adds to the treasured tradition of Puerto Rican anticolonial art," a tradition Rivera traces (in the use of word and image) from Francisco Oller, to Lorenzo Homar, to Antonio Martorell, to Elsa María Meléndez.[38] Delano's installation can also be called "decolonial," as it "not only seeks to overthrow colonialism, but also to remove and redress its lasting traces and legacies afterwards."[39] Indeed, the artist sees *The Museum of the Old Colony* as one of the projects in his "decolonial toolbox," and it certainly resonates with the tenets of "decolonial aesthesis" laid out by contemporary theorists. According to Walter Mignolo and Rolando Vázquez, such projects employ "techniques like juxtaposition, parody, or simple disobedience to the rules of art and polite society, to expose the contradictions of coloniality. [Their] goal, then, is not to produce feelings of beauty or sublimity, but ones of sadness, indignation, repentance, hope, and determination to change things in the future."[40] *The Museum of the Old Colony* brilliantly achieves this goal.

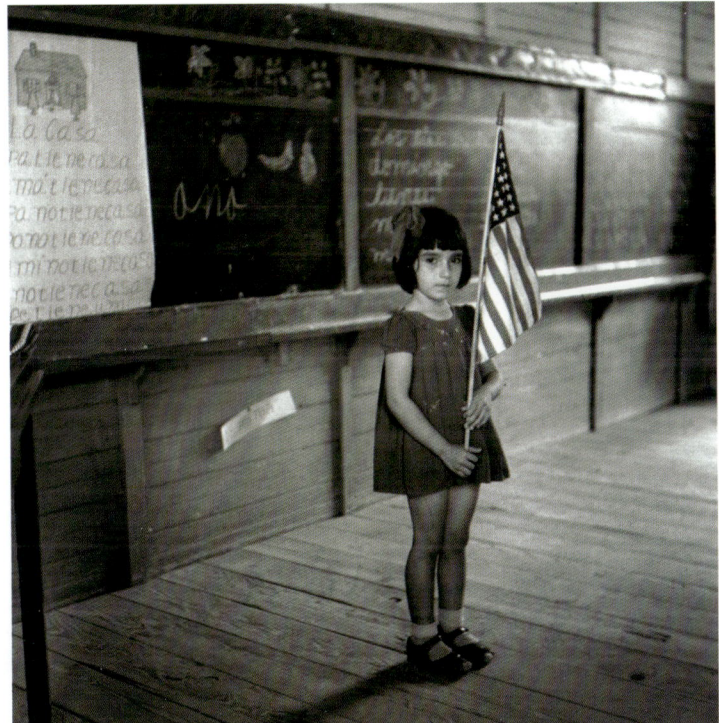

Figure 5. Jack Delano, *Pledging allegiance to the flag, in a school in Corozal.* Gelatin silver print, 1946. Jack Delano et al., *Puerto Rico mio: Four Decades of Change. Cuatro décadas de cambio*, Smithsonian Institution Press, Washington, D.C., 1990, 166. Courtesy of Pablo Delano and Laura Delano Duncan.

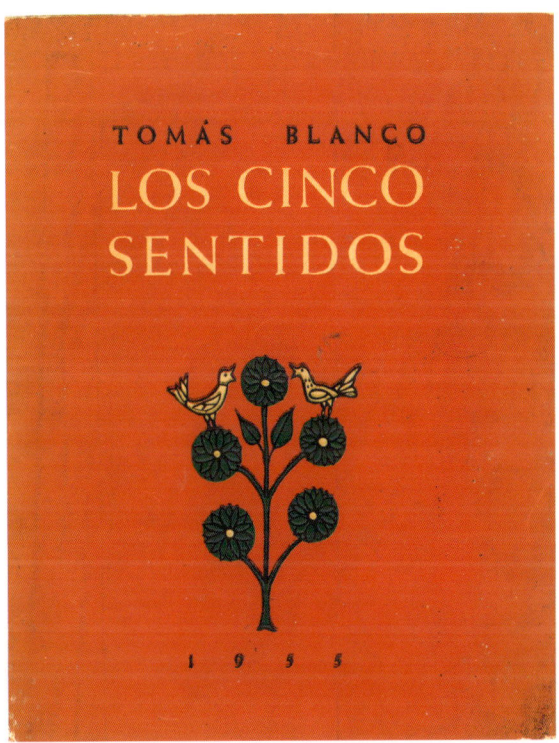

Figure 6. Irene Delano, cover design. Tomás Blanco, *Los cinco sentidos: cuaderno suelto de un inventario de cosas nuestras, con decoraciones de Irene Delano,* Pan American Book Company, San Juan, 1955. Courtesy of Pablo Delano and Laura Delano Duncan.

*The author expresses deep gratitude to José Roberto Martínez, Jorge Duany, Pedro Juan Hernández, and Arcadio Díaz Quiñones for lending their scholarly expertise to this essay.

1 The author takes this title from César J. Ayala and Rafael Bernabe, eds., *Puerto Rico in the American Century: A History Since 1898* (Chapel Hill: University of North Carolina Press, 2007), 1. Henry Luce declared in *Life* magazine on February 17, 1941: "The 20th Century is the American Century"; he implored the U.S. to prepare for a global leadership role in the midst of World War II. Ayala and Bernabe stated: "For some, the American Century had begun much earlier" with the Spanish-American War of 1898.

2 Quote from official website of *The Museum of the Old Colony*, accessed August 24, 2022, www. museumoftheoldcolony.org/about/about-the-museum/.

3 Maurice Berger, *The Museum of the Old Colony: An Art Installation by Pablo Delano* (Baltimore: Center for Art, Design and Visual Culture, University of Maryland, Baltimore County, 2020), 10.

4 See artist's website, accessed August 4, 2022, www.pablodelano.com/project/oisaida-1980-1984/. Key commissioned projects include a 1986 series on East 149th Street in the South Bronx, sponsored by Hostos Community Advisory Council, and a 1995 series, *Images of Washington Heights*, funded by the New York City Department of Cultural Affairs and the New York City School Construction Authority, Percent for Art Program.

5 Delano has returned to Trinidad and Tobago multiple times since 2008; he continued his coverage of Carnival in ways that he has said "offer a counterpoint to stereotypical notions of the Caribbean." See Andrew Boryga, "Carnival's Essence in Black and White," *New York Times Lens*, March 4, 2014, https://lens.blogs. nytimes.com/2014/03/04/carnivals-essence-in-black-and-white/.

6 Quote from artist's website, accessed August 4, 2022, www.pablodelano.com/on-the-wall/pr-urban-art-i/.

7 For the term "unseen," see Guillermo B. Irizarry, "Hartford Unseen," in *Hartford Seen: Photographs by Pablo Delano*, by Pablo Delano (Middletown: Wesleyan University Press, 2020), 1-7. On several of Delano's urban-focused projects, see Irizarry, "A Specific Beauty: Pablo Delano's Photography in New York City, Hartford, and Santurce." *Centro Journal*, 31, no. 1 (Spring 2019): 4-25.

8 First quote from Thomas G. Mathews, Kal Wagenheim, and Olga J. Wagenheim, "History of Puerto Rico," *Encyclopedia Britannica*, August 13, 2022, https://www.britannica.com/place/Puerto-Rico. Second quote from Jorge Duany, *Puerto Rico: What Everyone Needs to Know* (New York: Oxford University Press, 2017), 46.

9 Quotes from Duany, *Puerto Rico*, 66.

10 The U.S. Supreme Court "Insular Cases" (1901-1922), made distinctions between "incorporated" and "unincorporated" territories, based on specious reasoning that ignored ideals of the Declaration of Independence and the U.S. Constitution and that relied on racist beliefs that such lands were "inhabited by alien races." See Daniel Immerwahr, *How to Hide an Empire: A History of the Greater United States* (New York: Farrar, Straus and Giroux, 2019) and Sam Erman, *Almost Citizens: Puerto Rico, the U.S. Constitution, and Empire* (New York: Cambridge University Press, 2018).

11 For a brilliant exploration of *la brega* as a lens through which to examine Puerto Rican history, culture, and identity, see Arcadio Díaz Quiñones, *El arte de bregar: ensayos*, 2nd ed. (San Juan: Ediciones Callejón, 2003).

12 "Cultural expressions such as literature, music, and painting began to reflect a growing sense of Creole identity in Puerto Rico during the nineteenth century." Duany, *Puerto Rico*, 34.

13 The 2020 gubernatorial election in Puerto Rico saw a big shakeup of traditional party politics, with new parties emerging on the left and right, *Movimiento Victoria Ciudadana* and *Proyecto Dignidad*, respectively, which have siphoned support away from the PNP and the PPD, offering visions for a new future in the wake of urgent crises. The Puerto Rican Independence Party (PIP) saw the second-largest electoral results in its history. Two competing bills recently introduced in the U.S. Congress, the Puerto Rico Self-Determination Act, HR 2070, and the Puerto Rico Statehood Act, HR 1522, have been "reconciled" into a compromise bill, HR 8393, which is unlikely to be enacted. The author thanks José Roberto Martínez, Federico de Jesús Febles, Flavio Cumpiano, and Jorge Duany for sharing their expertise on this topic.

14 On this subject, see Laura Roulet's essay in this catalogue and the scholarship of Arlene M. Dávila.

15 See Díaz-Quiñones, "El 98: la guerra simbólica," in *El arte de bregar: ensayos*, 210–248; Duany, *Puerto Rican Nation on the Move: Identities on the Island and in the United States* (Chapel Hill: University of North Carolina Press, 2002), 87-121; Lanny Thompson, *Imperial Archipelago: Representation and Rule in the Insular Territories under U.S. Dominion after 1898* (Honolulu, University of Hawai'i Press, 2010); and Jorge Luis Crespo Armáiz, *Estereoscopia y sujeto colonial: la contribución de la fotografía estereoscópica en la construcción del otro puertorriqueño 1898-1930* (Gurabo: Universidad del Turabo, Sistema Universitario Ana G. Méndez, 2015).

16 "[T]he state-sponsored idea that Puerto Rican white and mixed-race identities operate separately from the U.S. racial framework is receding." See Isar Godreau and Yarimar Bonilla, "Nonsovereign Racecraft: How Colonialism, Debt, and Disaster are Transforming Puerto Rican Racial Subjectivities," *American Anthropologist* 123, no. 3 (September 2021): Abstract, 509-525. See also Carlos Vargas-Ramos, ed. *Race, Front and Center: Perspectives on Race Among Puerto Ricans* (New York: Centro Press, 2017).

17 Another major 20th century topic not addressed in the installation is the post-World War II "Great Migration" of Puerto Ricans to the U.S., who left their homeland mainly for economic reasons.

18 Frank Mitchell, *Art from Archive: Work by Lewis Watts and Pablo Delano* (Hartford: Widener Gallery, Austin Arts Center, Trinity College, 2017), 7.

19 Decades ago, Arcadio Díaz Quiñones discovered a vintage print of this photograph with the caption "Scaling the Palms for Cocoanut Water" in a private album in the McConnie Family Collection, Puerto Rico. With permission, he reproduced the work in the 2016 Portuguese translation of an anthology of his essays, *A memória rota: ensaios de cultura e política*, and in *Once tesis sobre un crimen de 1899* (San Juan: Editorial Luscinia C.E., 2019), 22.

20 Mitchell, *Art from Archive*, 7.

21 "Porto Rican Laundries" was taken around 1898 by the Canadian American Margherita Arlina Hamm, one of the few women who documented Puerto Rico at this time. A newspaper journalist, author, and suffragist, she covered the Sino-Japanese and Spanish-American Wars, and took great interest in women's work and their food traditions. How might Hamm's pioneering role and sympathetic approach affect viewers' interpretations of her photographs, even as her work circulated within a U.S. imperialist system—a system that she supported?

22 On photography in Puerto Rico before 1898, see Libia M González, "La ilusión del paraíso: fotografías y relatos de viajeros sobre Puerto Rico, 1898-1900," in *Los arcos de la memoria: el '98 de los pueblos puertorriqueños*, ed. Silvia Álvarez Curbelo, Mary Frances Gallard, and Carmen I. Raffucci (San Juan: Universidad de Puerto Rico; Mayagüez: Asociación Puertorriqueña de Historiadores, 1998), 275–276.

23 At least two exceptions in the installation are works by Jack Delano's New Deal friends: "Financiers," a 1949 photograph by Gordon Parks, and *Puerto Rico: Caribbean Crossroads*, a 1947 photo book by Charles Rotkin. A 1973 photograph by John Vachon has been shown in other venues. On OIPR photographers, see Laura Katzman et al., *Re-viewing Documentary: The Photographic Life of Louise Rosskam*, 2nd ed. (University Park: Pennsylvania State University Press, 2014) and the author's current book project on the OIPR photo-archive in the early *muñocista* era.

24 Pablo Delano, interview by Laura Katzman, Hartford, Connecticut, November 5-7, 2021, audio recording.

25 Delano remains interested in contemporary documentary photographers, such as Erika P. Rodríguez, noted for her striking coverage of social, political, and environmental conditions in Puerto Rico.

26 Delano, interview by Katzman. Delano draws broadly on appropriation practices that exploded in the art world in the 1970s and 1980s, with artists such as Roger Colescott, Richard Prince, and Sherrie Levine.

27 Delano includes other former PPD governors, less famous than Muñoz: Roberto Sánchez Vilella, Jesús T. Piñero, and the flamboyant former PPD mayor of San Juan, Felisa Rincón de Gautier (doña Fela). He includes several former PNP governors, but the current one, Pedro Pierluisi, is shown only in his previous role as resident commissioner. PNP Governor Ricardo Rosselló, ousted in 2019, does not appear in a photograph, but he and the civil protests against his administration appear in one of Delano's two video pieces. The shorter one brings viewers closer to the present than the photographs, which span from 1898 to the 1980s. The longer one, a sequenced montage of media perceptions of Puerto Rico, contains historical film and news footage, serving as a path into the installation.

28 Delano, interview by Katzman. César A. Salgado offers a different reading in his essay in this catalogue.

29 Delano, interview by Katzman. Delano recalls that in 1974, when enrolled in the New York Studio School summer study program, he found it more valuable to visit nearly every museum in Paris than to attend classes. He also noted a 2007-2008 museum exhibition that was influential for his installation: *Apartheid: The South African Mirror*, at the *Centre de Cultura Contemporània de Barcelona* in Catalonia, Spain.

30 Elisa Shoenberger, "What Does It Mean to Decolonize a Museum?, *Museum Next*, February 23, 2022, https://www.museumnext.com/article/what-does-it-mean-to-decolonize-a-museum/.

31 Berger, *The Museum of the Old Colony*, 7. Delano's project can be compared to the Jim Crow Museum of Racist Memorabilia, Ferris State University, Big Rapids, Michigan, founded by David Pilgrim to promote tolerance.

32 This is one of many controversies around displaying the Puerto Rican flag, a complex topic that goes beyond the scope of this essay.

33 Delano, interview with Katzman. Born Jacob Ovcharov, Jack Delano migrated to the U.S. as a child and grew up in Philadelphia; Irene Esser was born in Detroit to Ukrainian-Jewish immigrants and raised in Toronto. Both families fled antisemitism in their homelands. Pablo Delano speaks frankly about his identity as a Puerto Rican born in San Juan to North American parents of Jewish descent. He is proud of his Jewish heritage, but it was not a big part of his upbringing. He felt out of place when he moved to the U.S. in 1972, and like many in the diaspora, he remains strongly connected to the island and its local politics.

34 Delano, interview with Katzman. Contrary to popular perception, while tourism is significant to Puerto Rico's economy, it has never been a huge part of the nation's GDP. Manufacturing (capital-intensive industries) is the largest driver of the economy, followed by the service industry (of which tourism is but one part).

35 Delano's parents supported the PPD (though not uncritically) and were good friends and admirers of Governor (previously Senator) Muñoz and his wife Inés M. Mendoza de Muñoz. The Delanos respected the Muñozes' vision for improving economic conditions and promoting cultural nationalism. Along with the Rosskams and others, the Delanos launched cultural projects to combat rural illiteracy in the 1940s, such as the Division of Community Education (DIVEDCO), under the Piñero and Muñoz administrations. The Delano house was close to the Muñozes' home in the Trujillo Alto countryside and the families remained friends for decades. Pablo Delano's childhood not only coincided with the early Commonwealth years, but also with the fallout from the last major violent activities of the Nationalists and the mass government crackdown on suspected insurrectionists, including use of the so-called Gag Law, enacted in 1948. He was born the year of the Nationalist shooting in the U.S. Capitol on March 1, 1954. This was preceded by a series of coordinated armed assaults on October 30 and November 1, 1950, spawned by the actions leading up to the establishment of the Commonwealth. See Jack Delano's fair-minded portrayal of the 1950 uprising in *Photographic Memories* (Washington, D.C.: Smithsonian Institution Press, 1997), 123.

36 Even though Puerto Rico has exited from most of its bankruptcy-like debt restructuring proceeding, critics and activists argue that the resulting agreements do not cut enough of the debt to be sustainable and will hurt ordinary Puerto Ricans, given austerity measures required under the agreements. The Center for a New Economy (CNE), a non-profit think tank, declared PROMESA a "failed colonial experiment." See https://grupocne.org/wp-content/uploads/2021/06/2021.06.29-PROMESA-A-Failed-Colonial-Experiment.pdf.

37 Delano's work should be seen in the context of art that has responded to recent crises in Puerto Rico. See *no existe un mundo poshuracán: Puerto Rican Art in the Wake of Hurricane Maria*, Whitney Museum of American Art, November 23, 2022 to April 23, 2023; *Temporal: Puerto Rican Resistance*, Museum of Contemporary Photography, Chicago, July 7 to September 19, 2020; *Entredichos, Museo de Arte Contemporáneo de Puerto Rico*, December 2017 to July 2018; and Frances Negrón-Muntaner's "Arts of Catastrophe," a multi-authored dossier for *Small Axe* (forthcoming).

38 Nelson Rivera, in Rivera and Amy Halliday, *The Museum of the Old Colony: An Installation by Pablo Delano* (Amherst: Hampshire College Art Gallery, 2018), 17, 13–14.

39 Lydia Ayame Hiraide, "Postcolonial, Decolonial, Anti-Colonial: Does it Matter?," *New Voices Magazine* (Summer 2021): 14, https://newvoicespocostudies.wordpress.com/hiraide/.

40 Walter Mignolo and Rolando Vázquez, "Decolonial Aesthesis: Colonial Wounds/Decolonial Healings," *Social Text* (July 15, 2013), https://socialtextjournal.org/periscope_topic/decolonial_aesthesis/. Delano continues to fill his "decolonial toolbox," as seen in *Cuestiones Caribeñas/Caribbean Matters*, a new project that has grown out of *The Museum of the Old Colony*. By physically placing objects onto the space of the images, he creates more aggressive relationships between the former and the latter, which results in ensembles that are even more transgressive.

Plate 12: Installation view. *Tools of the Trade* (detail: Graflex 3A camera and reflections). *The Museum of the Old Colony*, Duke Hall Gallery of Fine Art, 2022. Checklist No. 22.

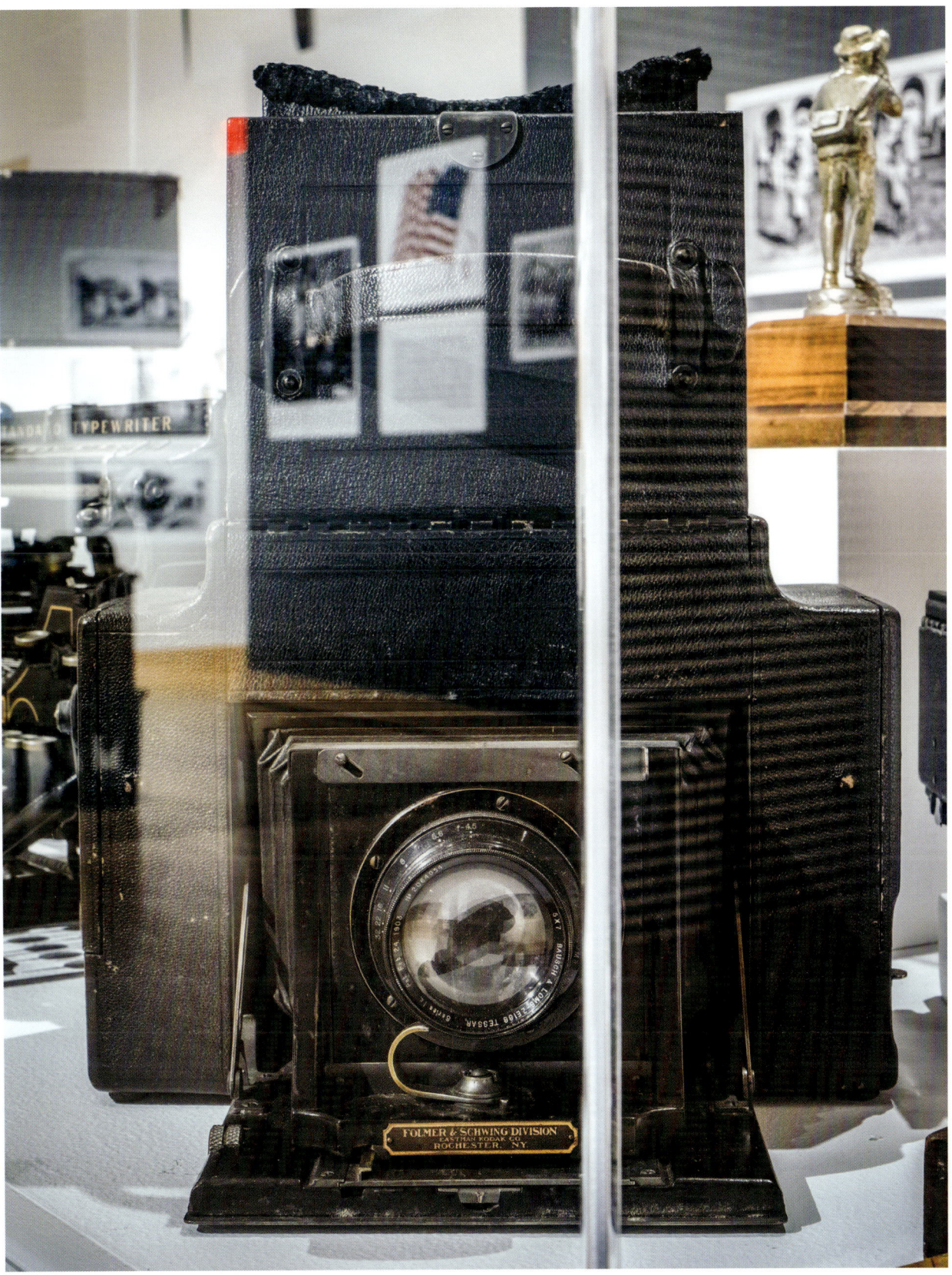

Plate 13. Installation view. *Platos y Cocos* (detail in foreground) and coconut-related photographs and captions. *The Museum of the Old Colony*, Duke Hall Gallery of Fine Art, 2022. Checklist Nos. 63, 72–79.

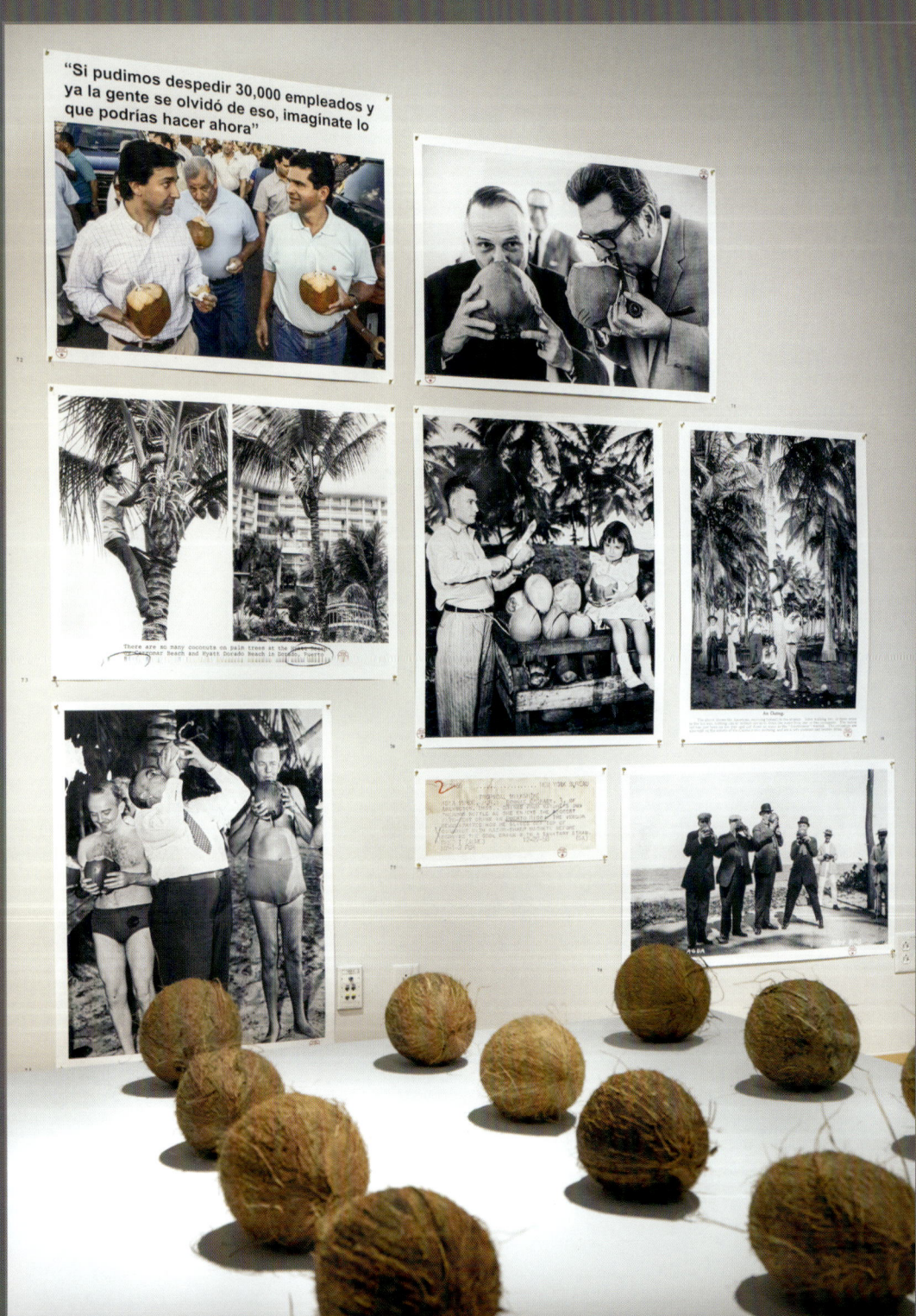

The *Museum of the Old Colony: An Art Installation by Pablo Delano* in the Duke Gallery of Fine Art is the latest and largest incarnation of this site-specific project to date. Making its debut at Alice Yard in Trinidad and Tobago, the installation had other Caribbean venues including the National Gallery of Jamaica in Kingston and the *Museo de Arte Contemporáneo de Puerto Rico* in San Juan. With a side tour to Tucumán, Argentina for the Biennial of Documentary Photography, the exhibition arrived in a paroxysm of irony at the King Juan Carlos I of Spain Center at New York University (NYU), before traveling north to Hampshire College (MA). Then in a progressively southerly fashion, it went from the University of Maryland Baltimore County (MD) to James Madison University (JMU/VA). With each venue aimed at a new audience, the installation has expanded, burgeoning in complexity and conflict.

The Museum of the Old Colony should not be mistaken for a history lesson, though it is very much about history, culture, and identity. Through his selections and artistic choices, Pablo Delano shapes a carefully considered narrative, which is open-ended, subject to multiple readings, and dependent on the frame of reference brought by the viewer. Each iteration has been reshuffled, molded to each new venue. In a 2017 interview on the Caribbean culture blog *Repeating Islands*, Delano comments: "Yes, definitely, each new venue requires reconceiving the installation; both the physical design and the tone or overall vibe of the image sequences… But what's more interesting, I think, is the way the location, or context, impacts actual choices of images and groupings. For instance, in Trinidad—a former British (and previously Spanish) colony which became independent in 1962—everyone is familiar with the concept of colonialism…. At NYU, in a city with a huge Puerto Rican population, I was sure to include images related to the diaspora."[1] For each audience, Delano determines the scale, the juxtapositions, and their sequencing within the gallery space. As may be anticipated, viewer reactions have ranged widely from indignant outrage at colonialism, to nostalgic recognition of familiar scenes or products, to snickering at the embedded humor. As the artist, Delano acknowledges that he is "muting his voice,"[2] removing himself as the maker of the objects—all the photographs and artifacts are appropriated—while at the same time asserting himself as the director and curator of the "museum." He assembles this ever-growing archive of photographs and objects through research and eBay purchases, all influenced by chance.

The most striking through line of *The Museum of the Old Colony* could be termed "the colonial gaze." Beginning with stereographs taken soon after the U.S. invasion of Puerto Rico, and illustrations from books intended for mainland audiences such as *Our Islands and Their People* (1899), a lineage of documentary photography unfolds. As a documentary photographer himself, and as the son of Jack and Irene Delano, who are credited with leading the development of 20th-century documentary photography, filmmaking, and graphic arts in Puerto Rico, the artist well understands the evidentiary power of photography. At first glance, even a sophisticated viewer assumes that "straight" or street photography represents a factual record. These turn-of-the-20th-century photographs with unedited captions present a shockingly condescending and objectifying view of the poverty and class disparities in the former Spanish colony, "Porto Rico," as the Americans referred to it in the early years after the 1898 invasion. The guise of the U.S. colonizer as intrepid anthropologist is reinforced slyly with a desk placed close to the entrance of the gallery, equipped with a pith helmet, stereograph viewer, magnifying glass, and other essential "tools" for overseeing the new "possession." Key source material including *National Geographic* and the alarmist *Dynamite at Our Doorstep* (1945) are ready at hand (plate 4).

Not unique to the Caribbean, but easily overlooked, are Puerto Rico's two layers of colonialism. Four hundred years of Spanish domination, which featured the near obliteration of the Indigenous population and introduction of the enslavement of Africans, has been followed by more than a century of U.S. interference. As Delano notes, "Puerto Rico hasn't been self-governing since 1493."[3] The pseudo-anthropological approach of early U.S. photojournalists belies their own ingrained racist and sexist biases. Pitting North American binary definitions of race (as it prevailed in the U.S., particularly in the American South) against pre-existing Spanish/Latin American *casta* colorism essentially meant laying one form of racism over another. In the U.S. context, one is either Black or White, whereas in the caste system one's status is based on a spectrum of skin tones from dark to light, mixed to less mixed.[4] U.S. photographers in Puerto Rico recognized a familiar White privilege on the island, as seen in the photograph of a staged tableau of wealthy women in flowing gowns, as well as Black poverty, as seen in "A Peon Cabin, San Turce, Porto Rico" (plates 41–42). The dehumanizing language of the photographs' captions reinforces the racial hierarchy in which poor Whites, Porto Rican or otherwise, are superior to poor Blacks. These racial and class hierarchies were later recognized (yet documented differently) in the American South and Appalachia by WPA-era photographers such as Dorothea Lange and Jack Delano.

While late-19th- and turn-of-the-20th-century imagery dominates the front gallery of the installation, with photographs taken mainly by North Americans, in the back gallery, viewers see that the colonial gaze was partly coopted by Puerto Rican photojournalists in the twentieth century. One of the more perplexing aspects of *The Museum of the Old Colony* is how it exposes the ways colonial sexism and racism have been perpetuated in Puerto Rico by beauty pageants, children's toys, and even by a 1970s-era blackface competition for a local coffee brand, one that still uses a Black mammy figure, *Mama Inés*, as its mascot. Puerto Rican cultural anthropologist Arlene Dávila might read this as the naturalization of colonialism through consumerism, entertainment, and the island's own tourist agency.[5] Others might implicate local political governance, business development, and education.

The more current the images that Delano selects (one video includes Donald Trump's despicable, post-Hurricane Maria, paper towel-throwing stunt), the more complicated the narratives.

Delano not only acts as *The Museum of the Old Colony's* director and curator, but also as its chief archivist. Beyond merely collecting images and objects, he gives the impression of assembling a definitive historical archive, implicitly acknowledging how the archive serves as a facet of public memory. As curator Okwui Enwezor notes in his introduction to the impactful 2008 exhibition *Archive Fever*, "artists interrogate the self-evidentiary claims of the archive by reading it against the grain."[6] Enwezor further unravels the (British) use of the data-gathered, surveilled, and classified archive as colonial power. He states: "Throughout the nineteenth century, the 'great game' of imperial expansion was an acquisitive game of spatial dominance but one invested with the superior capacity to control the flow of information through the archive."[7] In the case of Puerto Rico, *The Museum of the Old Colony* suggests that the archival construction and flow of information was one-way until well into the twentieth century. The first U.S. colonial documentation of the "Our Islands, Their People" ilk exists against a lacuna of visual information from the 400 years of Spanish control. Delano's own immigrant parents, with their perspective as sympathetic outsiders, contributed to creating a post-World War II counter-narrative with a Puerto Rican gaze.

Much postcolonial installation art is indebted to African American artist Fred Wilson's *Mining the Museum* exhibition. With this 1992 intervention at the Maryland Historical Society, Wilson undermined the foundations of museum practices by introducing slavery-era artifacts such as iron shackles into the "decorative arts" vitrines of fancy repoussé silverware (figure 7). By asking what is hidden and what is valued by museums and historical societies, he helped launch the era of institutional critique. Wilson created a situation of discomfort and tension for the viewer, one explicated by theorist Claire Bishop in her discussion of the role of antagonism within relational aesthetics, stating that "a democratic society is one in which relations of conflict are *sustained*, not erased."[8] With authoritarian censorship and content control as the implied alternative, Australian historian Alice Procter expands Bishop's argument by noting: "The worlds most of us live in are fundamentally hostile, defined by coping with aggressive and antagonistic experience and grappling with discrimination. This idea of antagonism is really important when we think about social art: any work that is trying to explore the ways people relate to each other needs to address the cruelty there, and to remember that interaction might be violent or hurtful to some of its audience."[9] In *The Museum of the Old Colony*, Delano deliberately creates an uncomfortable counter-narrative in which he lays bare not only the cruel legacy of colonialism in its turn-of-the-20th-century guise but also reveals how it became internalized well into the twentieth century. This revisionism reveals the pain of colonialism,

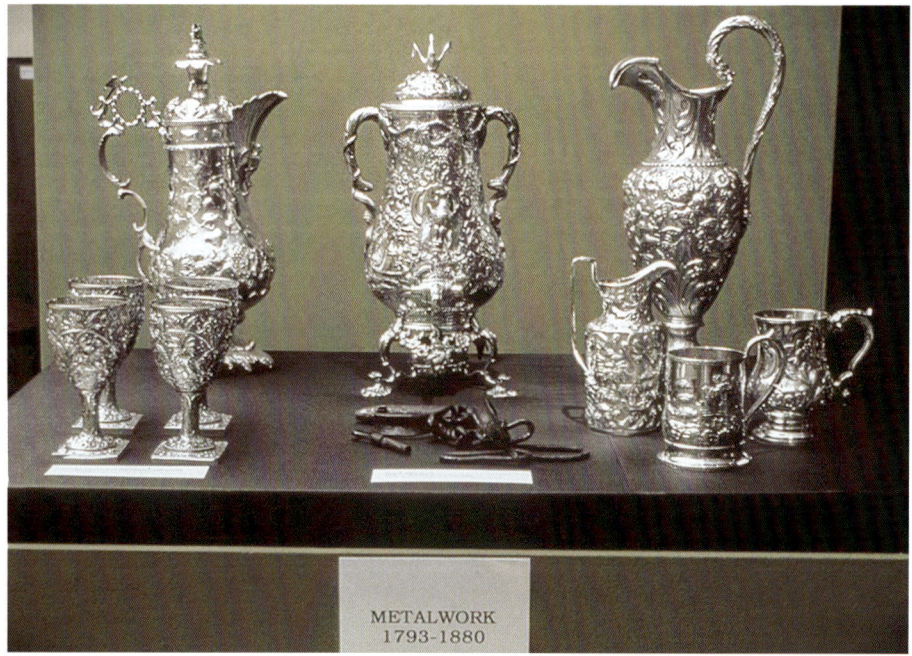

thus provoking greater understanding of Puerto Rico's current socio-political situation, and even encouraging empathy from various audiences. Of course, neither insight nor empathy can be forced, but artists may seek out every possible postcolonial opening.

Perhaps *The Museum of the Old Colony* provides space for the viewer's empathy for the colonizer? After all, U.S. condescension and ignorance towards other countries and peoples have often been mixed with the belief (however problematic) that spreading American-style culture and democracy around the world is an inherent good. How do we make sense of these democratic ideals in light of U.S. imperial ambition? At the turn of the twentieth century, Americans were still very much in the thrall of their former colonial master, Great Britain, which was then at its imperial apex. Everything from Victorian notions of sanitation and cleanliness to racist imperatives of imperialist duties was modeled on the British example. English writer Rudyard Kipling's infamous 1899 poem "The White Man's Burden" was directed at the U.S. and its newly "acquired" islands, the Philippines.

On the British Caribbean side, artist Hew Locke has been disrupting the colonial narrative for decades. Born in Scotland, his mother's homeland, he grew up in Guyana, his father's native country. This insider-outsider perspective led to Locke's early interrogation of the British colonial legacy, often with humor and pageantry.[10] In a series of embellished photographs, Locke fancifully dresses up historic figures, such as the notorious slave trader Lord Edward Colston, with cowry shells and trade beads. A bust of Queen Victoria

Figure 7. Fred Wilson, *Metalwork, 1793–1880*. Installation from *Mining the Museum*. Digitized 35 mm slide, 1992–1993. H. Furlong Baldwin Library, Maryland Center for History and Culture, Baltimore.

is festooned with imitation jewels, along with military badges for imperialist campaigns, in what is now known as the Benin Massacre and the Zulu Wars. In 2022, Locke was finally given center stage with *The Procession*, a spectacular installation at Tate Britain. The brilliantly decorated, Carnival-like scene, featuring 150 life-size figures, interplays with the dark underbelly of Tate Britain, namely its founder, Sir Henry Tate, whose fortune was built on slave labor and the sugar refining industry. As the artist has stated: "What I try to do in my work is mix ideas of attraction and ideas of discomfort—colourful and attractive, but strangely, scarily surreal at the same time."[11]

Regarding Puerto Rico's colonial narratives, among the more surreal historical episodes were several occasions between 1952 and 1955 when Felisa Rincón de Gautier (doña Fela), the flamboyant mayor of San Juan, brought planeloads of snow to the island. Inspired by his own bittersweet childhood memories of participation in these events, artist Antonio Martorell created *White Christmas* (1980), a farcical installation/happening at the *Liga de Arte* in San Juan. With invitations featuring tourist postcards of familiar tropical scenery that he covered with white paint to look like snow, Martorell urged guests to wear heavy clothing to the gallery, where they arrived to find a 1950s-era living room with North American Christmas carols playing in the background. While emphasizing the bizarre features of one of these episodes—a New Hampshire girl designated as *la princesa de nieve*, "Spanish" dancers presented as greeters at the airport, and Puerto Ricans engaged in a huge snowball fight in a baseball park—Martorell recalled how the mystification of the North through films, songs, and department store displays had been drummed into the popular imagination and how the warm tropical holiday was deemed somehow inferior to the snowy Northern version, the latter being "the white dreams of a *mestizo* people."[12]

With *White Christmas Revisited* (2015), Martorell adds another layer of absurdity to the construction of these postcolonial yearnings (figure 9). As part of his retrospective at the *Liga de Arte*, Martorell collaborated with an artist young enough to be his granddaughter, in an intergenerational historical revisionism. Although the legend of "when snow came to Puerto Rico" had been passed down from one generation to the next, good video documentation did not seem to exist, until 2007, when Sofia Gallisá Muriente, then a film student at NYU, happened upon the Paramount News 35-mm footage from 1955 at the National Archives in College Park, Maryland.[13] Her resulting two-channel video installation of 2014, *Lluvia con nieve (Rain with Snow)*, edits and massages the grainy black and white film, contrasting the ceremonial display at the airport with the subsequent public melee on the baseball field (figure 8). The revisited installation contrasts Martorell's personal memory with popular imagination and historic documentation. Irving Berlin's swoony "I'm Dreaming of a White Christmas" melds with Mon Rivera's downbeat salsa track. The cultural disconnect that emerges from this effort to construct historical memory through documentary media echoes another thread woven throughout *The Museum of the Old*

Colony. Delano, like Martorell and Gallisá Muriente, seems to delight in deciphering the surreal truths-stranger-than-fictions of his island, including those connected to the history and implications of Puerto Rico's political party system, which his installation addresses, if only obliquely.

Delano approaches Puerto Rican political status, which is a subject of endless debate on the island and a baffling enigma off the island, again with a slant. On the wall featuring photo ops of several generations of islanders and mainlanders enjoying fresh coconut water, straight from the source, Delano's selection of political leaders emphasizes one lineage from U.S.-appointed governors to pro-statehood governors of the *Partido Nuevo Progresivo* (PNP) (plate 13). This includes Luis A. Ferré, the first PNP governor, who is sharing the ceremonial *coco* with Roberto Sánchez Vilella, protégé of Luis Muñoz Marín, the first elected governor of Puerto Rico and primary founder of the *Partido Popular Democratico* (PPD), or the Commonwealth Party. The ensemble of leaders brandishing U.S. and/or Puerto Rican flags includes a triumphant-looking figure from a militant, pro-independence movement, Filiberto Ojeda Ríos,[14] and masked PNP Governor Wanda Vázquez, which brings *The Museum of the Old Colony* up to the pandemic era (plate 19).[15] In the spectrum of status possibilities from independence to statehood seen in the installation, the current status of Commonwealth (*Estado Libre Asociado* or ELA) is generally downplayed. Doña Fela, the legendary, snow-bringing San Juan mayor and a *popular*, appears, but Muñoz Marín does not. With a fairly light hand, Delano implicates one party in particular—the PNP—as being in cahoots with the U.S. colonizer. (The PNP has unsuccessfully introduced a bill in the U.S. Congress to become the 51st state multiple times.) The statehood message is that Puerto Rico will be safer and better off with even closer ties to the U.S., which is quite similar to the 1898 message from the colonizer. Radical *independentistas* like Lolita Lebrón and Ojeda are pictured in connection with their arrests. However, the viewer needs significant background knowledge of Puerto Rico's political personalities and dramas to gain insight into these figures and their actions. No political party gets off critique-free.

Each iteration of *The Museum of the Old Colony* is ethically fraught, as it should be. Each version gives ample space for viewers to engage memories and feelings. Outrage, humiliation, anger, pride, humor—all conflicting and uncomfortable emotions—are allowed here. In filling the vacuum of reliable postcolonial history, Pablo Delano constructs multiple narratives that shift and repeat over time. Each recombination of archival material creates an alternative, revisionist reading of its content. Each installation presents a new postcolonial history: *refreshed*.

1 Ivette Romero, "Pablo Delano: A Brief Interview with *Repeating Islands*," *Repeating Islands*, February 9, 2017, https://repeatingislands.com/2017/02/09/pablo-delano-a-brief-interview-with-repeating-islands/.

2 See artist statement, previous installations, and interviews on *The Museum of the Old Colony* website, accessed August 10, 2022, www.museumoftheoldcolony.org/.

3 Pablo Delano, telephone interview by Laura Roulet, April 22, 2022.

4 Racism is a complicated issue in the New World. The binary race delineation and "one drop of blood" laws once prevalent in the United States, particularly in the American South, contrast with the racist practices common throughout the Spanish colonies. *Casta* paintings, primarily created in colonial Mexico, display a hierarchy based on racial mixing between White Europeans, Indigenous people, and Black Africans. The meaning and usage of such paintings are still being researched by scholars, but they clearly indicate a racial hierarchy based on skin tones, closer to what is called "colorism" in the U.S., where lighter skin conveys higher status.

5 See *Roundtable Discussion*, February 16, 2017, held for *The Museum of the Old Colony* exhibition at the King Juan Carlos I of Spain Center, New York University, accessed August 10, 2022, www.museumoftheoldcolony. org/media/video/. See also Arlene M. Dávila, *Sponsored Identities: Cultural Politics in Puerto Rico* (Philadelphia: Temple University Press, 1997).

6 Okwui Enwezor, *Archive Fever, Uses of the Document in Contemporary Art* (New York: International Center of Photography, 2008), 18.

7 Enwezor, *Archive Fever*, 21. This quote comes from Enwezor's discussion of Thomas Richards, *The Imperial Archive: Knowledge and the Fantasy of Empire* (London: Verso, 1993).

8 Claire Bishop, "Antagonism and Relational Aesthetics," *October* 110 (Fall 2004): 66.

9 Alice Procter, *The Whole Picture, The Colonial Story of the Art in Our Museums and Why We Need to Talk About It* (London: Octopus Publishing Group Ltd, 2020), 207.

10 Delano is also interested in the Caribbean traditions of Carnival, and the use of masquerade by formerly enslaved peoples to subvert the colonial hierarchy. See Pablo Delano, *In Trinidad: Photographs by Pablo Delano* (Kingston, Jamaica and Miami: Ian Randle Publishers, 2008).

11 Hew Locke, quoted on Tate Britain website, accessed August 10, 2022, https://www.tate.org.uk/whats-on/tate-britain/hew-locke.

12 See Antonio Martorell's remembrance of *White Christmas* (1980) in Laura Roulet, *Contemporary Puerto Rican Installation Art: The Guagua Aérea, the Trojan Horse and the Termite.* (San Juan: Editorial de la Universidad de Puerto Rico, 2000), 37. Description is from Antonio Martorell, interview by Laura Roulet, artist's studio, New York City, January 16, 1999, audio recording. Martorell quote is from Foreword, *Blanca Snow in Puerto Rico* (New York: Hostos Center for the Arts and Culture, 1997), unpaginated.

13 Details from Sofia Gallisá Muriente, telephone interview by Laura Roulet, April 19, 2022. A re-edited version of *Lluvia con Nieve* (2014) was exhibited at the 2019 Whitney Biennial: https://whitney.org/collection/works/61477.

14 This Associated Press photograph of Filiberto Ojeda Ríos shows his release from U.S. federal prison, where he had been held for three years on charges related to the robbery of $7 million from a Wells Fargo armored truck. The Puerto Rican Nationalist group *Los Macheteros* took responsibility for the September 1983 heist in Hartford, Connecticut, where, coincidentally, Pablo Delano has taught at Trinity College since 1996.

15 Pro-statehood politician Wanda Vázquez was reluctantly thrust into the role of governor (2019-2021) after the first and only removal of a Puerto Rican governor by popular uprising. PNP Governor Ricardo A. Rosselló was forced out of office in July 2019, the culmination of public outrage over the Commonwealth government's handling of the Hurricane Maria disaster.

Figure 8. Sofía Gallisá Muriente, *Lluvia con nieve (Rain with snow)*, 2014. Two-channel video installation with sound. Courtesy of the artist.

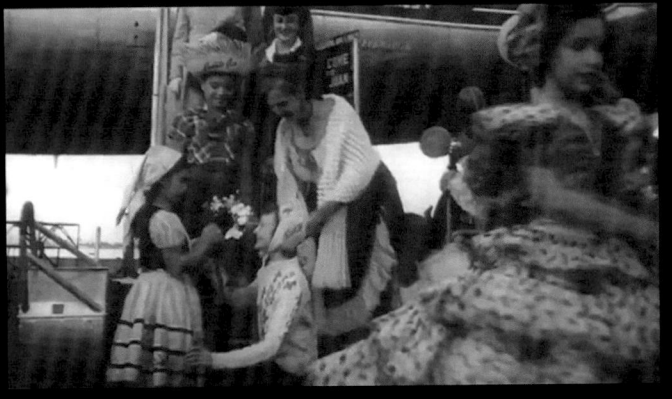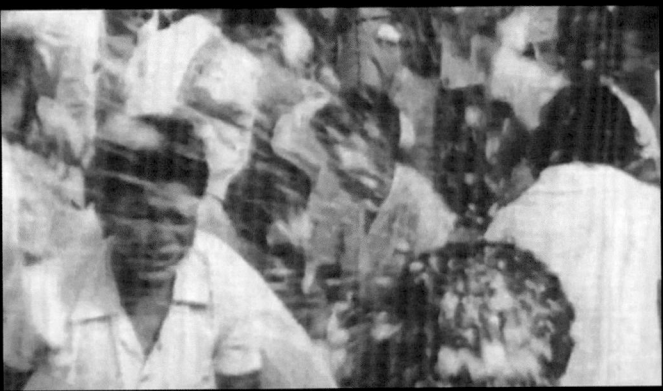

Figure 9. Antonio Martorell, *Old San Juan postcard.*
Acrylic on paper, 2015. From: *White Christmas Revisited*,
an installation of photographs, digital prints, new versions
of emblematic postcards of Puerto Rico, and a typical
piragua cart covered with snow. *Liga Estudiantes de Arte de
San Juan*, Puerto Rico. Courtesy of the artist.

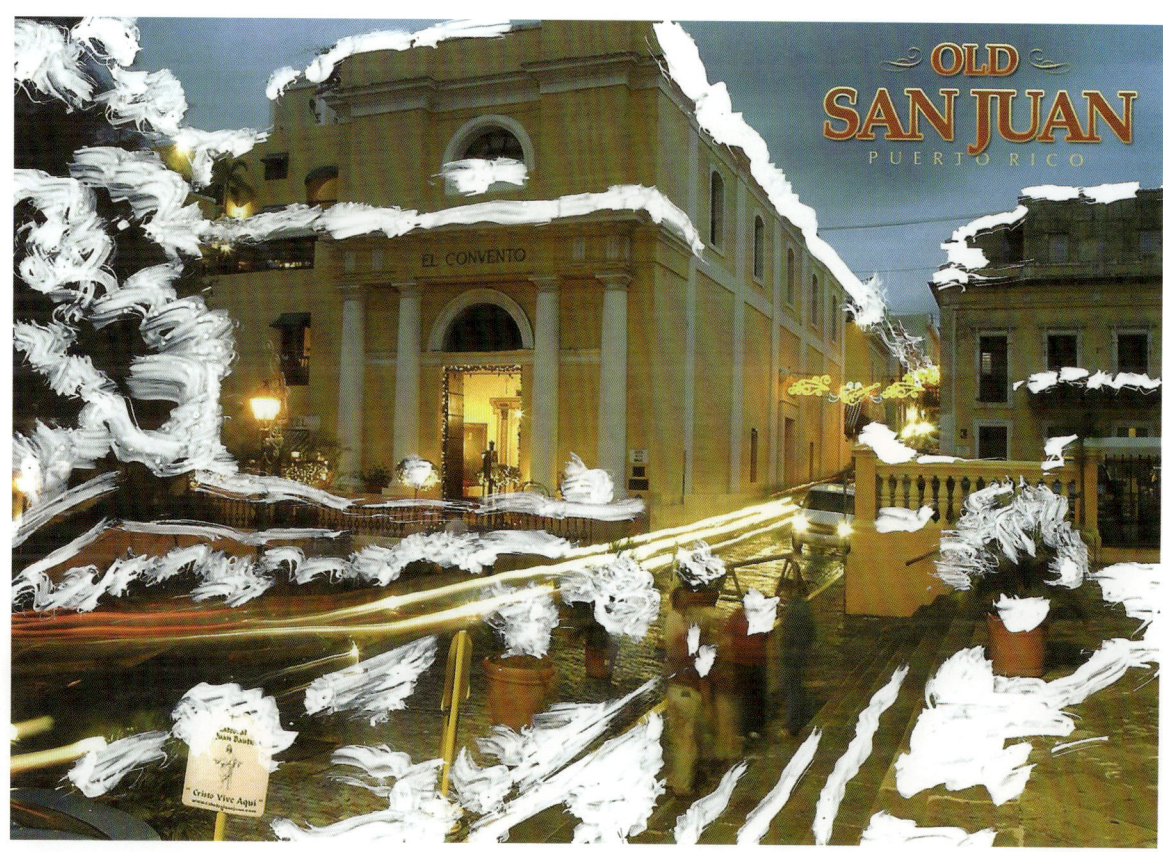

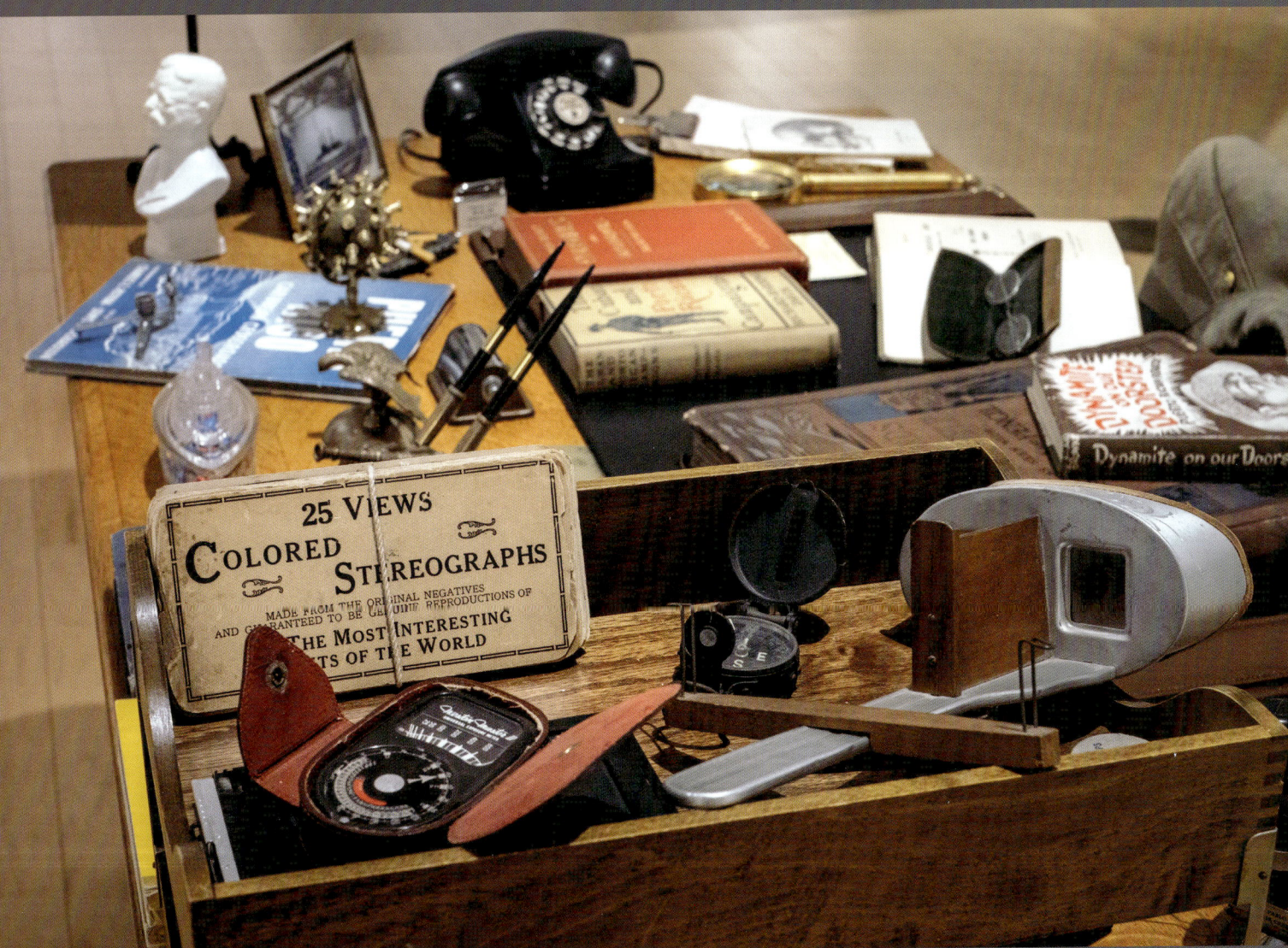

Challenging Curatorial Authority in Liminal Spaces:
The Museum Desk Piece as Orientation

When entering the *The Museum of the Old Colony: An Art Installation by Pablo Delano* in the Duke Gallery of Fine Art, visitors are confronted with "The Museum Desk," described simply in the exhibition checklist as a "Sculptural assemblage of found objects," collected between 2020 and 2022 (plate 3). Yet a close analysis of this object, which this essay aims to provide, reveals this standard wooden desk to be something much more meaningful. It is a dense material meditation on institutions, governments, and museums, and on the ways objects have historically served as symbols of national power, instruments of academic documentation, and forms of intercultural representations. The desk's installation site employs, in the words of Sandra Ruiz, "the aesthetic as intervention" and "shifts us beyond dread and despair, reorienting subjects often lost in history" in portraying a past and present Puerto Rico characterized by intersecting, looping processes of crisis, debt, and death.[1]

"The Museum Desk"—in presence, content, and arrangement—tangibly sketches a curation of positionality, that is, curation from a point of view, if only obliquely expressed; hence, Delano's disorienting counterpoint to the typically neutral voice of the museum curator. Despite its neat and ordered presentation, the desk offers no clear expression of ownership or explanatory narration to the visitor. With this, Delano acutely reimagines his audience and its potential engagement with his art installation as "an *exchange* of knowledge with publics, rather than *broadcasting* [knowledge] to them."[2] At first glance, the desk feels out of place in this art space, as it is glaringly emblematic of the mundane administrative infrastructure of museum work (from planning to installation) that produces exhibitions and exists outside of public view. After detailed inspection, the piece even takes on an almost voyeuristic aura, as one observes a pair of glasses in an open case, an army tan military jacket hung over the back of the desk chair, extinguished cigarette butts in an ash tray, and crushed-up papers in the adjacent trash bin. It is as if the visitor has walked in on an office scenario while the desk occupant is momentarily away.

The Museum of the Old Colony might thus be best defined as a liminal space that exists at the crossroads of the normative practices of museum display and transgressive artistic production. This liminality is echoed in the present-day political status of Puerto Rico and its connection to the United States, which one of Delano's small, framed narrative texts describes as "an old and unequal power relationship" whereby "Puerto Ricans may be U.S. citizens, but do not receive the full benefits conferred by citizenship." With the desk left unoccupied, there arises an active opening for a conversation between the artist and his audiences about this relationship, as well as about the creation and interpretation of Delano's installation.

In a literal sense, the desk presents thematic previews of object groupings that visitors will encounter in the varied material holdings exhibited throughout the installation—on the walls, in plexiglass cases, and on open tables. On one end of the desk is a group of objects symbolizing the American government and military, including a gold eagle statue; an Avon aftershave bottle in the form of a Theodore Roosevelt bust; a picture of the Battleship USS Iowa, which bombed San Juan, shown in a flag-decorated frame; and a pen holder in the shape of cannons. Such examples of nationalistic iconography recur across the installation, from the miniature U.S. and Puerto Rican flags atop a Libby's Corned Beef can to the American flags arranged like a wreath on the bicycle of its proud owner in a photograph on display.[3] On top of the desk organizer lies a group of tools including a compass and a stereoscope. These devices, associated with travel course-plotting and recording images, respectively, correspond to a nearby display case entitled "Tools of the Trade," comprising different types of measuring instruments and cameras. In the center of the desk, facing the chair, are assorted and mostly bright-colored publications: popular magazines such as *National Geographic*; "Reports of the Auditor of Porto Rico"; and Richard Harding Davis' *The Cuban and Porto Rican Campaigns* (1898), an illustrated textbook on the new colonial land possessions seized by the U.S. in the Spanish-American War (plates 14, 30).

The legacy of such public narrations of Puerto Rico in U.S. publications is amplified in the open table composed of U.S. schoolbooks about the island. Arranged around the table's borders, the books frame four rows of Kool-Aid tropical punch bottles, whose bright red and blue colors are matched by the similarly hued M&M's candies and plastic house pieces from a Monopoly board game (plates 61–62). Returning to the desk, one can then see it is not merely a dormant historical reference aimed at linear storytelling, but rather a prelude to Delano's exploratory installation approach, that is, an art practice based on acquiring and assembling materials in order to make historically grounded, politically assertive articulations.

Materializing Island Protest:
Artistic Practice and Curatorial Process as Sites of Pleasure

The desk and in its placement within *The Museum of the Old Colony* can be seen in relation to the genre of Caribbean life writing, as described by Jocelyn Fenton Stitt. Such writing enables us see how Delano's installation "stretch[es] our understanding of what archives might look like…memorializ[ing] lives and events not contained within traditional repositories" and "showing how the project of Caribbean memorialization tells multiple histories in a variety of forms."[4] Museum curation has historically valued traditional, "high art" materials, and the physical "presences" produced or left behind by dominant cultures. And it is from these kinds of objects that curators have written authoritative narratives. More inclusive interpretative strategies might instead emphasize, or at least be conscious of, the weight of the "absences" of various cultures—the material culture and the narratives of those whom the historical record has forgotten or those whom dominant cultural thinking (and academic research) has deemed unworthy of study.

Delano attends to such absences in his artistic practice. He does this, for example, with his scans, enlargements, and public display of troubling historical stereograph images, which are typically only encountered by researchers in archival settings, and with his acquisition of Puerto Rican tourist memorabilia (made by both the imperial power and its "territory").[5] Such objects, acquired through alternative commercial repositories like eBay, have not been traditionally valued or collected by museum institutions. "Tourism" has long been an area of absence in museum collecting because souvenir materials were viewed as popular, non-traditional objects not necessarily made by or for the culture or country in which the objects were sold. In *The Museum of the Old Colony*, Puerto Rican souvenirs take on charged meanings in Delano's tableaus, such as *"Platos y Cocos,"* an assemblage of souvenir plates and actual coconuts that are lined up in rows by type, reminiscent of the slogan on the *Farmacia Colonial* business card sitting on the museum desk that reads "For the Service You Deserve." The implication here is that Puerto Rico exists as a site for external consumption, a perception reinforced by the nearby series of color photographs featuring the tourist leisure landscapes of beaches and hotels that remain ubiquitous in countless Caribbean vacation advertisements and postcards (plate 15).

Regarding the museum desk as a generative, imagined space for decentering curatorial authority, Delano not only appropriates old and new "found" objects as would-be museum pieces, but he also uses the site of the museum itself (both physical and conceptual) for new purposes. On the surface, *The Museum of the Old Colony* has all the expected trappings of a historical exhibition in a mainstream institution: the groupings of images and objects according to observable themes, an introductory wall text authored by a curator, and a clearly presented object checklist. Yet upon closer inspection, visitors might question the presence of gold-tipped push pins attaching the unframed photographs to the gallery walls in lieu of hidden hardware typically used to hang works in standard frames. They might also question the presence of a circular stamp (bearing Delano's logo for his fictionalized museum) that appears on all the photographs and on the artist's gold-framed narrative texts. The museum desk announces these practices and asserts the artist's intentions in making such material choices, as it features aspects of his process: the push pins used for the photographs are pierced into a miniature globe and the artist's stamps are resting nearby in their holders (plates 14, 69).

Delano's symbolic appropriations of museum space used for critical commentary find their parallel beyond the site of the gallery, in Puerto Rican protest culture. In the fall of 2016, activists plastered the *Charging Bull* statue on Wall Street in New York City with black and white Puerto Rican flags in response to the U.S. federal establishment of an external fiscal board to oversee the island's debt repayments. In the summer of

2019, islandwide protests calling for the resignation of then-Governor Ricardo Rosselló saw Spanish colonial-era street names, such as *Calle Cristo*, be changed to "Street of the Corrupt." The red logo for "Decolonize This Place," an action-oriented collective, indexes the group's demands for greater transparency and care in art museums—in their community collaborations, exhibition designs, and funding practices. The migration of the sticker form of their logo, commonly used in tagging New York institutions, to the Puerto Rican capital of San Juan signifies a diasporic flow of decolonizing practices of questioning, interrupting, and transforming space through artistic production.

Through his nuanced material choices, Delano literally and figuratively breaks from the pristine ideal of the gallery space and the curator's traditional role as sole trustworthy arbiter and narrator of historical truths. His humorous, irreverent handling of selected stereograph reproductions and other photographic appropriations, along with his use of gold-colored push pins and gold-painted frames, highlights the artist's awareness of audience expectations of institutional *ways of knowing*. His installation suggests that visitors might too readily accept the flawed value systems of museums that judge the authenticity and value of the objects and voices they deem worthy of inclusion in exhibitions.

Delano makes apparent his artistic interventions in multiple ways. This appears in the temporal disjunction, for example, between the historical date and *The Museum of the Old Colony* artwork date of the source material listed on the exhibition checklist, in the artist's stamping of the appropriated historical photographs, and in the latter's altered scale. It is also visible in his use of mid-20th-century plastic resin wall decor plaques to activate the different installation sections, as the plaques share little historical or geographic context with the photographs or objects assembled in each section. These seemingly incongruous decor plaques echo the U.S. military symbols on the desk and their cheap shiny materials resonate with the gold-colored curatorial devices used throughout the installation— the push pins and small frames mentioned above. In his installation, Delano does not shy away from showcasing "process," not only his own process but also the process of others, including that of earlier historical actors who created, altered, and manipulated photographs and objects to construct the popular production of Puerto Rico in the American imaginary. This is exemplified by the photographs that show their original crop marks and notes with printing instructions (plates 40, 60).[6]

The institutional collection and documentation of ethnographic material culture have traditionally entailed the acquisition of exemplary "types" or diagnostic specimens that, according to Hannah Turner, "were found in the field" and deemed "useful for research"— around which arose networks of museum "administrative and bureaucratic structures" that "would enable and solidify these interpretations" centered in "presumed European primacy and progress."[7] Museum curation has thus never been neutral or objective in its cultural practices despite claims to the contrary—claims addressed in *The Museum of the*

Old Colony. The cover of a stereograph collection on the museum desk, for example, reads: "Made From The Original Negatives And Guaranteed To Be Genuine Reproductions Of The Most Interesting Sights Of The World." The ethnographic "type" concept is best represented in the installation by the plexiglass case of Old Colony bottles and cans lined up in a timeline dated 1940s to 2017. This tableau has featured in multiple iterations of Delano's installation, which he named after the popular soft drink shown in the case (plate 1).

Another reference to the way museums have displayed ethnographic material culture is found in the plexiglass case tableau entitled "Artifacts of the Aborigines," which confronts the visitor with a dizzying display of popular, stereotypical representations of Puerto Rican (and U.S.) indigeneity (plates 17, 44). In addition to Native American figures from the continental U.S. shown in sculptural form, on a *botánica* candle, and on a *Cerveza* India beer can, this case includes figures of a *Taíno* Indian and a Spanish conquistador in a mythic harmonious encounter on a Budweiser beer mug from Puerto Rico. In front of this mug and placed unceremoniously in one corner of the case is an ancient ceramic sherd, specifically a diagnostic decorated portion of a sherd, resting on sand in a glass specimen container topped with petroglyph symbols.[8] Conflating aspects of real and imagined Indians, this tableau enmeshes past and present materialities in a complex celebration of messy object legacies. Such objects encapsulate issues of Puerto Rican colonial domination by both the Spanish and American empires, the visitor's acknowledgment of which can be a starting point for visualizing more egalitarian futures. Marisol LeBrón has noted that in "a society based on racial, sexual, and gendered dominance structured through colonial capitalism, the creation of spaces where oppressed populations can *live* and experience joy is critical for actualizing a society where all Puerto Ricans are valued in their difference."[9]

The Storytelling Possibilities of Counter-Archives: New Orientations and Puerto Rican Futures

Following Delano's curatorial path in *The Museum of the Old Colony*, visitors end where they began—at a desk that has framed and guided a critical look back at a difficult history and aside at an ever-complex present. The installation therein arguably participates in "One of the agendas of Caribbean studies…to create archives—or, more accurately, counter-archives"—that offer "new possibilities, possibilities for seeing connections previously unexamined and for reordering our ontological taken-for-granteds."[10] The material selections and groupings throughout Delano's art installation demonstrate the many ways in which asymmetrical logics and dynamics between the U.S. and the Commonwealth of Puerto Rico actively remain structured, taught, codified, and represented as natural and fixed across related yet distinct objects, actors, landscapes, and temporalities. For instance, the plexiglass case tableau labelled "Better Living Through Better Banking," with its colorful and playful pop-culture objects like piggy banks, domino game pieces, and a toy Uncle Sam cash register slyly decorated with a Bitcoin logo, addresses these unequal dynamics between the U.S. and Puerto Rico. Such relations are also apparent in related cartoons and photographs showing belittling depictions of Puerto Ricans as perpetually needy colonial subjects seeking handouts from American business or government (plates 16, 46).[11] The entire banking and adjacent tourism sections of the installation reference the present-day economic landscape and the current contention in Puerto Rico over cryptocurrency traders and real estate investors. Largely from the U.S., and often hostile to the concerns of local communities, they have been buying up properties on the island as privileged tax havens of economic opportunity.[12]

The museum desk, with its multilayered focus on material manifestations of power and inequality, speaks to the complicated and continually unfolding trajectory of Puerto Rico's relationship with the U.S. Despite the matter-of-fact presentation of objects on the desk, Delano's presentation is anything but straightforward, as he has embedded it with irony and critique rather than commemoration. The desk thus offers visitors an analytical lens through which to navigate the whole installation, offering a thematic series of diverse material engagements in which artistic presentation supplants and subverts expectations of traditional curatorial authority. Objects, individually and collectively, emerge as access points for visitors and serve to activate the gallery as a transformative site for Delano's alternative history telling. The installation is therefore as unsettling as it is informative. It refuses tidy endings, it favors asking questions over providing answers; and it forces viewer confrontation of stark realities over passive acceptance of simplistic stereotypes.

Ultimately, Delano may be imploring his audiences to consider under what conditions new, life-affirming, intersectional, post-Hurricane Maria Puerto Rican "futures" might be possible. Such conditions would allow for visions of the island beyond the violent images, infantilizing tropes, and limited "types." They would make possible more expansive narratives that value Puerto Rican authorship and lived experience over standard mainland documentations and conventional arguments grounded in ideas of American exceptionalism. They would move past a careless, dangerous attitude that sees Puerto Rico merely in terms of what it offers tropical beach-seeking vacationers, and on to consideration of the well-being and survival of Puerto Rican people. This requires an empathetic appreciation of the contemporary circumstances in which Puerto Rico exists—circumstances that are the legacy of the historical conditions referenced in the cultural appropriations indexed, arranged, and displayed in *The Museum of the Old Colony*. According to Mimi Sheller, "[t]he coloniality of climate calls for attention to repair, care, and reparations. We need to ask: Who is responsible, who is harmed, and who should be accountable?"[13] With its small moments of defiant gazes and larger moments of revolutionary action by historical actors,[14] Pablo Delano's *The Museum of the Old Colony* stands not as a static or complete requiem but rather as a shifting, emergent call to action for more just "futures."

1 Sandra Ruiz, *Ricanness: Enduring Time in Anticolonial Performance* (New York: New York University Press, 2019), 170.

2 Laura Raicovich, *Culture Strike: Art and Museums in an Age of Protest* (London and New York: Verso, 2021), 167.

3 See, for example, "Real Yankee Doodle Dandy, Mayagüez, Puerto Rico." Official Puerto Rico Government Photo, via Hamilton Wright Org., Inc., New York, April 1948 (Artwork date: 2019).

4 Jocelyn Fenton Stitt, *Dreams of Archives Unfolded: Absence and Caribbean Life Writing* (New Brunswick: Rutgers University Press, 2021), 117, 140.

5 See, for example, the stereograph "Porto Rican Boys in their Sunday Dress, Near Aibonita [sic]." Strohmeyer & Wyman, Underwood & Underwood Publishers, New York, 1900 (Artwork date: 2019) and the tourist memorabilia "Souvenir handkerchief from Puerto Rico." Found vintage souvenir, mid-20th century (Artwork date: 2019).

6 See, for example, "Cash on the line is acknowledged by a teller in the mobile bank. The depositor is Señora Teresa González Rivera whose 100-year-old mother is also one of the banking unit's customers." International News Photos, 1952 (Artwork date: 2021) and "Tropical Contrast, Punta Salinas, Puerto Rico." ACME Photo, January 12, 1940 (Artwork date: 2019).

7 Hannah Turner, *Cataloguing Culture: Legacies of Colonialism in Museum Documentation* (Vancouver and Toronto: University of British Columbia Press, 2020), 29.

8 This *Taino* sherd was among the items Pablo Delano found in his parents' collections after his father died in 1997.

9 Marisol LeBrón, *Against Muerto Rico: Lessons from the Verano Boricua/Contra Muerto Rico: lecciones del Verano Boricua*, transl. Beatriz Llenin Figueroa (Cabo Rojo: Editora Educación Emergente, 2021), 45.

10 Deborah A. Thomas, "Caribbean Studies, Archive Building, and the Problem of Violence," *Small Axe* 17, no. 2 (41) (July 2013): 27.

11 See, for example, "The Closed Door." *Life* 35, no. 909, April 12, 1900 (Artwork date: 2020) and "Federal Aid is a Staple." Photograph by Gary Williams, Associated Press Newsfeatures Photo, July 22, 1980 (Artwork date: 2019).

12 Pushing up home prices and displacing local residents, such crypto activity has met with resistance, as Puerto Rican activists have called out the inequitable wealth distribution on the cash-strapped island, which has only recently exited most of its bankruptcy-like proceeding with regard to the restructuring of massive public debt.

13 Mimi Sheller, *Island Futures: Caribbean Survival in the Anthropocene* (Durham and London: Duke University Press, 2020), 166.

14 See "Porto Rican Laundries." Photograph by Margherita Arlina Hamm, *Neely's Panorama of Our New Possessions*, F. Tennyson Neely Publisher, New York & London, 1898 (Artwork date: 2019) and "Lolita Lebrón Arrested." Associated Press Photo, March 1, 1954 (Artwork date: 2019).

Plate 15. Installation view. *Platos y Cocos* (foreground) and
tourism and coconut-related photographs, objects, and
captions. *The Museum of the Old Colony*, Duke Hall Gallery
of Fine Art, 2022. Checklist Nos. 63–79.

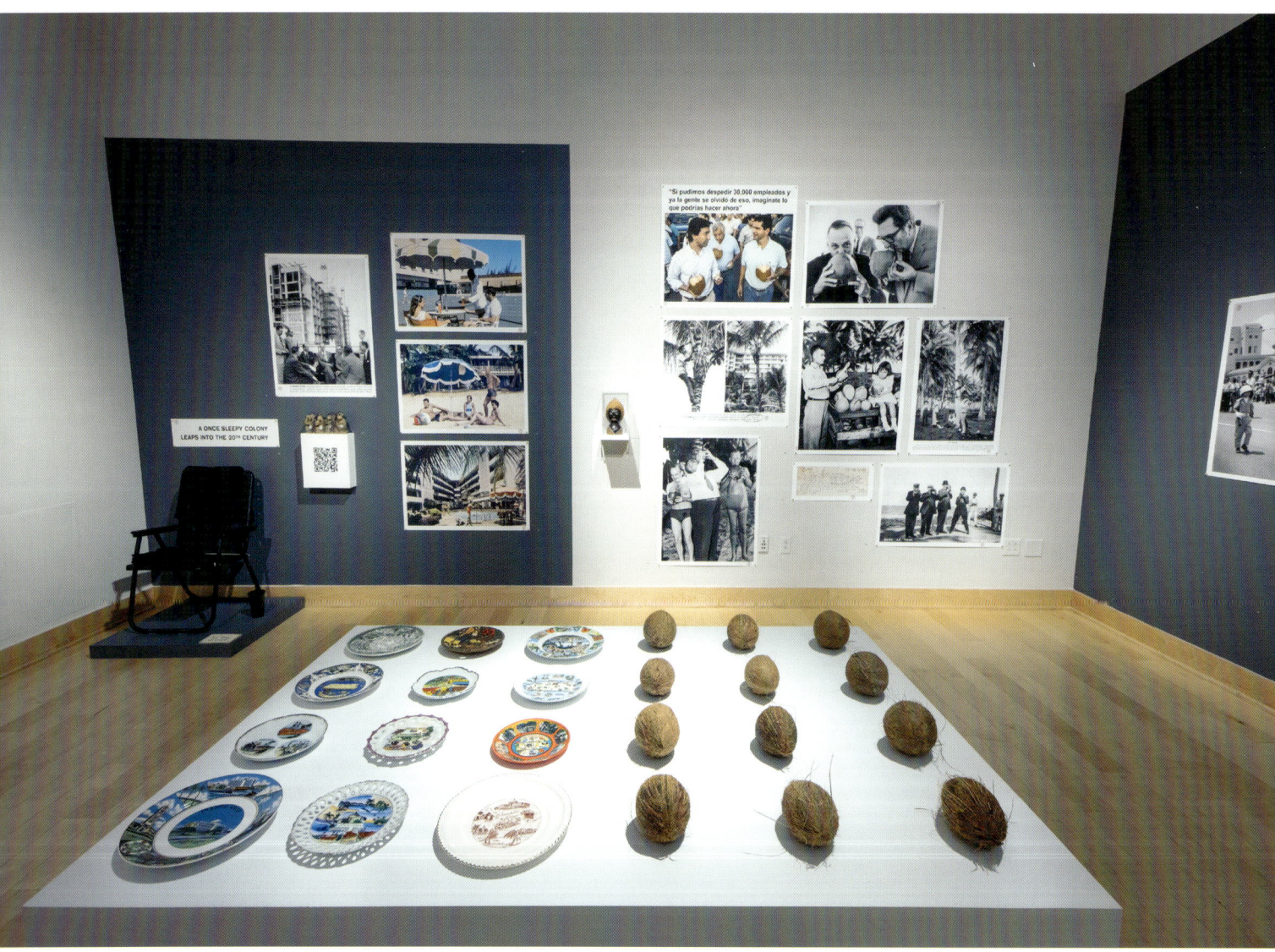

Plate 16. Installation view. *Better Living Through Better Banking*. Assemblage of found objects | 2021. *The Museum of the Old Colony*, Duke Hall Gallery of Fine Art, 2022. Checklist No. 62.

Plate 17. Installation view. *Artifacts of the Aborigines* (detail). *The Museum of the Old Colony*, Duke Hall Gallery of Fine Art, 2022. Checklist No. 34.

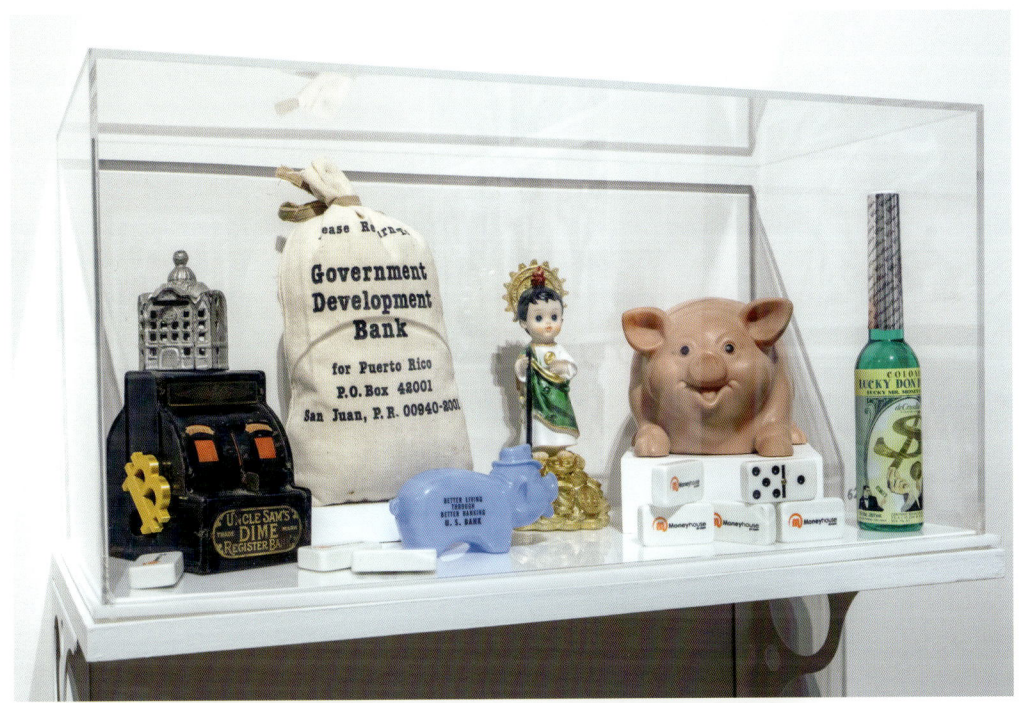

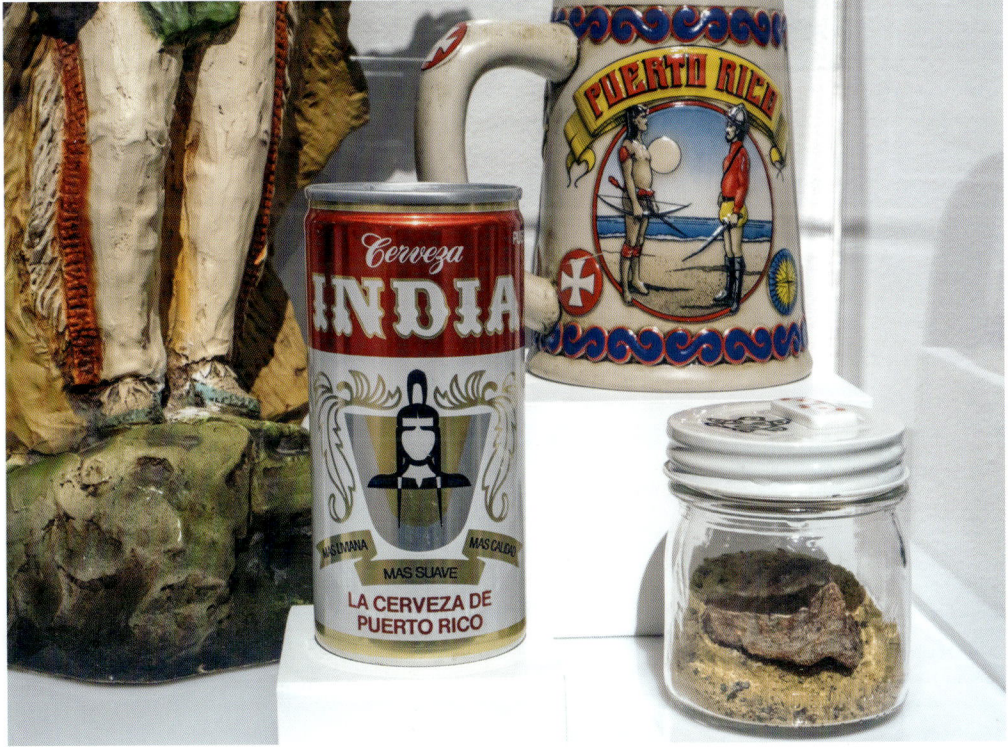

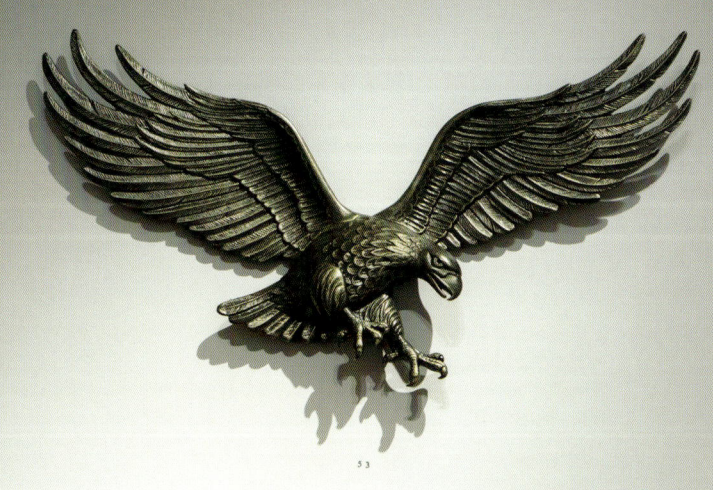

53

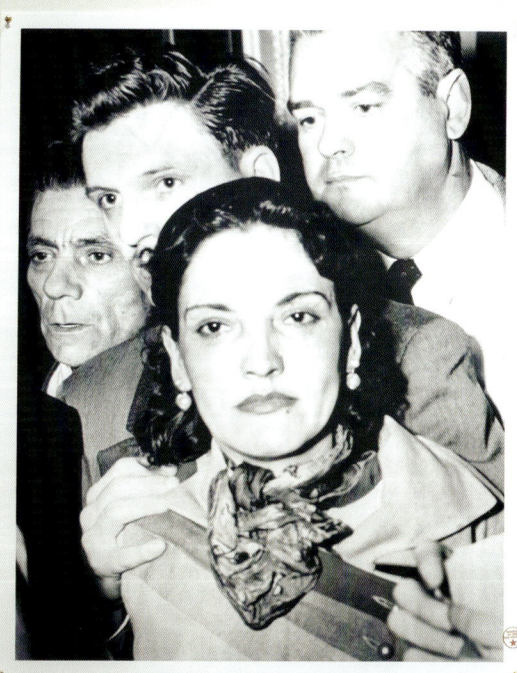

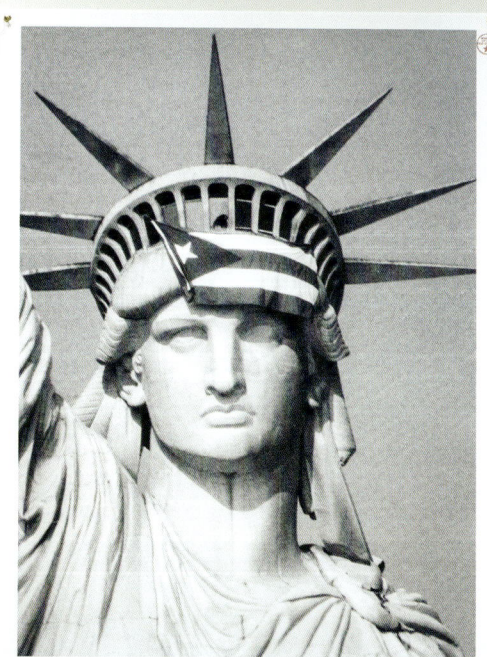

A Tale of Two Icons

In the 1940s, two logos were circulating in the political and commercial arenas of pre-Commonwealth Puerto Rico. Like twins separated at birth, these trademarks were similar in design, but stood for different ideas of nationhood. On the labels of Old Colony soda, licensed and bottled in Mayagüez by the Valdés family, the profile of an American Revolutionary War-era figure sporting a red tricorn hat evoked a forward-looking George Washington. Similarly, the bright red emblem on the rally flags and voter ballots of the *Partido Popular Democrático* (Popular Democratic Party or PPD), with the silhouette of a *jíbaro* (landless rural worker) wearing the *pava* (straw hat) of a hard sugar harvest, symbolized the core electoral franchise of Luis Muñoz Marín, who, as PPD founder in 1938, would dominate Puerto Rican politics for decades to come (figures 10–11).[1]

The PPD was founded in response to a governmental crisis and to the great social unrest and rampant poverty of the 1930s. After the United States took over Puerto Rico in the Spanish-American War of 1898, American sugar companies began to shift the Puerto Rican economy from one based largely on coffee to one based on sugar, forcing landless farmers to adjust to the hardships endemic to cutting cane. In an attempt to quell potential rebellion and increasing discontent with American colonial rule, the U.S. Congress passed the Jones Act in 1917.[2] The act gave islanders U.S. citizenship and a bicameral legislature but left unchanged Puerto Rico's status as a territorial possession without voting representation in Washington, D.C. Labor, liberal, and pro-statehood Puerto Rican statesmen, who were aligned with mainland interests, built odd alliances to appease all-powerful colonial governors on the island. In 1934, organized cane workers sided instead with the anti-American Nationalist Party president, Pedro Albizu Campos, to stage massive strikes and defy extractive imperialism. U.S.-appointed Governor Blanton C. Winship used police state tactics to harshly suppress the Nationalists. This climaxed in the 1936 federal sentencing of the party's leadership for seditious conspiracy and in the 1937 police killing of 19 unarmed Nationalists in a peaceful civilian march, known as the Ponce Massacre.

As a well-connected freshman senator for the Liberal Party in 1932, Muñoz had joined forces with New Deal strategists in the U.S. to extend to Puerto Rico federal plans for subsidizing farm workers and reining in absentee sugar corporations. Expelled from the Liberal Party, Muñoz founded the PPD with like-minded independence supporters who, unlike Albizu, were careful not to antagonize the U.S. In 1940 the party gathered enough votes among the landless peasantry and other groups to make Muñoz president of the Senate. The PPD passed legislation that instituted land reform, a government bank and planning board, and expanded worker rights. It sought to undo sugar company dominance by launching in 1947 an industrial development program based on export manufacturing. Named "Operation Bootstrap," it would attract big-name corporations with the promise of tax havens, aggressively modernize the island's public services, and spawn a professional middle class.

The PPD's success laid the groundwork for Muñoz to become the first elected governor in 1948 (he had already abandoned independence as a viable option for Puerto Rico and sought a "third way" between independence and annexation to the U.S. as a state). That same year, after Albizu's release from prison and return to Puerto Rico, and in response to several Nationalist conflicts, the Puerto Rican legislature enacted the so-called "Gag Law," modeled after the U.S. Smith Act, which "prohibited the expression of ideas and acts against the U.S. government and in favor of Puerto Rico's independence."[3] By July 25, 1952, Governor Muñoz signed the proclamation by which the Puerto Rican Constitution came into effect, inaugurating the U.S. Commonwealth of Puerto Rico (*Estado Libre Asociado* or ELA).[4] This new "political status" avowedly recast the U.S.-Puerto Rico territorial relation, establishing a "decolonizing" formula for "prosperity under two flags." Muñoz would win three more elections and serve as governor through January 1965, all under the banner of the *jíbaro-with-pava* icon.

Thanks to the incentives facilitated by Operation Bootstrap, the Valdés company would expand and remain the most prosperous brewery and bottler in Puerto Rico.[5] Acquiescence to the PPD model of "self-perpetuating hyper-dependence" on the U.S. probably led the family to keep the colonial patriot on its bottles as a pro-U.S. symbol that could consort well with the omnipresent *jíbaro-with-pava*.[6] As an artificially flavored sugary drink, Old Colony could also be read as a metaphor for the PPD vision, offering instant gratification but long-term health consequences to those who consumed it. The logos for both—as the head and tail of Puerto Rico's newly minted Commonwealth status—can be seen to represent what historians César J. Ayala and Rafael Bernabe have called the PPD's "Janus-faced vehicle for constructing Puerto Rico as both distinct from and subordinate to the United States."[7] Together, they anticipate the profile of Boricua Broadway wunderkind Lin Manuel Miranda—as a *jíbaro* Hamilton from rural Vega Alta, his family's native town.

Principles of Colonial Iconology

The Museum of the Old Colony: An Art Installation by Pablo Delano at James Madison University's Duke Gallery of Fine Art is both an exposé and an exploration of how icons such as the Old Colony patriot and the PPD *jíbaro* have been complicit in camouflaging and perpetuating U.S. colonialism in Puerto Rico. *The Museum of the Old Colony* is an installation of appropriated images—all marked with Delano's ironic curatorial stamp—which the artist has been collecting since the late 1990s. Delano was first inspired by scholarly studies of the triumphal, exhortatory media culture behind the U.S. imperial moment, published around the time of the 1898 centennial commemorations.[8] Still, as a project following a conceptual path charted by artist Marcel Duchamp and with inspiration from political philosopher Frantz Fanon, it did not come together until 2016.

At that time, after two decades of junk bond issuance to cover bloated state spending while corporate tax exemptions meant to revive the Commonwealth's industrial program

Figure 10. *Old Colony Soda*. Found object: Old Colony soda bottle, Mayagüez, Puerto Rico, circa 1940s | 2018. *The Museum of the Old Colony.*

Figure 11. *Vergüenza Contra Dinero*. Poster for *Partido Popular Democrático/*Popular Democratic Party, circa 1940s. Courtesy of *Fundación Luis Muñoz Marin*, San Juan, Puerto Rico.

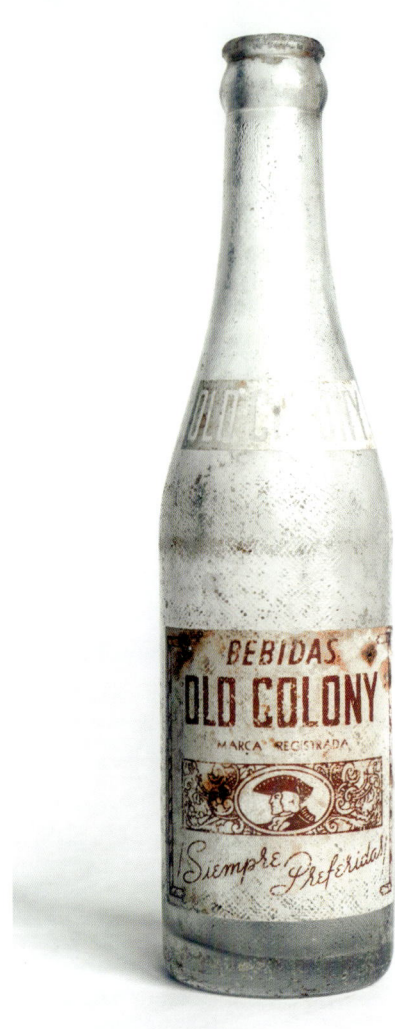

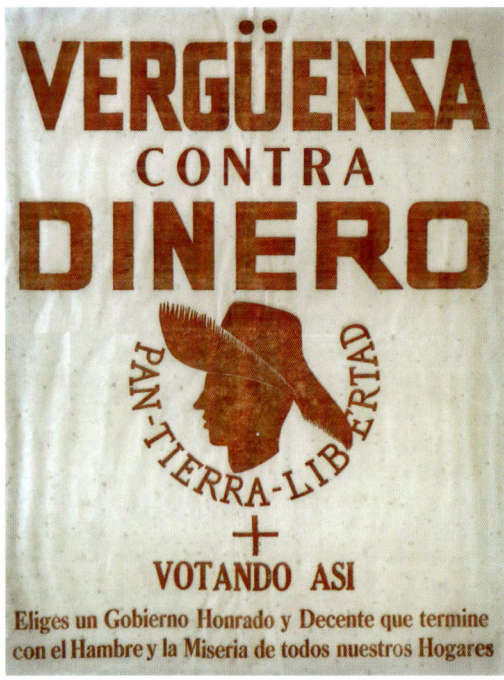

were phased out, PPD Governor Alejandro García Padilla declared unpayable a fiscal debt of $72 billion. In response, the U.S. Congress passed the Puerto Rico Oversight, Management, and Economic Stability Act (PROMESA), appointing a fiscal board that superseded local governance on the island, as it imposed extreme austerity measures in restructuring the debt. PROMESA dispelled any pretense of post-1952 constitutional self-determination in Puerto Rico, triggering massive discontent islandwide. *The Museum of the Old Colony* can thus be seen as Delano's personal vision of the bankruptcy of the Commonwealth's claims of sovereignty, democracy, and solvency under the "benevolent" protection of the U.S. In the installation, we witness the dissipation of the PPD legacy as a 70-year-old procession of colonial simulacra.

In 2017, the federal mismanagement of the enormous suffering caused by hurricanes Irma and Maria in Puerto Rico showed how U.S. dominance has condemned the Commonwealth to seemingly endless imperial modes of disaster extractions, racial stereotyping, and dehumanization. Delano said in 2017: "I was struck by how similar the 1899 pictures [of the devastation from Hurricane San Ciríaco] looked to the ones we're seeing from Hurricane Maria.... It was difficult to look at because to me it suggested visually maybe we were back where we started."[9] By matching and contrasting 1898-era images with more contemporary ones, Delano's installation reveals how—like the stylish redesigns of Old Colony bottles and cans across time—the empire carefully upgrades its inventory of weaponized clichés. The more times change, the better U.S. colonialism deploys new visual resources to intensify its strategies of dispossession.

From my perspective, *The Museum of the Old Colony's* genius lies in the way it shows how seven decades of legal, rhetorical, and media mystifications of ELA—as "the best of two worlds," "a compact among equals," and "a showcase of democracy"—can be visualized as a replay of the pre-Commonwealth years. To move from the first part of the installation, which focuses on U.S. plans for harnessing the resources of its new "possession," to the second part, which deals with the Commonwealth servility to U.S. military, financial, and civic interests, is to move through a time-warped house of mirrors. Delano opens with an image of "The Star Spangled Banner" from a children's book of 1900 with propagandistic content; the flag is described as "Puerto Rico's Flag," thus expressing the arrogance of the age. In a later section, the flag motif reappears, refracted in a wall of photographs of political and civilian personalities from *independentistas* to *populares* to *estadistas* who wave flags in a kaleidoscope of cacophonous patriotism (plate 19).

Stereograph images from 1898 to 1900 of Puerto Rican "washerwomen" in Ponce are echoed in a later press photograph of 1948 showing blue-collar women in a school for training maids for U.S. jobs and in images of women deluded by the beauty industry during the Commonwealth's halcyon years (plates 61, 65). The colonial officer's desk with its colorful array of Spanish-American War-era books and mementos—a "Remember the Maine" glass candy dish, a mini-bust of Theodore Roosevelt, and a cracking colonial pith helmet—finds parallels on a table where U.S. books on Puerto Rico's charms and ills are swarmed by an army of plastic toy soldiers and in nearby images of military parades for July 4th or July 25th (Commonwealth Day) commemorations and surveillance activities from the World War II and Cold War years (plates 51–53).

Reversing the Optics of Imperial Entitlement

Maurice Berger likens Delano's installation to those of Fred Wilson, Mark Dion, and Pepón Osorio.[10] Berger foregrounds Delano's affinity to Wilson since both enjoy juxtaposing hegemonic artworks to bitingly reveal the white supremacy lurking behind purportedly disinterested museum collecting and exhibition practices. For his celebrated *Mining the Museum* installation, Wilson relied on the Maryland Historical Society's reservoir of respectable artifacts.[11] For his part, Delano acts more like an archeologist of the digital age, creating his critique with "lowbrow" objects acquired via eBay and other sources, from a made-in-China "Patriot Economy Eraser" with the Puerto Rican flag to the latest Old Colony aluminum cans.

As a teenager and with the advice of his father Jack Delano (a renowned documentary photographer of the New Deal era), Pablo Delano started taking professional pictures for a book on devotional objects by Teodoro Vidal (Puerto Rico's most influential collector of folkloric art).[12] The younger Delano claims this made him "appreciate the power of objects."[13] In contrast to Vidal's quest for one-of-a-kind votive offerings, Delano rummages the internet seeking Puerto Rican-related kitsch that is mass produced for the racist delectation of the U.S. imperial gaze. Aunt Jemima-inspired figurines re-merchandised as Puerto Rican souvenirs show how cartoonish blackface representations of Afro-Puerto Rican women (as in *Café Yaucono's "Mamá Inés"* promotional mascot) are aligned with media denigrations of African American bodies from the post-U.S. Reconstruction era. Cutesy dolls and Halloween costumes of *jíbaros* spoof the self-congratulatory middle-class complacency of the beneficiaries of Commonwealth progress (plates 39–40, 58–59). An assemblage of products branded with stock images of North American Indians shows how symbols that trivialize the genocide of Indigenous peoples have gradually displaced the memory of the native *Taíno* inhabitants in Puerto Rico's historical imagination.[14]

These products shine with the glint of colonial reductionism. Rather than humbly revere the figures they depict, as is the case with Vidal's hand-carved *ex-votos* and *santos*, they bastardize and demean them. In short, Delano curates—and mordantly critiques—images and objects that impudently debase Puerto Rican dignity. Following W.J.T. Mitchell, we could say that Delano appropriates such objects as "'hypericons,' figures of figuration, pictures that reflect on the nature of images," in a critical iconology that "restores the provocative, dialogic power of these dead images."[15] In the spirit of Jean Baudrillard, Delano also reveals this material culture as grotesque, hyper-real simulacra—invasive modes of representation that displace and annihilate all that they signify as they follow the most "murderous" rules of market exchange.[16]

In his impishly witty juxtapositions, Delano follows a montage syntax that parodies ethnographic and devotional visualities. In the first part of the exhibition, groupings of photographs from the early years of U.S. occupation are completed by an assemblage of objects that embody the material implications of the colonial and sociracial dynamics pinned on the wall. A box of Nabisco National Sodas topped with a Libby's Corned Beef can with miniature U.S. and Puerto Rican flags specifically mocks the adjacent photograph of the luxurious dinner table of a White, Puerto Rican, ruling class family and a political cartoon boasting post-1898 U.S. munificence in the Caribbean and the Pacific (plate 38). In the second part of the exhibition, a display of 12 actual coconuts, plus one refashioned as a degrading Puerto-Rican Black mammy souvenir, spoofs a wall of photographs showing several generations of politicians, tourists, and children posing while drinking from coconuts. Nearby, a surprising ensemble of a pitch-black beach chair, towel, and flip flops, called "An Orgy of Color," counters the more expected colorful tourist brochure-type photographs of vacationers enjoying the waterfront amenities of luxury hotels built during the post-World War II economic upturn (plates 49–50).

Through all this, Delano unravels the "proprietary effect" crystalized by the optical apparatus of the stereoscope, an example of which sits on the colonial officer's desk. The artist's ensembles are hyperbolic reversals of the duplicitous visual rhetoric of turn-of-the-20th-century U.S. stereographs of Puerto Ricans, many of which feature racialized, semi-naked children who are used to signify the territory's destitution and incapacity for self-rule. According to Jorge Luis Crespo-Armáiz, the stereoscopic "double viewing" of such pictures—always captioned with paternalistic messages about the "new possession"—was meant to generate a three-dimensional, seemingly tactile, reassuring chimera of proprietary realism—of *being-there-in-our-possession* and of *our-possession-being-here-at-hand*—for the privileged mainland spectator.[17] To call out the colonial machinations behind such tricks of spatial illusionism, Delano installs tourist trinkets, toys, uniforms, sugary beverages, and tacky home ornaments as if they were hilarious stereoscopic projections of the U.S. territorial hegemony pictured on the walls. *The Museum of the Old Colony* thus exposes and deconstructs the optics of U.S. imperial entitlement.

Refacing Lady Liberty

Delano's sardonic assemblages of colonial hypericons could be seen in contrast to his father's celebrated photography, especially to Jack Delano's *Puerto Rico mio: Four Decades of Change* (1990), also based on photographic juxtapositions. In many ways, *The Museum of the Old Colony* is a profound revision of *Puerto Rico mio*. With his wife Irene as his research and design collaborator, Jack Delano colligated photographs taken in the 1940s for the U.S. and Puerto Rican governments with ones taken decades later, so as "to compare with what we had seen forty years before."[18] In the late 1970s and early '80s, the Delano team poured over the earlier photographs of struggling sugar, tobacco, dock, and factory workers with the aim to revisit people, sites, and themes. Then they documented better-nourished workers next to cutting-edge mechanical equipment, shoppers in megamalls and fast-food joints, and college-educated professionals in business offices and labs. By carefully pairing before-and-after photographs, the Delanos remarked on the persistent qualities of Puerto Rican people—what anthropologist Sidney Mintz praised as "the intense, enduring nobility and serenity of a people triumphantly untransformed...."[19] At the same time, the project confirmed the spectacular industrial progress and higher standards of living achieved under the Commonwealth.[20] Before the work was complete, Muñoz passed away, which led the Delanos, who had befriended the PPD politician in the 1940s and helped launch his government's ground-breaking Division of Community Education (DIVEDCO), to incorporate into the book pictures of grieving mourners at Muñoz's apotheotic funeral.

Pablo Delano's caustic vision of how official, commercial, and press photography has colluded to keep the island subservient qualifies Jack Delano's more hopeful belief in the reformist potential of documentary photography under the PPD government.[21] The younger Delano's work suggests that such visual media may in fact have served to maintain Puerto Rico *suyo* (theirs, the empire's possession) rather than *mío* (mine, ours, belonging to a native community). We can further measure the wide distance between Pablo and Jack Delano's visualities in the section of the installation showing the Nationalist insurrections of the 1950s. Viewing the Commonwealth as a trap for Puerto Rican sovereignty, Albizu and his followers planned for armed insurgencies. On October 30, 1950, Nationalists attacked police stations in several cities and towns and the governor's mansion to "cause a political crisis" and denounce Public Law 600 as "a sham," an illegitimate tool for decolonialization. Likely alerted by spies, local police and the Puerto Rican National Guard, backed by the U.S. Air Force, quickly suppressed the rebellion.[22]

In his installation, Delano features press images of armed officers rounding up Nationalist suspects—images that highlight the sizable role women played in the plots. One woman stands out among them all: Lolita Lebrón, a militant in New York's branch of the Nationalist Party, who organized an armed attack in Washington, D.C. to spotlight international attention on Puerto Rico at a time when decolonization processes were sweeping the globe. On March 1st, 1954, Lebrón led three men to the visitor's gallery in the U.S. Capitol, from which they opened gunfire onto the House floor while Lebrón waved the Puerto Rican flag shouting "*¡Viva Puerto Rico libre!*" Five congressmen were wounded and the attack made headlines in world media.[23] Lebrón's alluring poise, impeccable attire, unrepentant position, and clear-minded eloquence earned her great iconic stature as a symbol of resistance to her supporters but also as a villain—as *the terrorist who wore lipstick*—to her critics.[24]

It is thus not surprising that the wall in *The Museum of the Old Colony* dedicated to Nationalist activities focuses on the polarizing figure of Lebrón (plate 18). As with the pairings in *Puerto Rico mío*, two pictures taken decades apart are aligned according to a visual resemblance that invites deep historical connections. Delano matches the famous news photograph of Lebrón's arrest in 1954 with an aerial photograph from October 25, 1977 of another icon of freedom, the Statue of Liberty, which strangely appears with a gigantic Puerto Rican flag across its crown. This United Press International picture was taken at the time of another daring *independentista* action, when some 30 members of the Committee to Free the Five Puerto Rican Nationalists took the monument hostage for eight hours, again, to command international attention for Puerto Rican independence.[25] Citing "humanitarian considerations," President Jimmy Carter commuted the sentences of Lebrón and her co-assailants in 1979.

After 1954, Lebrón became a national Puerto Rican symbol as complex and far-reaching as Albizu and Muñoz. The strong-willed daughter of a coffee plantation foreman from Lares, a town legendary for a failed revolt against Spanish colonial rule in 1868, she migrated in the 1940s to New York City, where she found backbreaking work as a seamstress. Seeing how Puerto Ricans were abused in sweatshops reinforced her nationalistic views and led her to take Albizu's creed to heart and join his movement.[26] Sandra Ruiz has described Lebrón's behavior during the 1954 attack as a "Rican" performance of womanly sacrifice, combining selflessness and candor, couture and hauteur. Unlike her companions, she shot at the ceiling, declaring: "I didn't come here to kill, I came to die," with moral clarity and in style.[27] While in prison, Lebrón found strength in a brand of rapt Catholic piety and Marian mysticism common among Nationalists, which she expressed in a book of poems.[28] After her release, she adopted more pacifist tactics in her tireless fight for independence, later joining the civil disobedience protests of U.S. Navy bombing exercises in Vieques. As mystic "mother-of-the-nation" and stalwart of female power, the late Lebrón continues to inspire feminists, like the anti-colonial collective "*Las Lolitas* NYC," whose members don her famous "rainbow" skirt suit and lipstick in celebratory marching drills.[29] Some believe that the Bronx-Queens congresswoman, Alexandria Ocasio-Cortéz, pays covert homage to Lebrón with her signature Stilo lipstick in the shade of Beso.[30]

Rather than stressing her sartorial flair or femme fatale looks, Delano focuses our attention on Lebrón's defiant eyes and facial architecture, reinforced by the chiseled visage of the Statue of Liberty. The blank gaze of the idealized, classical monument contrasts with the fiery yet calm stare of the rebel *Boricua* who looks as determined as Che Guevara does in Alberto Korda's iconic portrait of the Argentinian revolutionary. Delano highlights Lebrón's stately stance over her glamour, the juxtaposition making her petite physique seem as large as the enormous monument and rendering her an embodiment of freedom, not unlike the Statue's symbolism as a beacon for immigrants escaping hardship and oppression. This self-possessed, ready-to-die Puerto Rican Lady Liberty, unlike the Old Colony patriot and the PPD *jíbaro*, confronts the world head-on and does not look away. Pablo Delano thus chooses Lebrón as a key political icon over Jack Delano's admired Muñoz. *The Museum of the Old Colony* seems to say that Puerto Ricans require more decisive forms of protest, especially those that are female-powered, to transcend the colonial plight of their nation, than those proposed by Muñoz and the Commonwealth vision.

To conclude, we can look to the philosopher Emmanuel Lévinas, who wrote of the sacredness of the face as the locus for acknowledging foreign "others" in their full dignity.[31] It follows then, that when visualizing colonized peoples, imperial powers will often obliterate the majestic uniqueness of faces through caricature, typecasting, racialization, and infantilization. With *The Museum of the Old Colony's* striking presentation of Lolita Lebrón's rebellious singularity, Pablo Delano manages to reverse nearly 125 years of defacement of Puerto Rican national identity in U.S. media and politics.

---

1 See Nathaniel T. Cordova, "In his image and likeness: The Puerto Rican *jibaro* as political icon," *Centro Journal* 17, no. 2 (Fall 2005): 170-191.

2 On other reasons for the Jones Act, see Harry Franqui-Rivera, "National Mythologies: U.S. Citizenship for the People of Puerto Rico and Military Service," *Memorias: Revista Digital de Historia y Arqueologia desde el Caribe*, Año 10, no. 21 (September-December 2013): 5-21.

3 Jorge Duany, *Puerto Rico: What Everyone Needs to Know* (New York: Oxford University Press, 2017), 56. For a full study, see Ivonne Acosta Lespier, *La Mordaza (The Gag Law): The Attempt to Crush the Independence Movement in Puerto Rico (1948-1957)* (Rio Piedras: DS Editores, 2018).

4 In 1950, the U.S. Congress and President Harry S. Truman approved Public Law 600, providing for the organization of a constitutional government in Puerto Rico. After the law was accepted by a majority of Puerto Rican voters via referendum, a constitution was drafted by a Puerto Rican Convention, whose elected members reluctantly accepted significant congressional amendments to the constitution.

5 Carla Minet, "Cervecera de Puerto Rico," *Mayagüez sabe a mangó*, accessed July 24. 2022, http://mayaguezsabeamango.com/index.php?option=com_content&view=article&id=524.

6 César J. Ayala and Rafael Bernabe, *Puerto Rico in the American Century: A History Since 1898* (Chapel Hill: University of North Carolina Press, 2007), 190.

7 Ayala and Bernabe, *Puerto Rico in the American Century*, 210.

8 See Silvia Álvarez Curbelo, Mary Frances Gallart, and Carmen I. Raffucci, eds., *Los arcos de la memoria: el '98 de los pueblos puertorriqueños* (San Juan: Universidad de Puerto Rico; Mayagüez: Asociación Puertorriqueña de Historiadores, 1998) and Arcadio Diaz-Quiñones, "El 98: la guerra simbólica," in *El arte de bregar: ensayos*, 2nd ed. (San Juan: Ediciones Callejón, 2003), 210-248. Lanny Thompson's pioneering work is also critical for understanding representations of U.S. territories circa 1898.

9 David Gonzalez, "The New Museum for an Old Colony, Puerto Rico," *New York Times Lens*, November 15, 2017, https://lens.blogs.nytimes.com/2017/11/15/a-new-museum-for-an-old-colony-puerto-rico/.

10 Maurice Berger, *The Museum of the Old Colony: An Art Installation by Pablo Delano* (Baltimore: Center for Art, Design and Visual Culture, University of Maryland, Baltimore County, 2020), 4, 7.

11 Lisa G. Corrin, *Mining the Museum: An Installation by Fred Wilson* (Baltimore: Contemporary; New York: New Press, 1994).

12 Teodoro Vidal, *Los milagros en metal y en cera de Puerto Rico* (San Juan: Ediciones Alba, 1974).

13 Pablo Delano, Zoom interview by César A. Salgado, April 17, 2022.

14 The presence of North American Indians as revered figures on votive objects in *botánicas* and in popular culture also speaks to how Caribbean people have used symbols and myths associated with U.S. Native Americans for their own spiritual purposes.

15 W. J. T. Mitchell, *Iconology: Image, Text, Ideology* (Chicago: University of Chicago Press, 1986), 158.

16 Jean Baudrillard, *Simulacra and Simulation*, trans. Sheila Faria Glaser (Ann Arbor: University of Michigan Press, 1994), 5.

17 Jorge Luis Crespo Armáiz, *Estereoscopia y sujeto colonial: la contribución de la fotografía estereoscópica en la construcción del otro puertorriqueño, 1898-1930* (Gurabo: Universidad del Turabo, Sistema Universitario Ana G. Méndez, 2015).

18 Jack Delano et al., *Puerto Rico mío: Four Decades of Change. Cuatro décadas de cambio* (Washington, D.C.: Smithsonian Institution Press, 1990), 28.

19 Sidney W. Mintz, "The Island/*La Isla*," in Delano et al., *Puerto Rico mío*, 5.

20 See Yolanda Martínez-San Miguel, *Caribe Two Ways: cultura de la migración en el Caribe insular hispánico* (San Juan: Ediciones Callejón, 2003), 51-84.

21 On this topic, see Laura Katzman et al., *Re-viewing Documentary: The Photographic Life of Louise Rosskam*, 2nd ed. (University Park: Pennsylvania State University Press, 2014), 27-35, 36-47, and 102-143.

22 On November 1, 1950, Nationalists also made an attempt on the life of President Truman. On the 1950 insurrections, see Ayala and Bernabe, *Puerto Rico in the American Century*, 165-167, and Miñi Seijo-Bruno, *La insurrección nacionalista en Puerto Rico: 1950*, 2nd ed. (Río Piedras: Editorial Edil, 1997).

23 Olga Jiménez de Wagenheim, *Nationalist Heroines: Puerto Rican Women History Forgot, 1930s-1950s* (Princeton: Markus Weiner Publishers, 2017), 242-278.

24 Manuel Roig-Franzia, "When Terror Wore Lipstick," *Washington Post Magazine*, February 22, 2004, https://www.washingtonpost.com/archive/lifestyle/magazine/2004/02/22/a-terrorist-in-the-house/293c52cd-8794-47bd-9960-9c7a871e009c/.

25 Mary Breasted, "30 in Puerto Rican Group Held in Liberty I. Protest," *New York Times*, October 26, 1977, 30, https://www.nytimes.com/1977/10/26/archives/30-in-puerto-rican-group-held-in-liberty-i-protest.html.

26 Margaret Power, "If People Had Not Been Willing to Give Their Lives for the *patria* or There Had Not Been the Political Prisoners, Then We Would Be Nothing.': Interview with Lolita Lebrón," *Radical History Review* 2017, no. 128 (May 1, 2017): 37–45.

27 Sandra Ruiz, *Ricanness. Enduring Time in Anticolonial Performance* (New York: New York University Press, 2019), 37, 35-72.

28 Lolita Lebrón, *Sándalo en la celda* (Cataño: Editorial Betances, 1975).

29 Frances Solá-Santiago, "A Celebration of Lolita Lebrón at the 2019 Puerto Rican Day Parade," *Emperifollá*, June 11, 2019, https://emperifolla.com/2019/06/11/lolita-lebron-puerto-rican-day-parade/.

30 See Benigno Trigo, "AOC's Lipstick," *Los Angeles Review of Books Channel Project*, April 1, 2019, https://thephilosophicalsalon.com/aocs-lipstick/.

31 Emmanuel Lévinas, *Totality and Infinity: An Essay on Exteriority*, trans. Alphonso Lingis (Pittsburgh: Duquesne University Press, 1969).

Plate 19. Installation view. Flag-related photographs and caption. *The Museum of the Old Colony*, Duke Hall Gallery of Fine Art, 2022. Checklist Nos. 93-101.

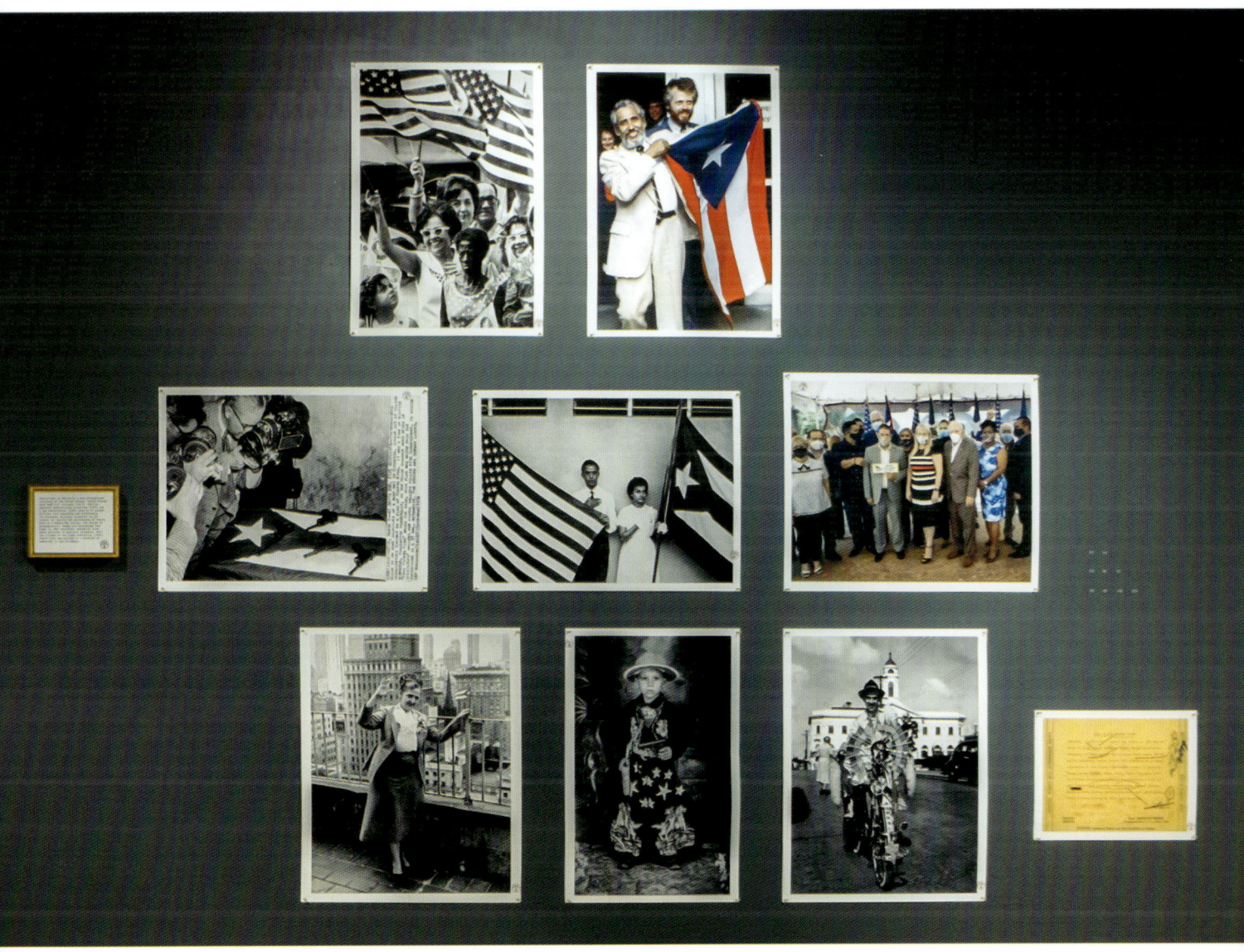

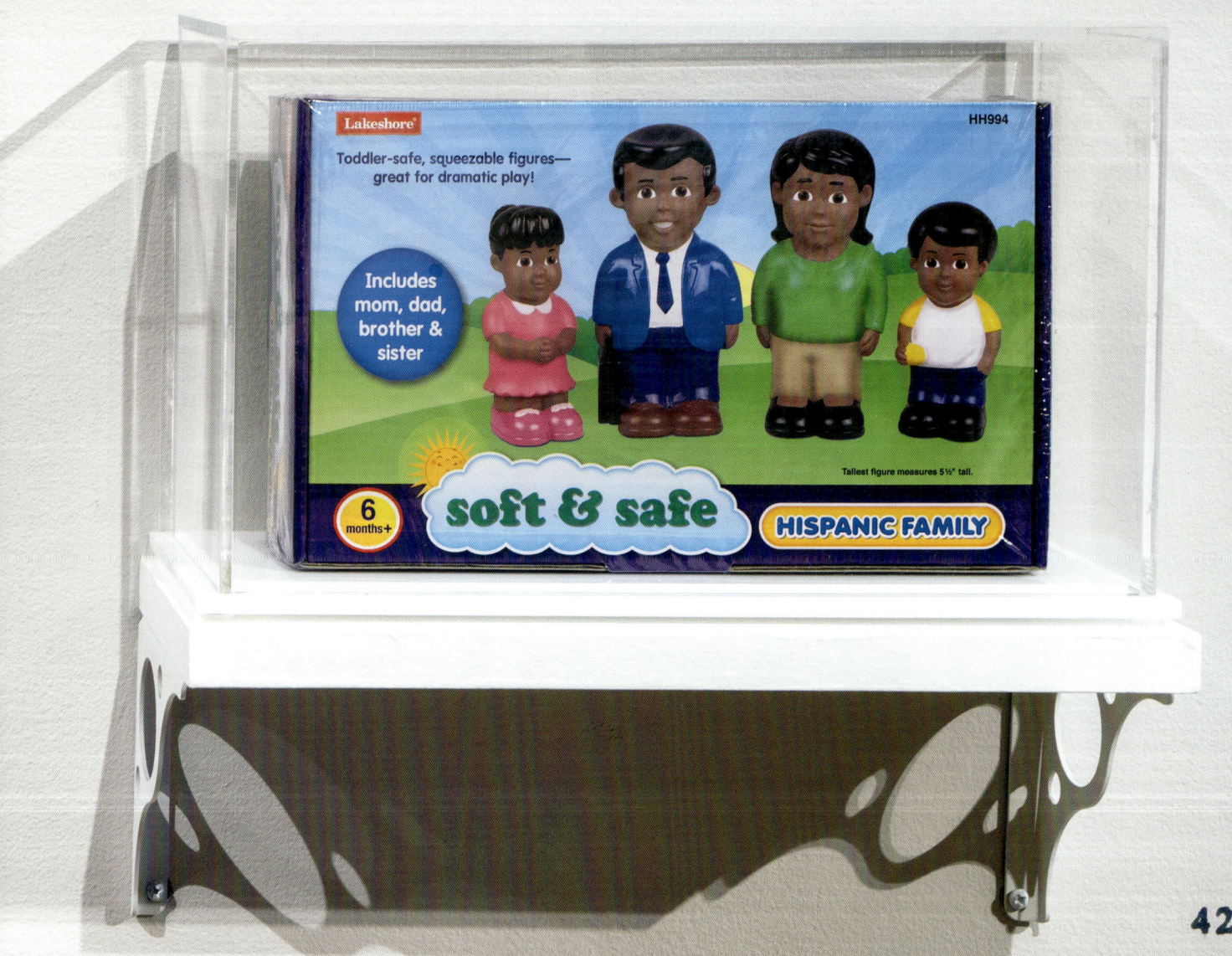

The *Museum of the Old Colony: An Art Installation by Pablo Delano* gives the fields of museum studies and contemporary art theory much to consider. A large wooden desk close to the entrance of the exhibition appears to be awaiting the return of its resident occupant, who has seemingly sat there for long hours smoking cigarettes (the butts of which dirty the ashtray), looking at stereographic images, and perusing an assortment of books about Puerto Rico and other colonial possessions "won" by the United States in the Spanish-American War of 1898 (plates 3, 27). A collection of rubber stamps sits on the desk, including one embossed with *The Museum of the Old Colony* logo that Pablo Delano has stamped on the photographs and documents in the exhibition. The pith helmet and khaki coat with brass buttons appear to be the property of a colonial officer, the likely occupant of this military desk. But could this desk not also belong to a museum director, whose archiving of colonial plunder sought to hide the violence of acquisition with narratives that justified enslavement, colonialism, and other forms of oppression and racism? After all, the colonial officer and the museum director are twin figures, historically bound together in ways worthy of the famous line from Charles Baudelaire's 1857 poem *Au Lecteur, "—mon semblable,—mon frère!"* In his installation, Delano points out the resonances between these two identities with a dry humor that makes his critique of colonialism even more impactful.

The desk chair is empty—a warning that the ongoing project of colonialism still hides its evil under the guise of day-to-day banalities. Did the military officer/museum director just step away momentarily? Is his briefcase, which is adjacent to the desk, full and heavy? What was he writing before crumpling up a letter and throwing it in the nearby trash bin? What did he think of Theodore Roosevelt when looking at the eerie grin on the white plastic bust of the 26th U.S. president that sits on the desk? (plate 21). Further, what motivated 1970s' consumers to buy this bust, which is actually a bottle of Avon aftershave? Did they feel "presidential" when wearing its "Wild Country" scent? Were they transported back to the "glory" days of "Rough Riders" and their romanticized battles? The stubborn entrenchment of such mythic narratives is revealed by Delano's interrogation of the colonial archive, which shows how they have appeared and reappeared and have been packaged and repackaged to U.S. consumers for over a century.

The officer/director desk is but one object among many in *The Museum of the Old Colony* that convey these messages. To its right hangs a wall vitrine entitled "Soft and Safe Hispanic Family," which is the name of the contemporary boxed children's doll set featured in the case (plate 20). Looking more like a toy from an earlier era than one made today, the father wears a business suit and tie and carries a briefcase, while the mother smiles gently with her hands by her side. The daughter is dressed in pink; the son in blue, holding a baseball. Advertised as "Toddler-safe, squeezable figures—great for dramatic play!", the "soft and safe" family poses no threat to its potential users. This "educational" toy stands out against the many colonial devices Delano has assembled in his "museum"

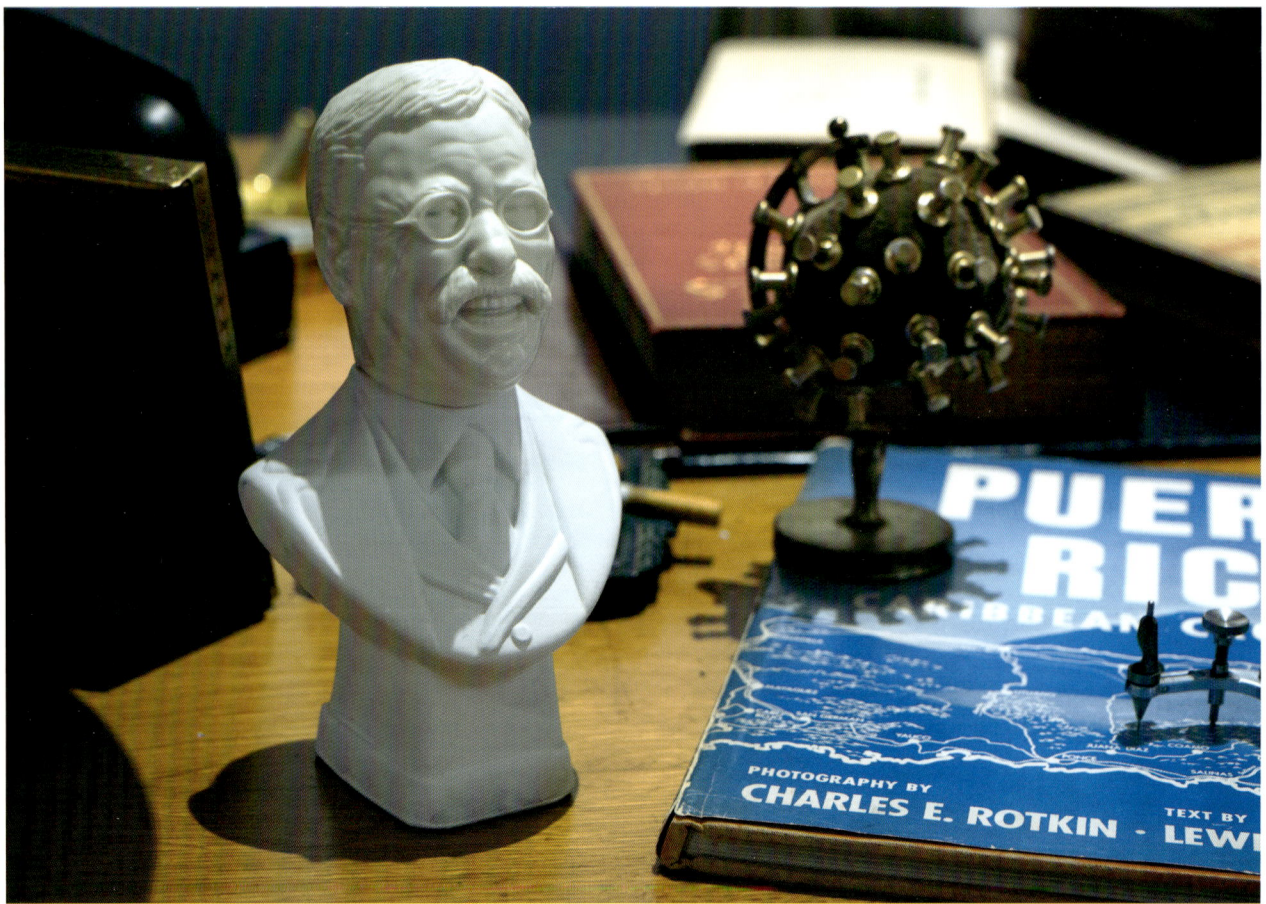

that have surveilled, classified, dominated, and punished its subjects: anthropometric tools such as calipers for measuring skull sizes, skin tone charts, and denigrating photographs of colonized people portrayed as infantile. The introduction of the "soft and safe" Hispanic family into this classificatory scheme symbolizes both the pinnacle of colonialism's taxonomic logic and the destruction of its authority, veracity, and regulatory capacity. And if it represents the kind of toys that were collected by the colonial officer/museum director, then in the context of the installation, it parodies coloniality's goals, smiles in the face of the official archive's intelligence failures, and refuses to be animated within its strictures.

The Museum of the Old Colony challenges the twinned colonial officer/museum director on his home base, as if to hold him accountable for the crimes apparently committed at his desk, while implicating the audiences who pursue its contents and those of the entire installation. The museum in Western society has sanitized imperial plunder for too long. In his foundational essay *Discourse on Colonialism*, Aimé Césaire attacked the legitimacy of the museum, which for him was an irredeemable institution. He wrote, "the museum by itself is nothing; that it means nothing…when smug self-satisfaction rots the eyes, when a secret contempt for others withers the heart, when racism, admitted or not, dries up sympathy….in the scales of knowledge all the museums in the world will never weigh so much as one spark of human sympathy."[1] The audiences of Delano's "museum" are compelled to confront the racist colonial structure of the museum that Césaire

Plate 21. Installation view. *The Museum Desk* (detail). *The Museum of the Old Colony*, Duke Hall Gallery of Fine Art, 2022. Checklist No. 4.

77

condemns. Are they smugly self-satisfied or sympathetic to seeing how colonization has been at the root of so much historical and ongoing harm to humanity?

Throughout *The Museum of the Old Colony*, the visitor finds that sparks fly when the colonial archive is read against the grain. A "Patriot Economy Eraser" with a Puerto Rican flag on its label, which appears to have erased the writing on a blackboard, is a cipher of liberation from the attempt at enforcing the English language in Puerto Rican schools in early decades of the twentieth century. It may also represent the pervasive imperial push to "erase" the culture as a whole in favor of U.S. assimilation, especially through financial means (i.e., debt). An altar entitled "At the Crossroads"— which holds secular and religious objects important in Puerto Rico, from a necklace worn by a devotee of *Eleguá* (an *orisha* from the Afro-Caribbean religion *Santeria*), to a bottle of Manischewitz wine, to a jar of Vicks VapoRub—suggests the strength and traditions of those who have endured colonialism (plate 23). Across the gallery, a wall vitrine called "*Madamas*" houses the devotional figure with strong Cuban roots, *La Madama*, which honors a group of spirits of enslaved women of African descent with conjure and healing abilities, who are venerated in *Espiritismo* practices.[2] *La Madama* rests next to a coffee pot adorned with an image of *Mamá Inés*, a longtime figurehead for the popular *Café Yaucono* brand that derived in part from the Black mammy stereotype introduced to Puerto Rico after the U.S. invasion in 1898 (plate 24).

La Madama, in her red skirt and kerchief head wrap, may look similar to *Mamá Inés*, especially to a continental U.S. viewer. Their origins are intertwined in complex ways, yet they represent different world views. *La Madama* is an invaluable and much esteemed helper in the afterlife, aiding those who honor her as an adopted ancestor. Shown alongside a mammy figure, she reveals how museum techniques of classification and presentation can control interpretation and meaning, and in this case, obscure the viewer's recognition of important traditions within colonized cultures that are sources of self-determination and cultural sovereignty. *La Madama* confronts the racism inherent in those who deny her identity and deem her a mammy. Those who do so repeat the same projection of metropole racism onto colonial sites, ironically mirroring the initial imposition of the mammy stereotype onto Puerto Rican popular culture.

Within the context of *The Museum of the Old Colony*, *La Madama* holds the potential to guide viewers, who honor her with recognition, in acknowledging the need for transformation of museums from colonial echo chambers into forums of conversation. With the absence of the colonial officer and museum director from the desk, visitors to the installation can converse with and challenge the different forms of authority on display. As the field of museum studies struggles to decolonize its practices, *The Museum of the Old Colony* offers guideposts, signs, and symbols to shape new paths. *La Madama*, in particular, can lead visitors down the road of re-imagining and rebuilding a "softer and safer" museum. Her gifts turn small sparks into raging conflagrations.

1 Aimé Césaire, *Discourse on Colonialism*, transl. Joan Pinkham (New York: Monthly Review Press, 2001), 71-72. The essay was originally published as *Discours sur le colonialisme* in 1955.

2 While a majority of Puerto Ricans identify as Catholic, other belief systems (Christian and non-Christian) are important, including various Protestant sects. *Espiritismo*, which combines spiritual-religious practices of European Spiritism with African elements, remains a strong influence on the island. *Santeria* is based on Yoruba beliefs brought to the Americas by enslaved people who found ways to keep their banned religion alive by syncretizing it with Catholicism. See Margarite Fernández Olmos and Lizabeth Paravisini-Gebert, *Creole Religions of the Caribbean: An Introduction*, 3rd. ed. (New York: New York University Press, 2022).

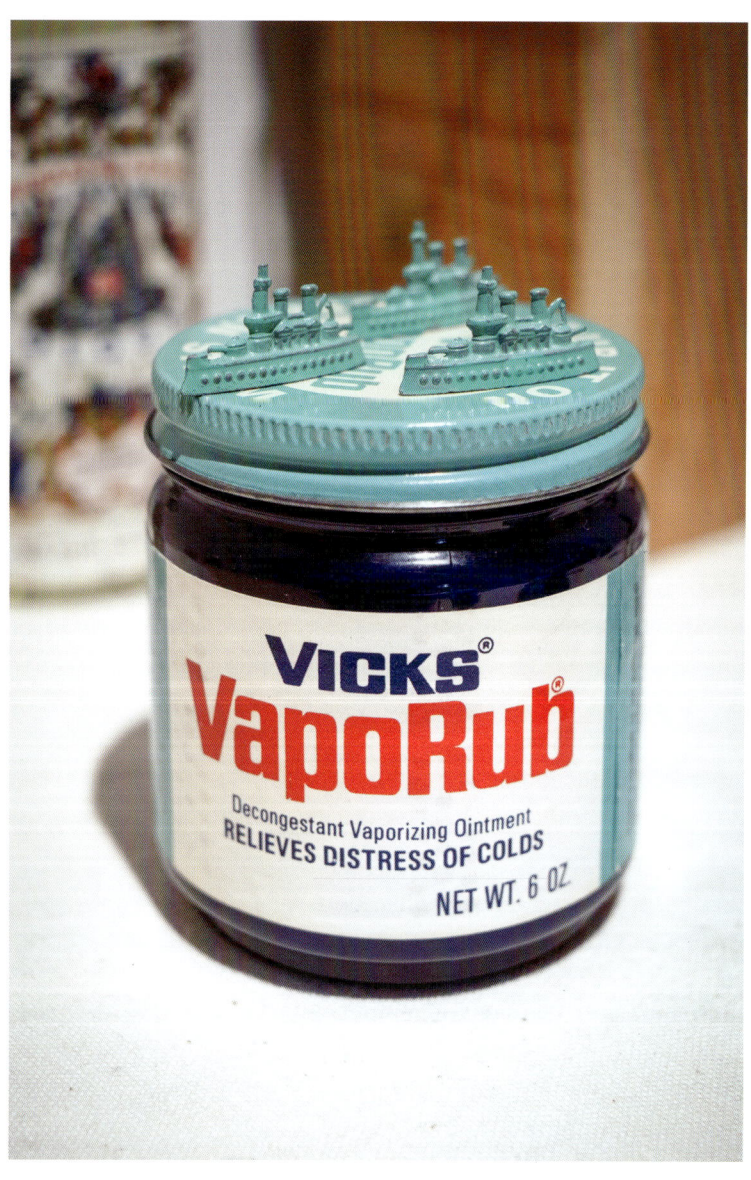

Plate 23. Installation view. *At the Crossroads*. Assemblage of found objects | 2021. *The Museum of the Old Colony*, Duke Hall Gallery of Fine Art, 2022. Checklist No. 3.

Plate 24. Installation view. *Madamas*. Assemblage of found objects | 2021. *The Museum of the Old Colony*, Duke Hall Gallery of Fine Art, 2022. Checklist No. 29.

79

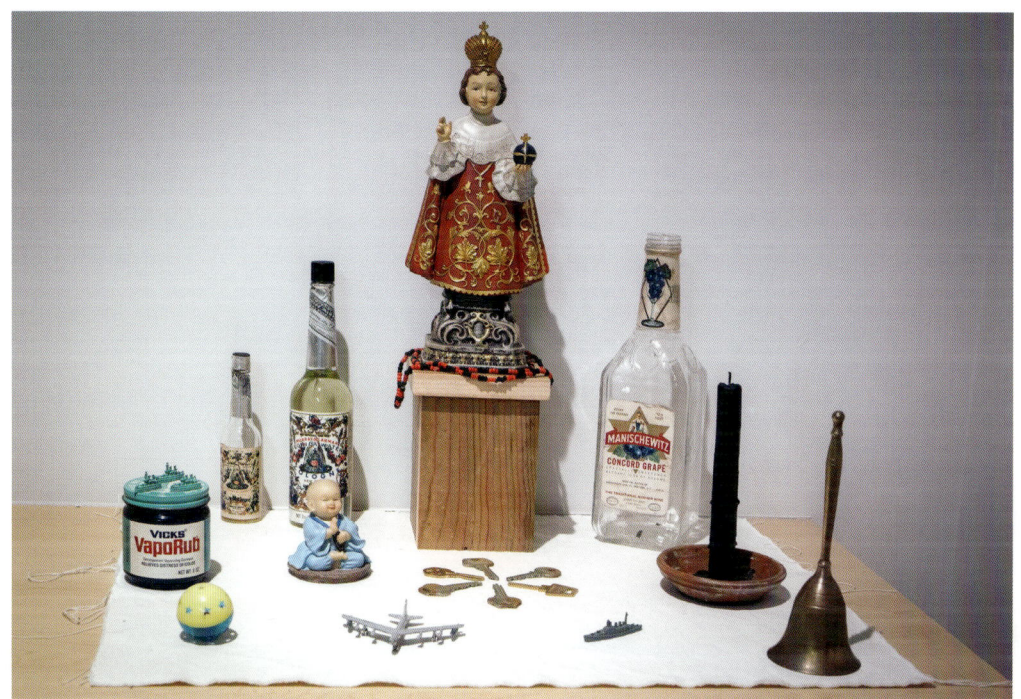

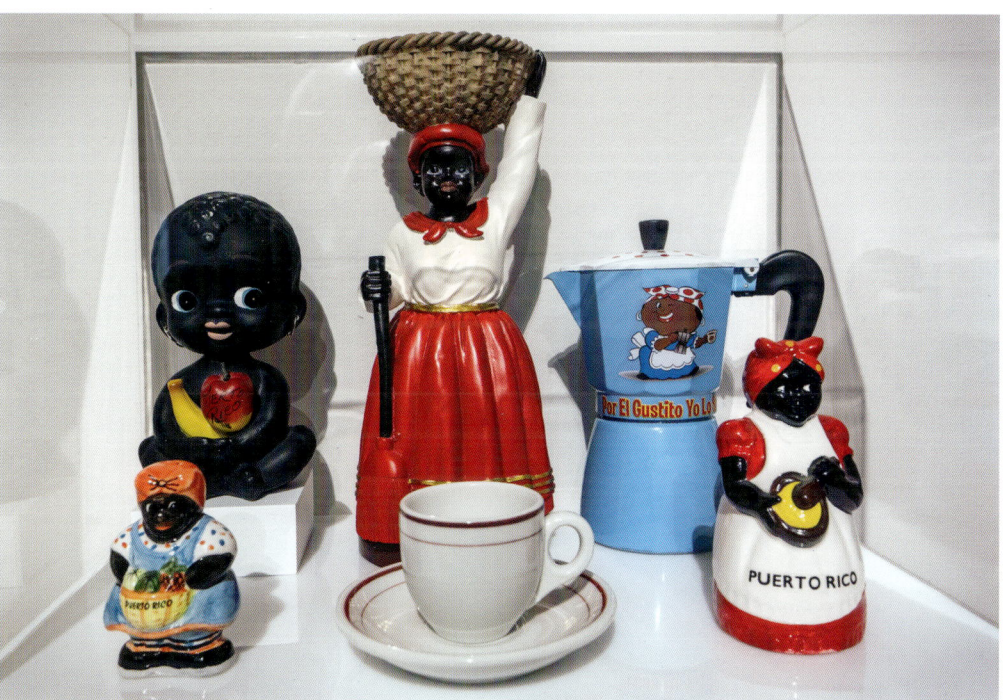

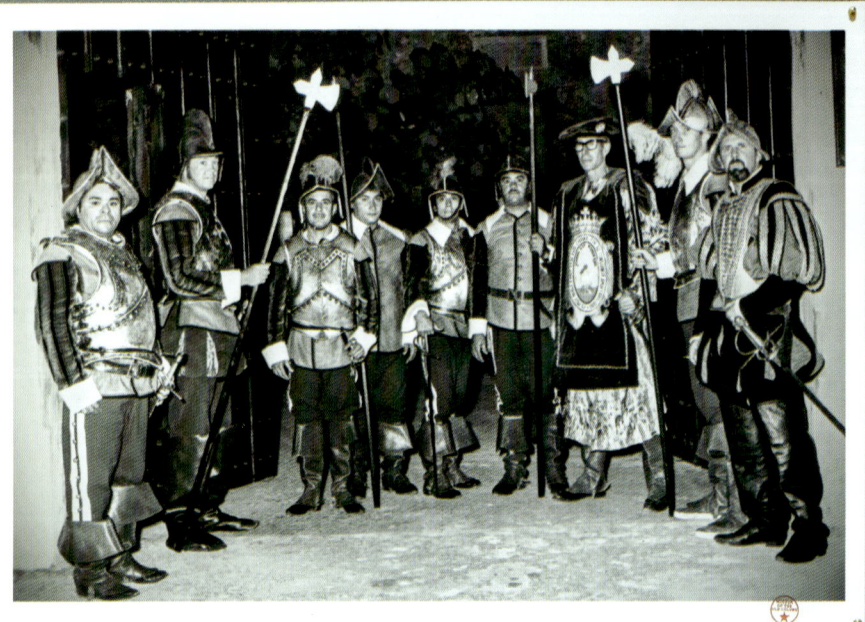

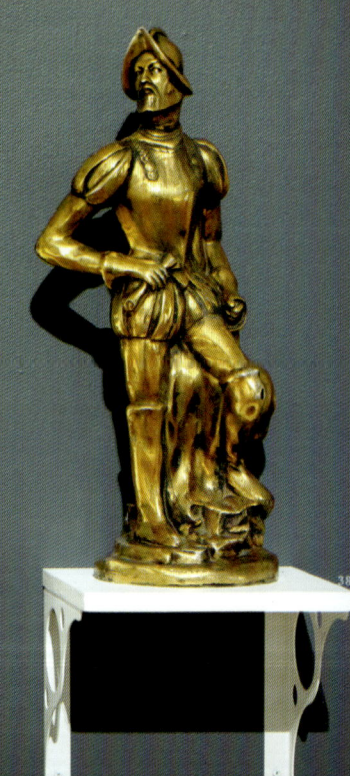

36

38

The history of Porto Rico is a strange, romantic and, in many respects, awful story. From the date of its discovery by Christopher Columbus in 1493 until it came under the American flag in 1898, the island was continuously a Spanish possession. Being a small country, only three times the size of our smallest State, Rhode Island, the Spaniards were able to keep it under the iron heel of subjection through four centuries. The people who colonized it were a mixture of criminals and peasant stock and accustomed to a harsh form of government. There were no general revolutions such as made Cuba often a great battlefield, although Porto Rico sympathized with the sister island. Once a liberating army from South America reached Porto Rico, but it was unsuccessful.

37

Exhibition Catalogue

Installation Views by Pablo Delano

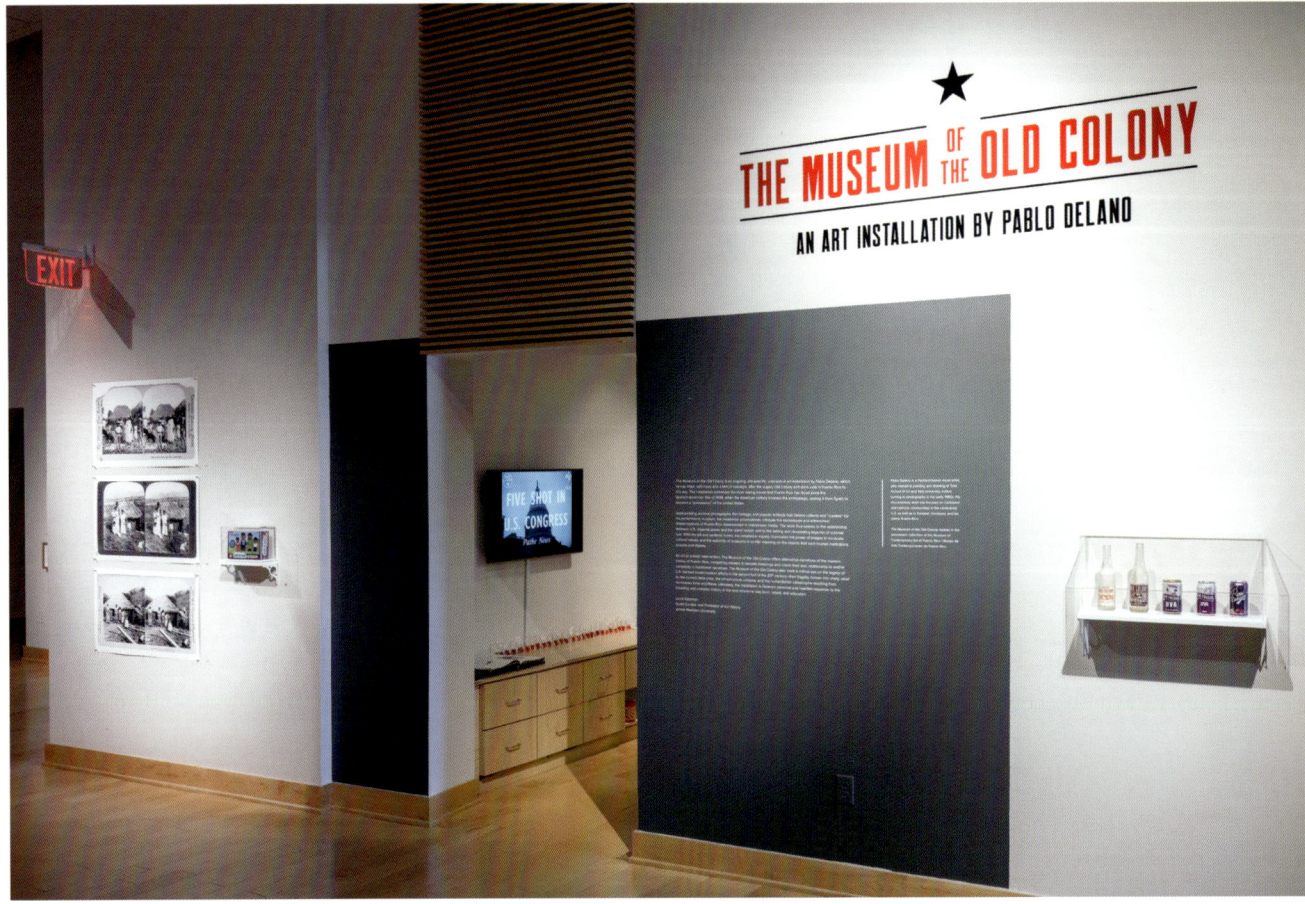

Plate 27. Installation view. View from *The Museum Desk*
across the front gallery. *The Museum of the Old Colony*, 2022.

83

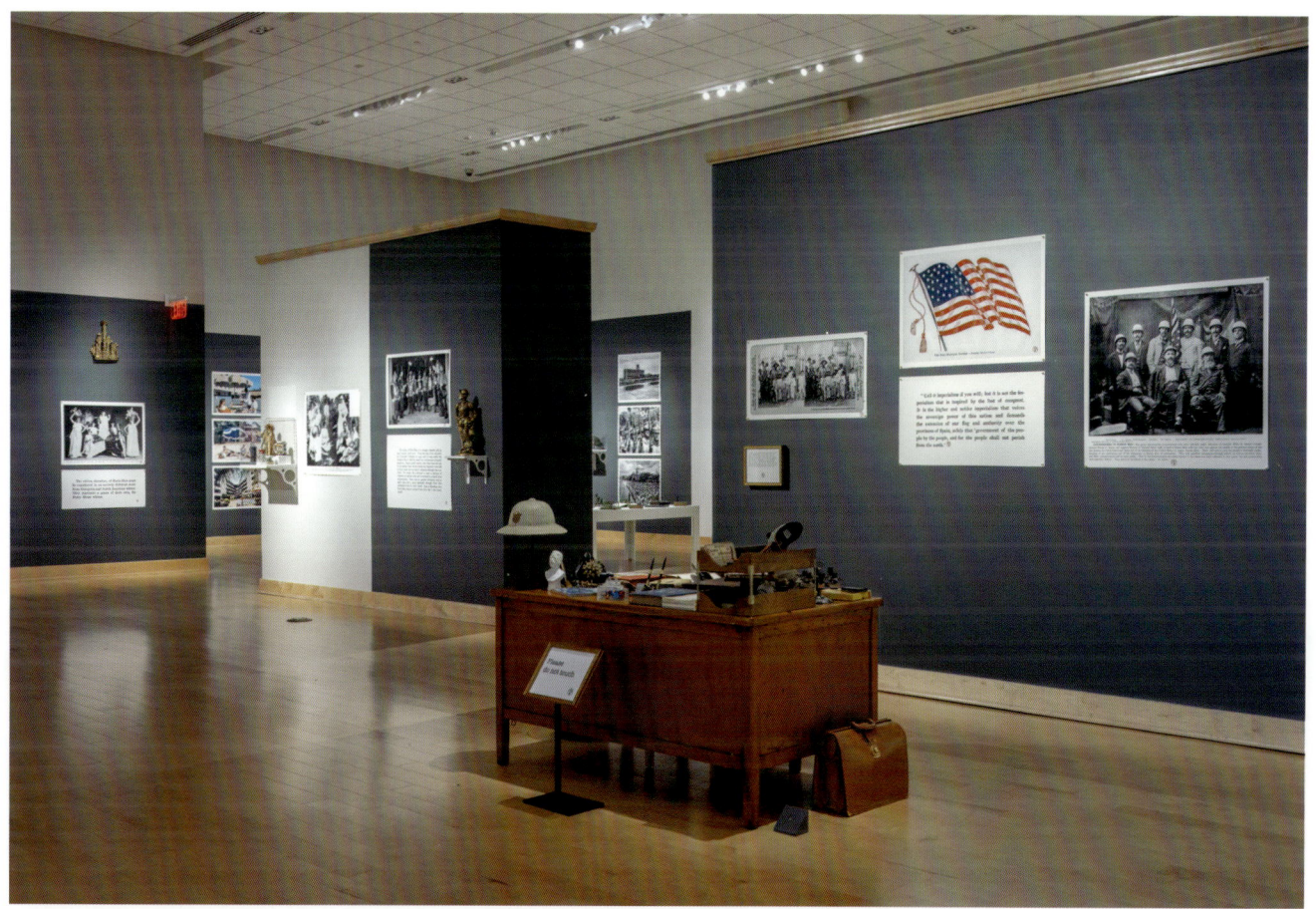

Plate 28. Installation view. *The Museum Desk* and U.S. empire-related photographs and captions. *The Museum of the Old Colony*, 2022. Checklist Nos. 4, 6–8.

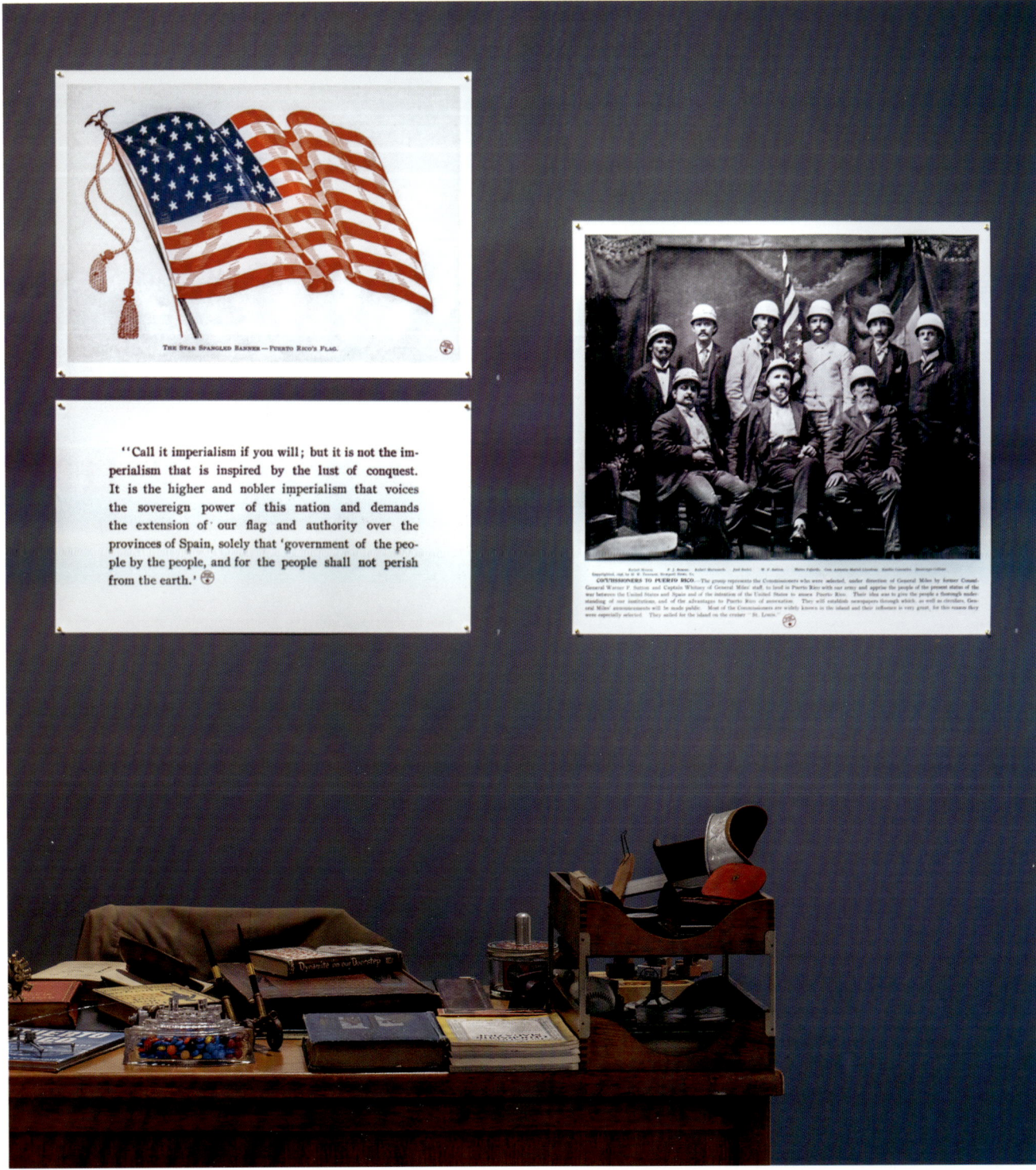

Plates **29–30**. Installation views. *The Museum Desk* (details: "Remember the Maine" candy dish and vintage books and objects). *The Museum of the Old Colony*, 2022. Checklist No. 4.

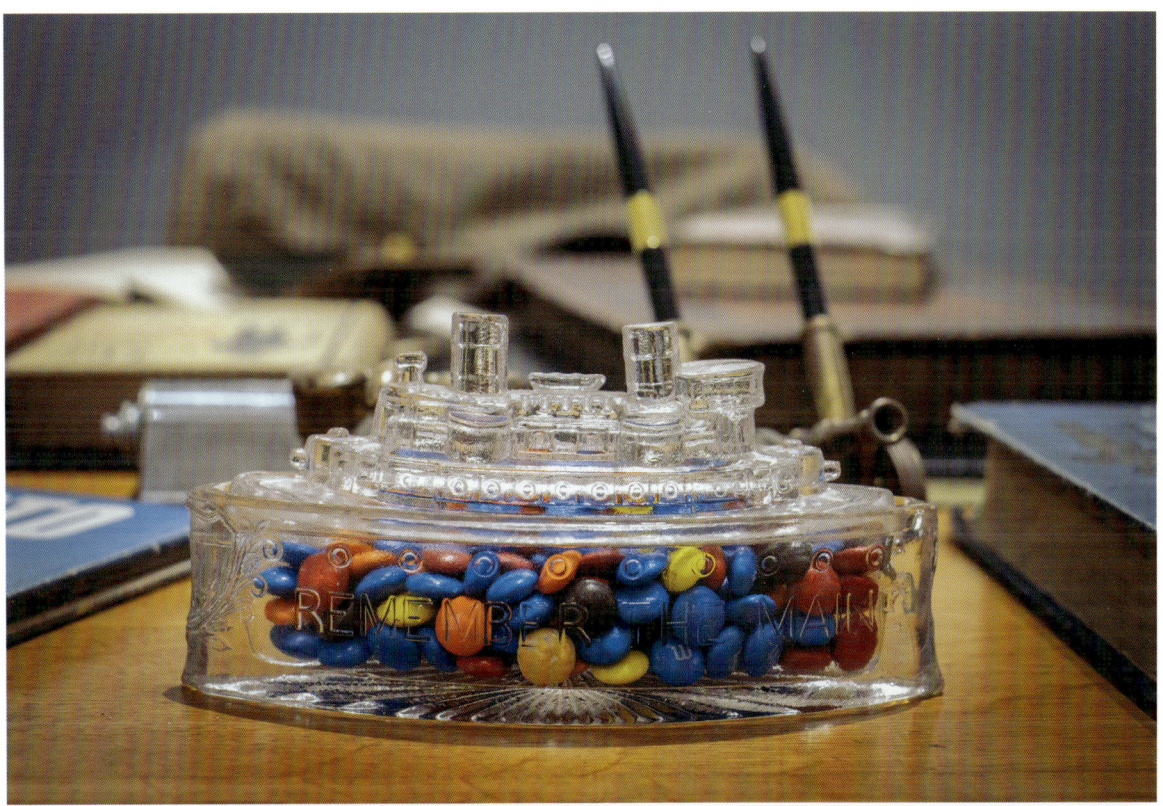

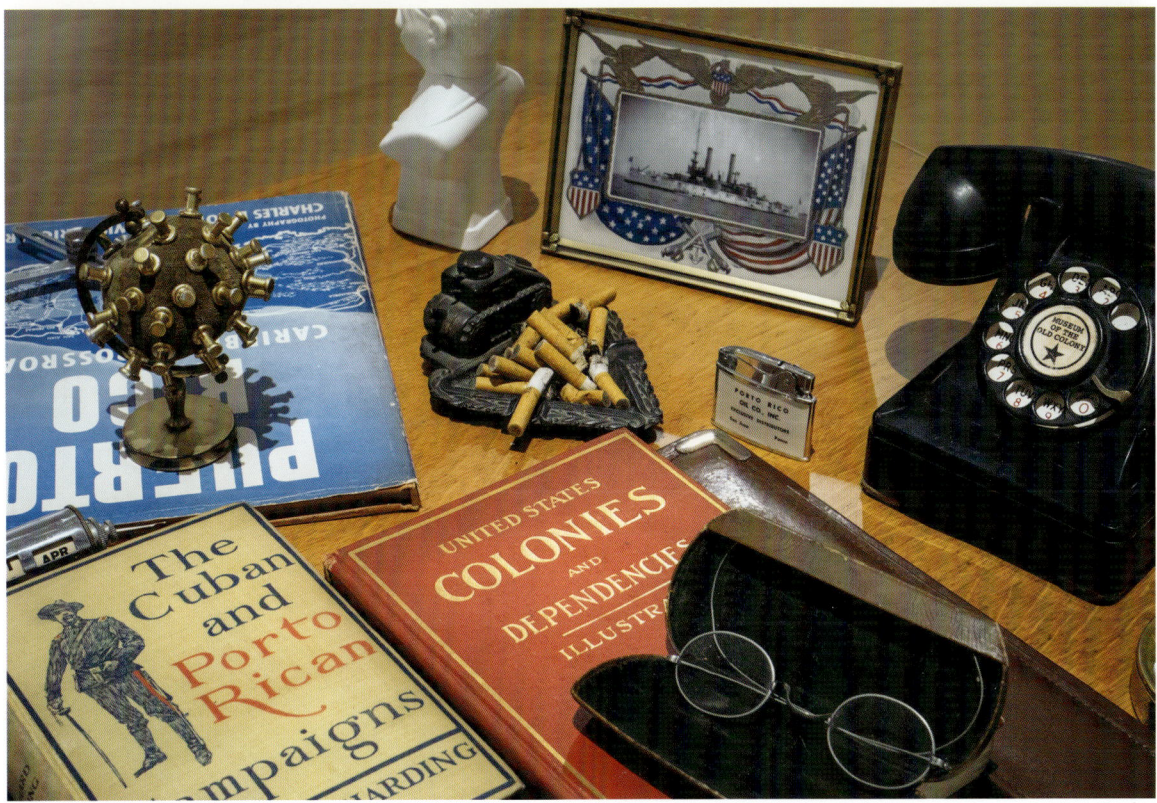

Plates 31–32. Installation views. *"Plantation Joe"*;
At Work in the Cane Field; and *White Jesus with the
Orishas* (including detail). *The Museum of the Old
Colony*, 2022. Checklist Nos. 9–11.

Plate 33. *Cupid.* Found object, 20th century (set of two) |
2020. *The Museum of the Old Colony*, 2022. Checklist No. 12.

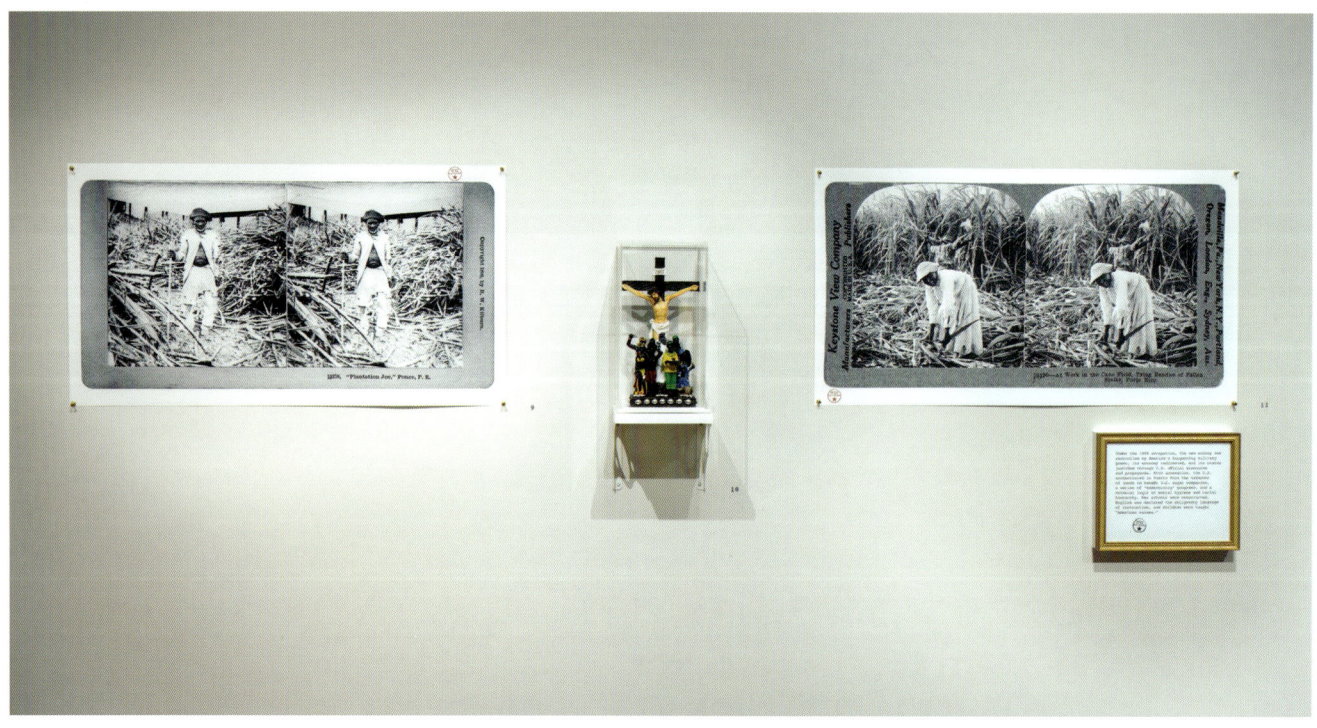

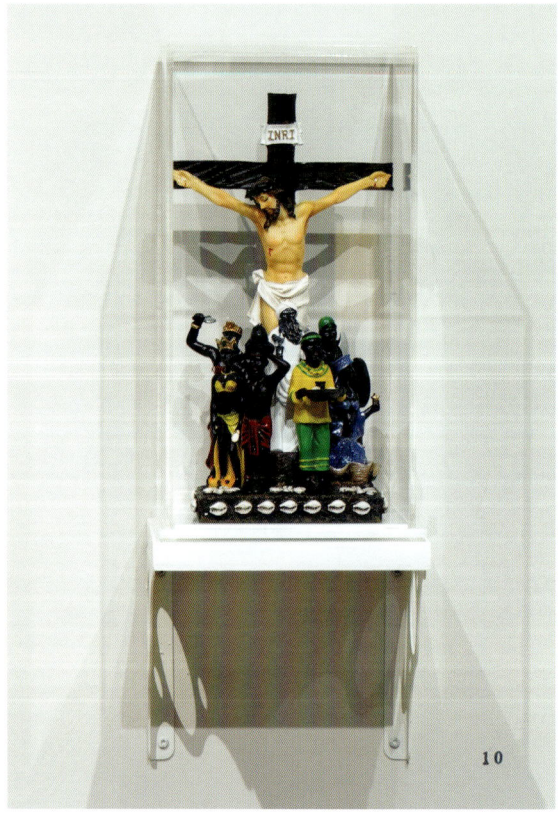

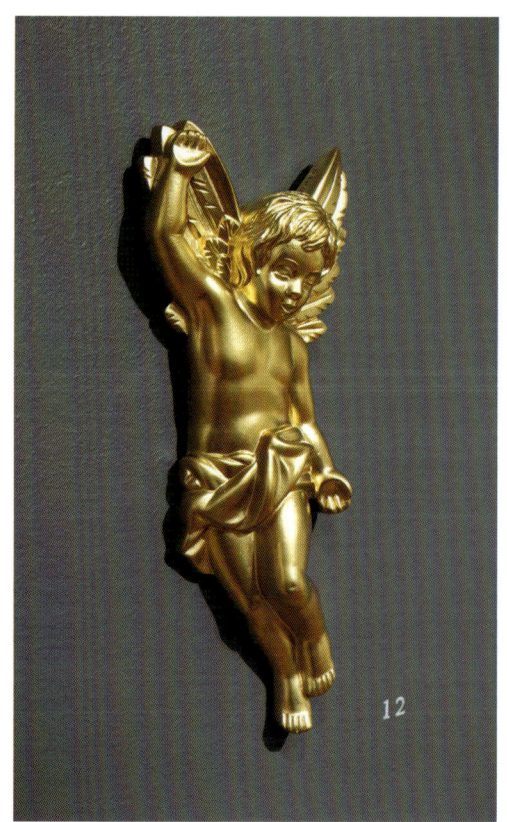

Plates 34–35. Installation view. Stereographs of Puerto Rican children and *Waiting for Uncle Sam* caption (verso). *The Museum of the Old Colony*, 2022. Checklist Nos. 13–18.

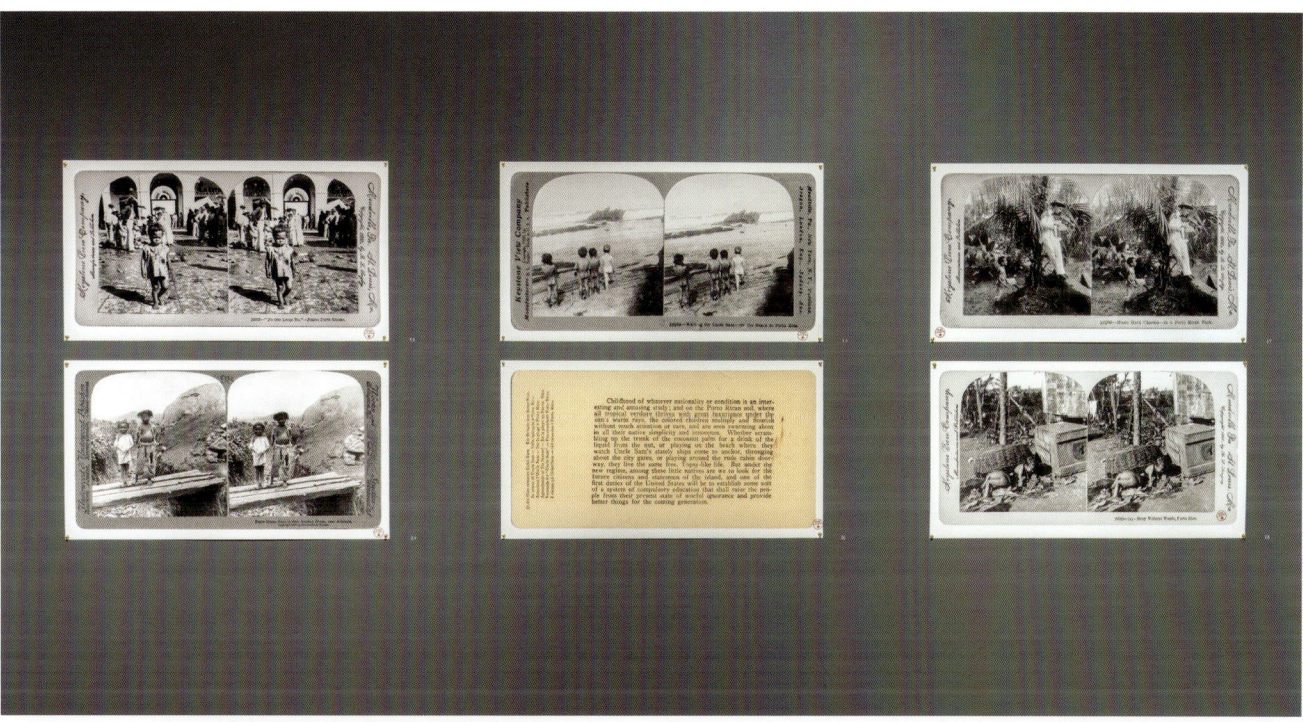

Childhood of whatever nationality or condition is an interesting and amusing study; and on the Porto Rican soil, where all tropical verdure thrives with great luxuriance under the sun's warm rays, the colored children multiply and flourish without much attention or care, and are seen swarming about in all their native simplicity and innocence. Whether scrambling up the trunk of the cocoanut palm for a drink of the liquid from the nut, or playing on the beach where they watch Uncle Sam's stately ships come to anchor, thronging about the city gates, or playing around the rude cabin doorway, they live the same free, Topsy-like life. But under the new regime, among these little natives are we to look for the future citizens and statesmen of the island, and one of the first duties of the United States will be to establish some sort of a system of compulsory education that shall raise the people from their present state of woeful ignorance and provide better things for the coming generation.

10,262 Man erwartet Onkel Sam.
In attesa di Uncle Sam —
Attendant l'Oncle Sam —
Aguardando al Tio Samuel —
Ventende for "Uncle Sam" —
Un Gestade von Porto Rico.
Sulla spiaggia a Porto Rico.
Sur la plage à Porto Rico.
En la playa en Puerto Rico.
Paa stranden i Porto Rico.
I väntan på Onkel Sam — vid stranden i Porto Rico.

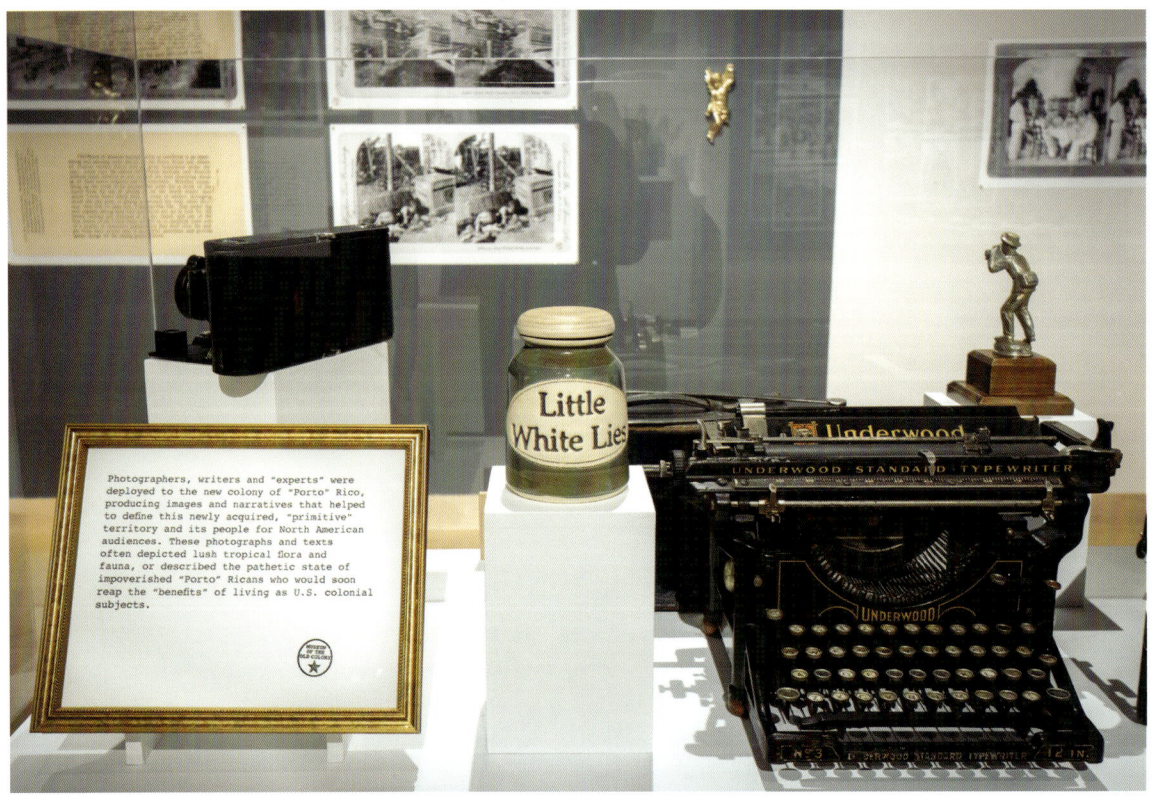

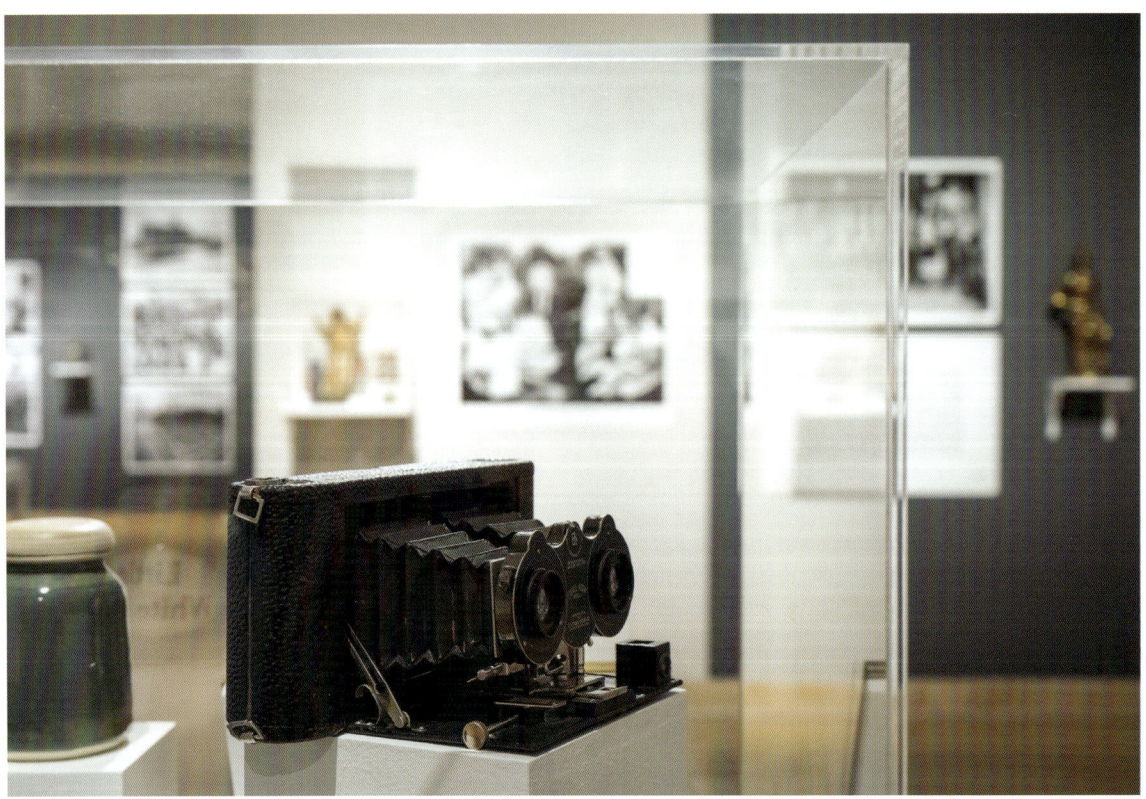

Plate 38. Installation view. *Plum Pudding* and *Plenty of Room at the Table*. The Museum of the Old Colony, 2022. Checklist Nos. 20–21.

89

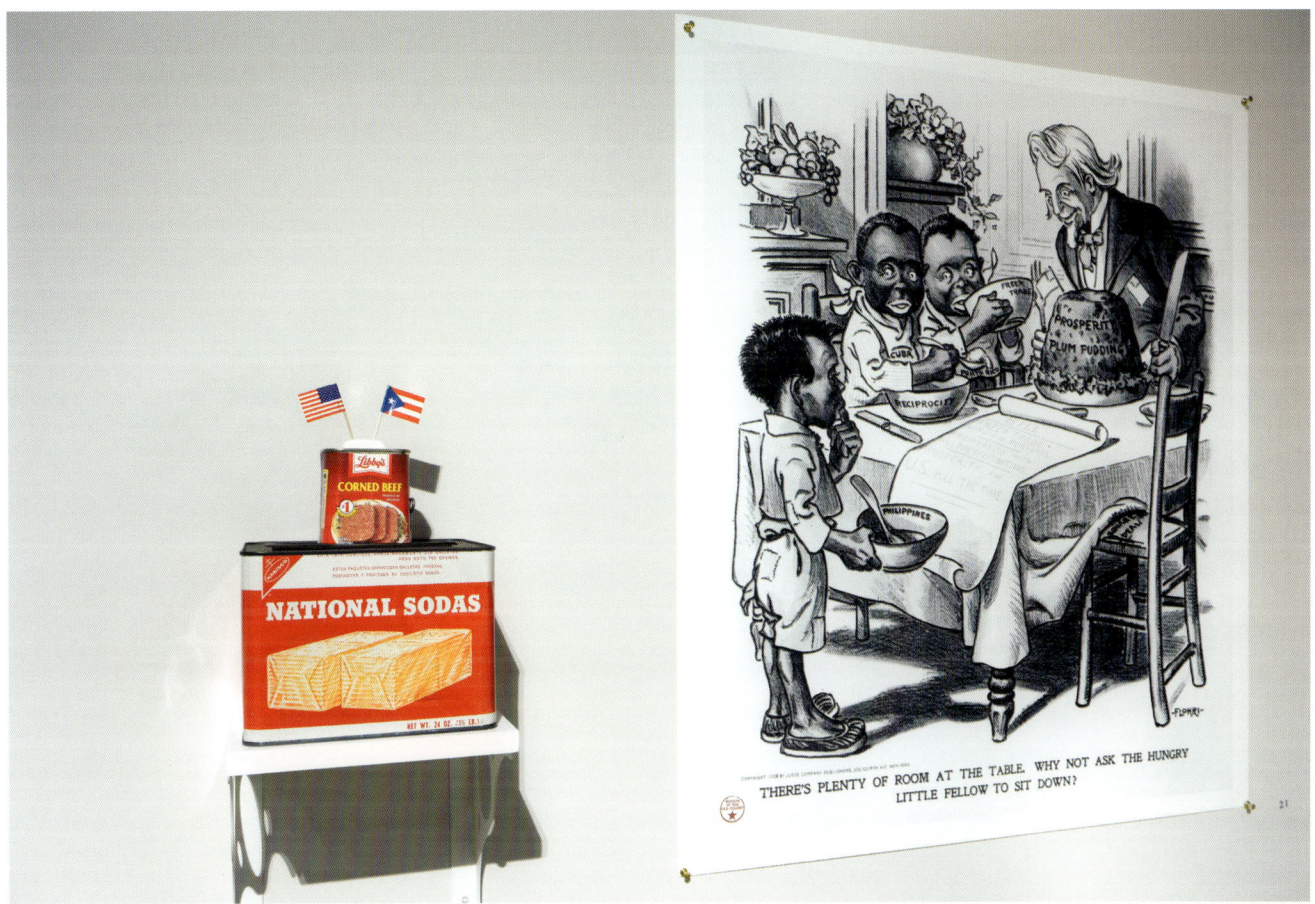

Plate 39. Installation view. *Porto Rican Laundries; Danaide;* and photographs of Ponce washerwomen. *The Museum of the Old Colony*, 2022. Checklist Nos. 23–27.

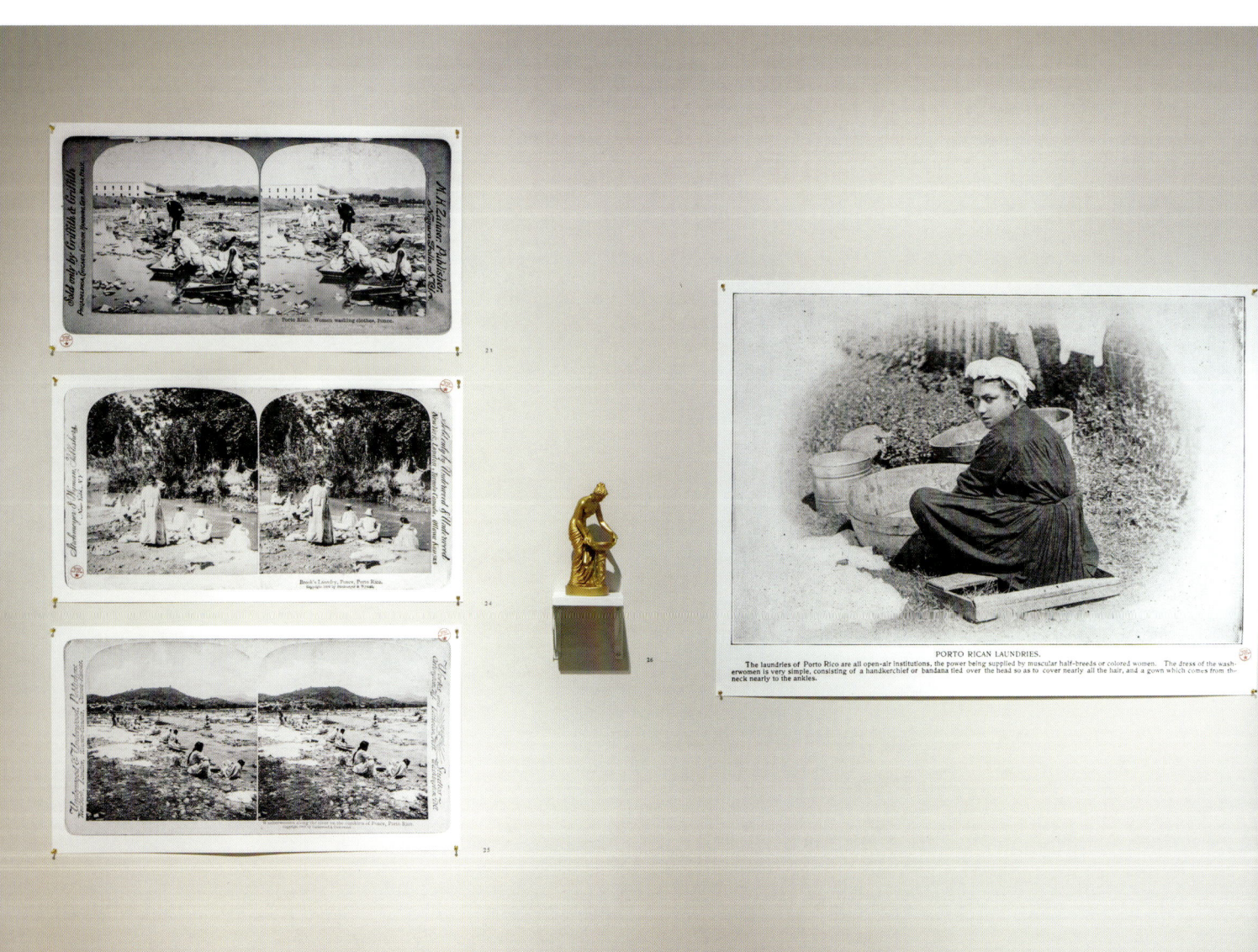

Plate 40. Installation view. *A Colored Belle of Porto Rico;*
Madamas; and *Mamá Inés lookalike contest. The Museum of*
the Old Colony, 2022. Checklist Nos. 28–30.

91

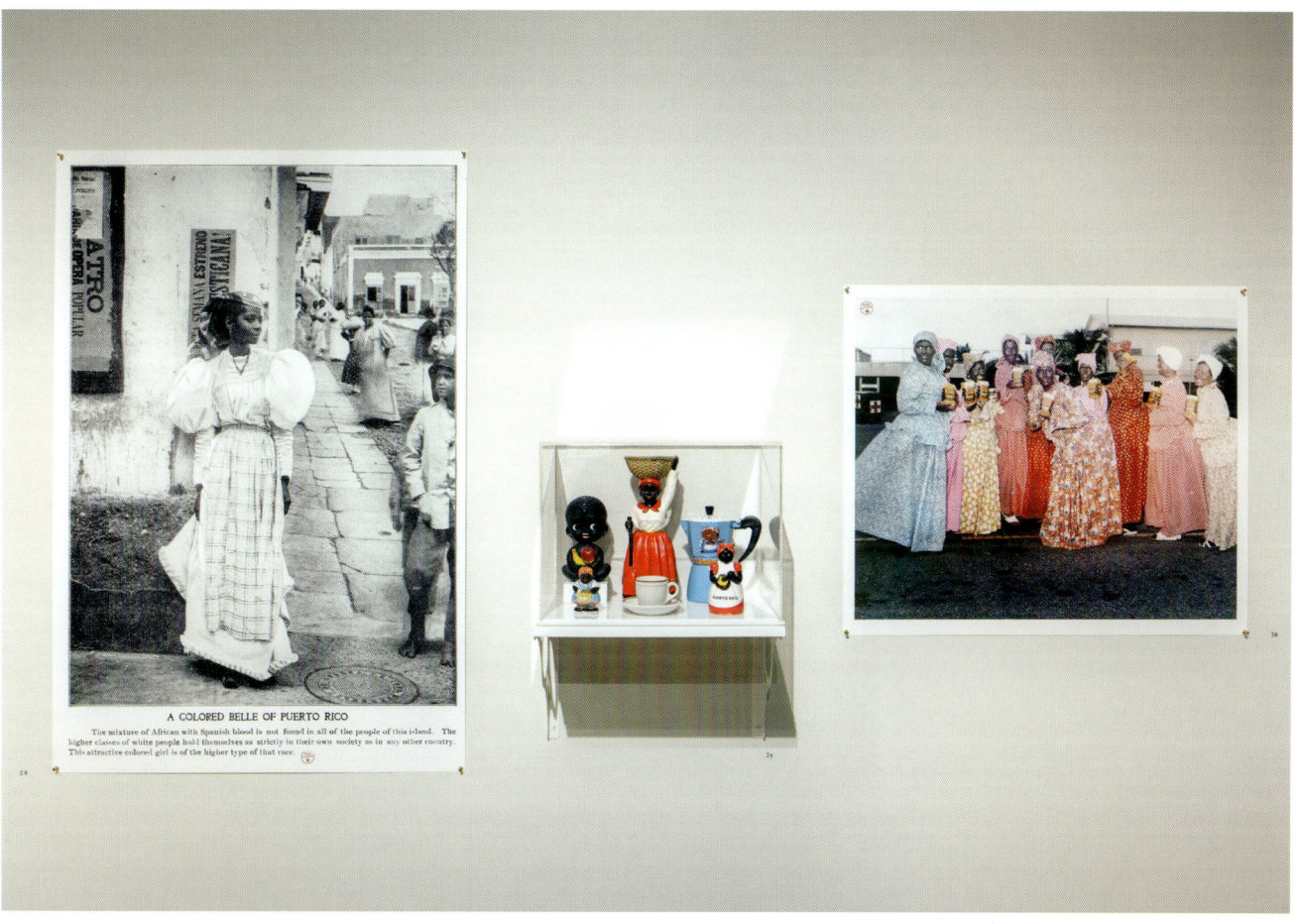

Plate 41. Installation view. *Remnant of the 20th Century;
Cuadro Plástico de la "Estrella de Oriente";* and *The whites,
therefore, of Porto Rico....The Museum of the Old Colony,*
2022. Checklist Nos. 31–33.

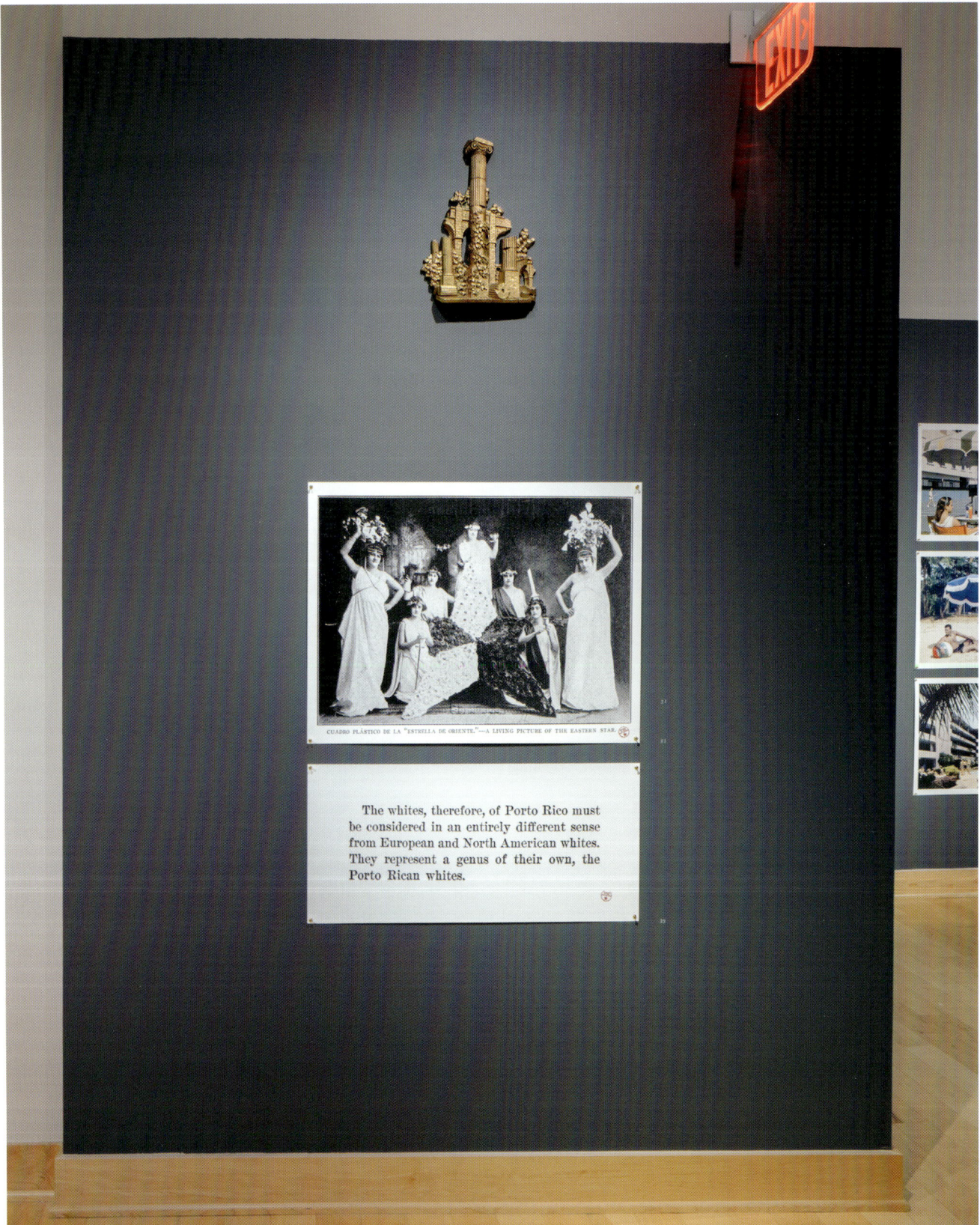

Plate 42. Installation view. *Soft and Safe Hispanic Family*
and photographs of Puerto Rican families next to *bohíos*.
The Museum of the Old Colony, 2022. Checklist Nos. 39–42.

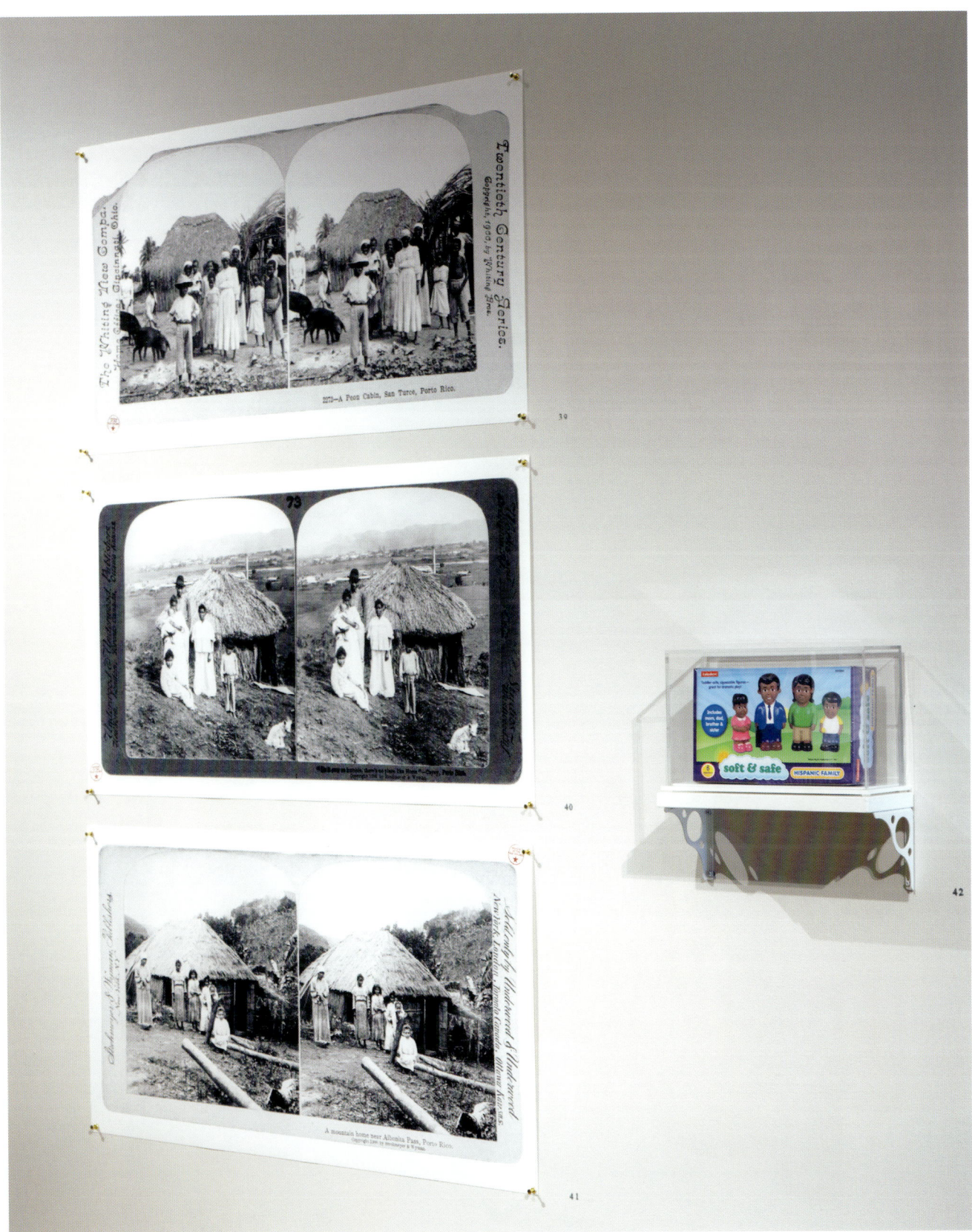

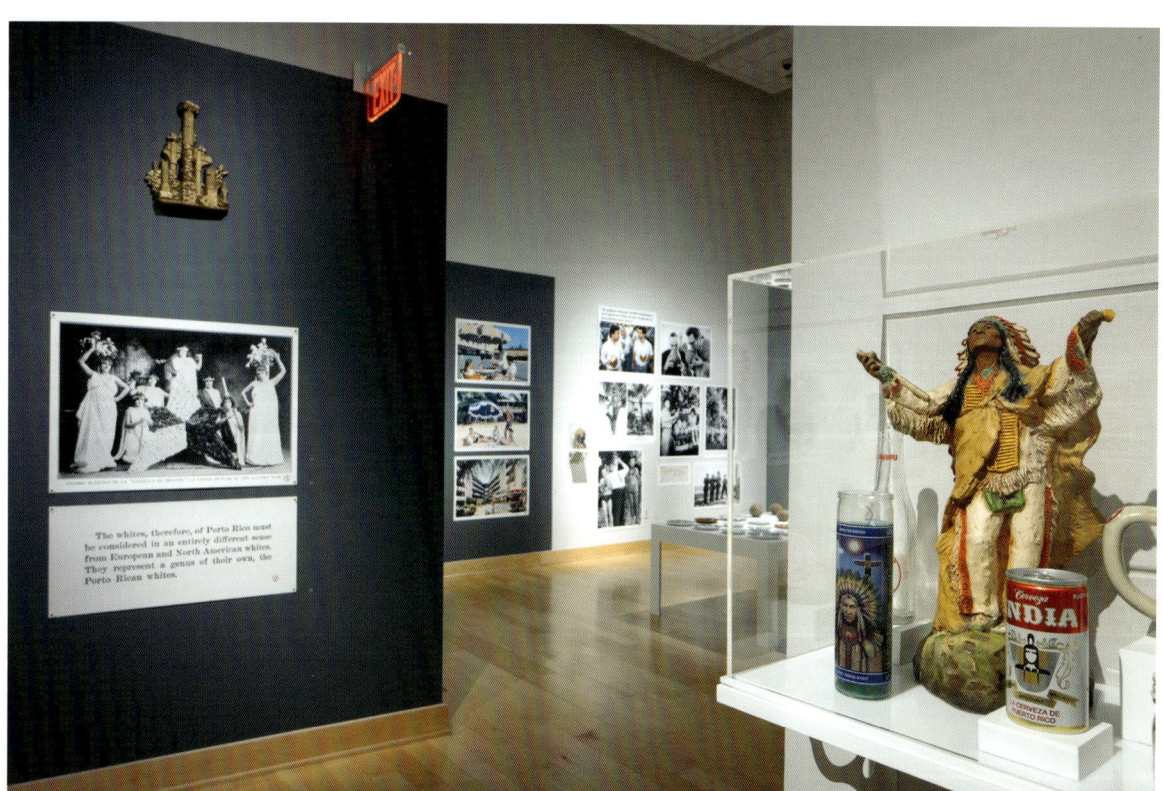

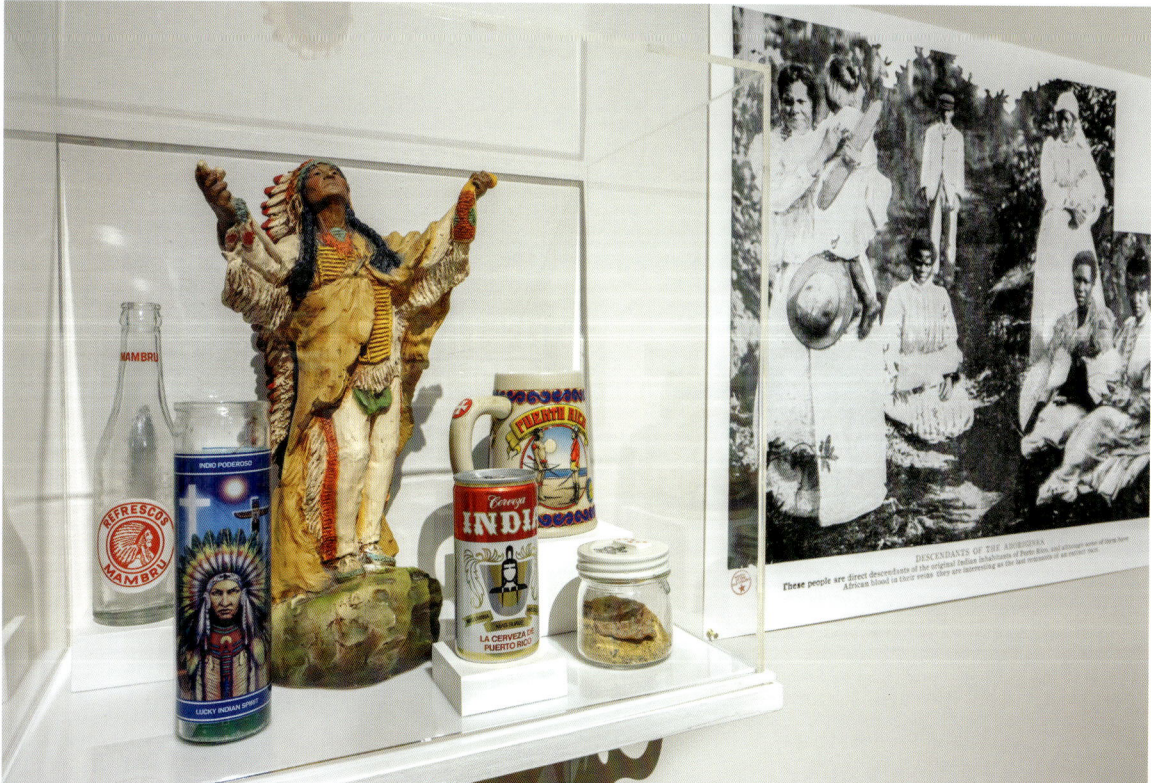

Plate 45. Installation view. *Hombres representando a soldados españoles de la época colonial; The history of Porto Rico is...*; and *The Golden Conquistador* (foreground); flag-related photographs (background). *The Museum of the Old Colony*, 2022. Checklist Nos. 36–38.

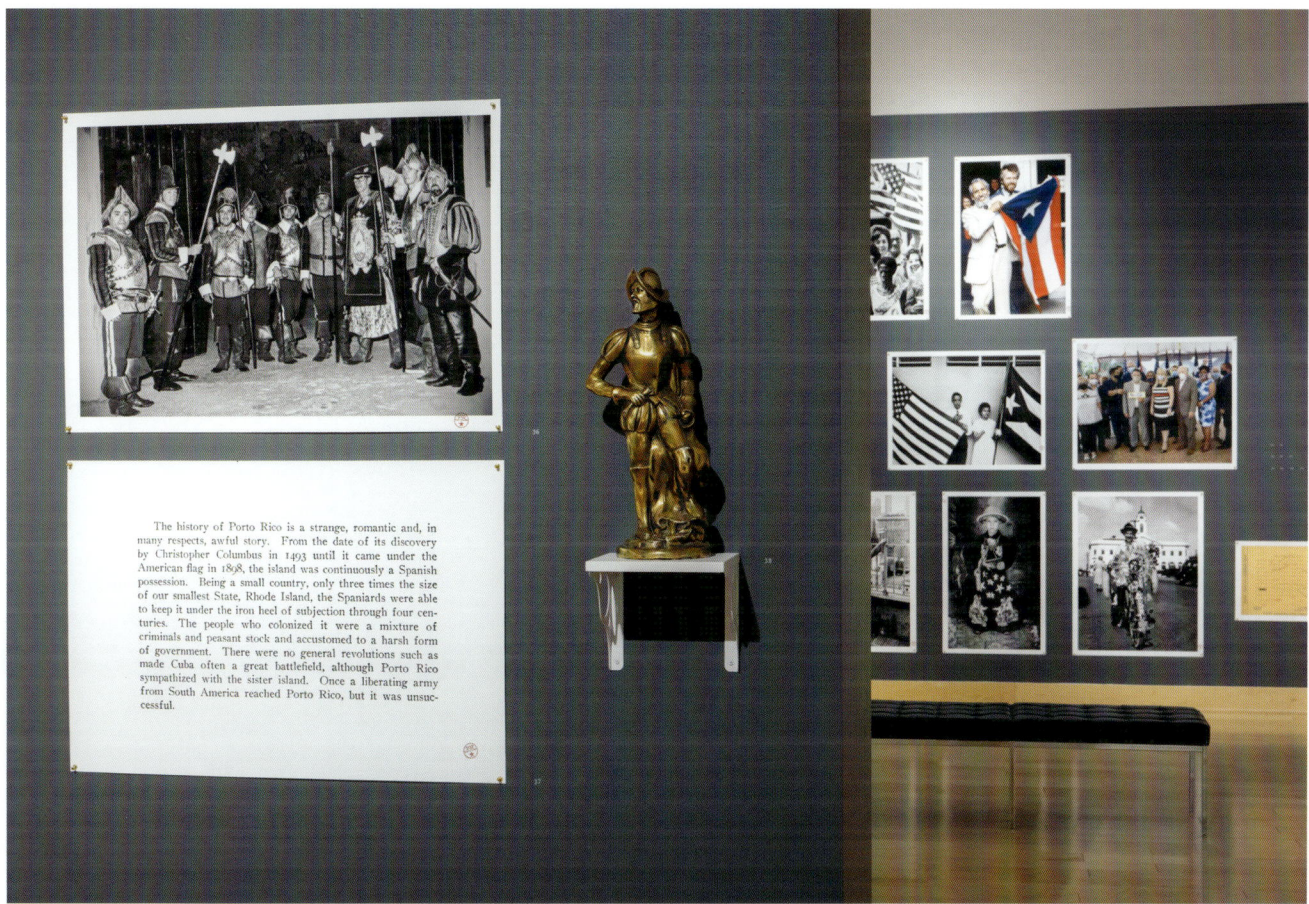

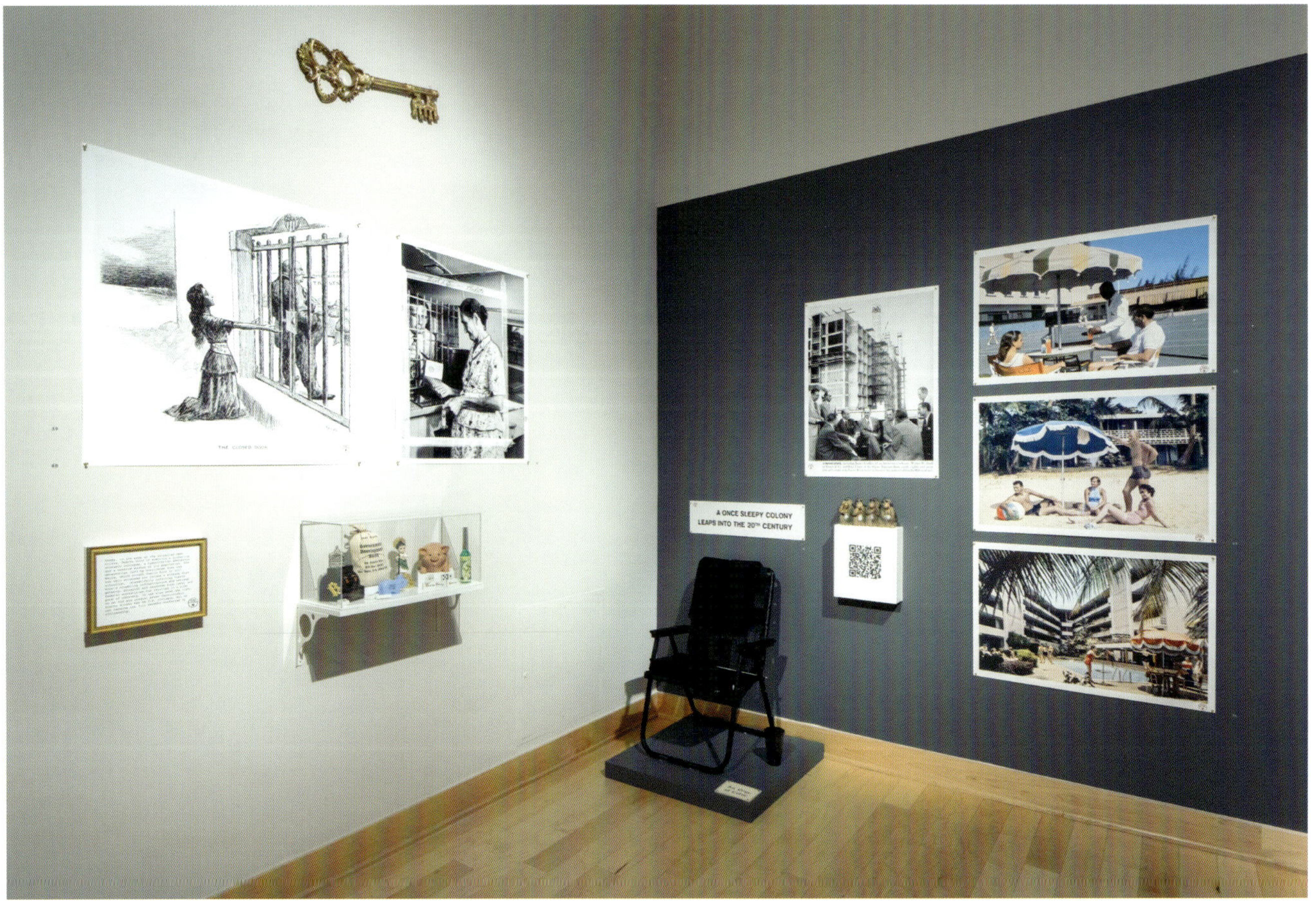

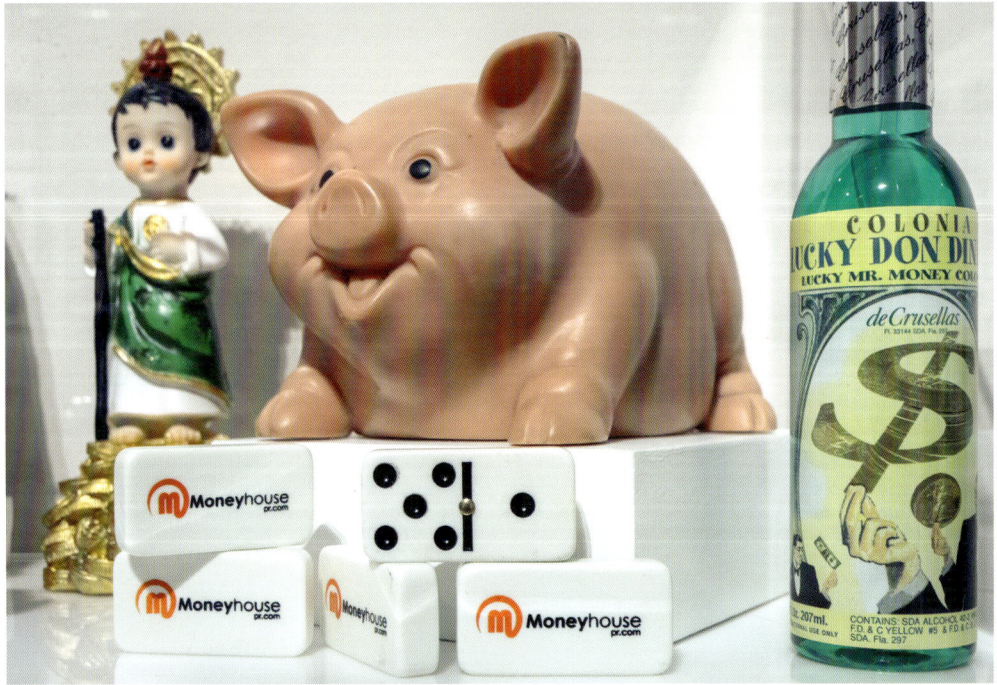

Plate 48. Installation view. Found object and video: *See No Evil, Hear No Evil* and tourism-related photographs. *The Museum of the Old Colony*, 2022. Checklist Nos. 65, 67–68, 70.

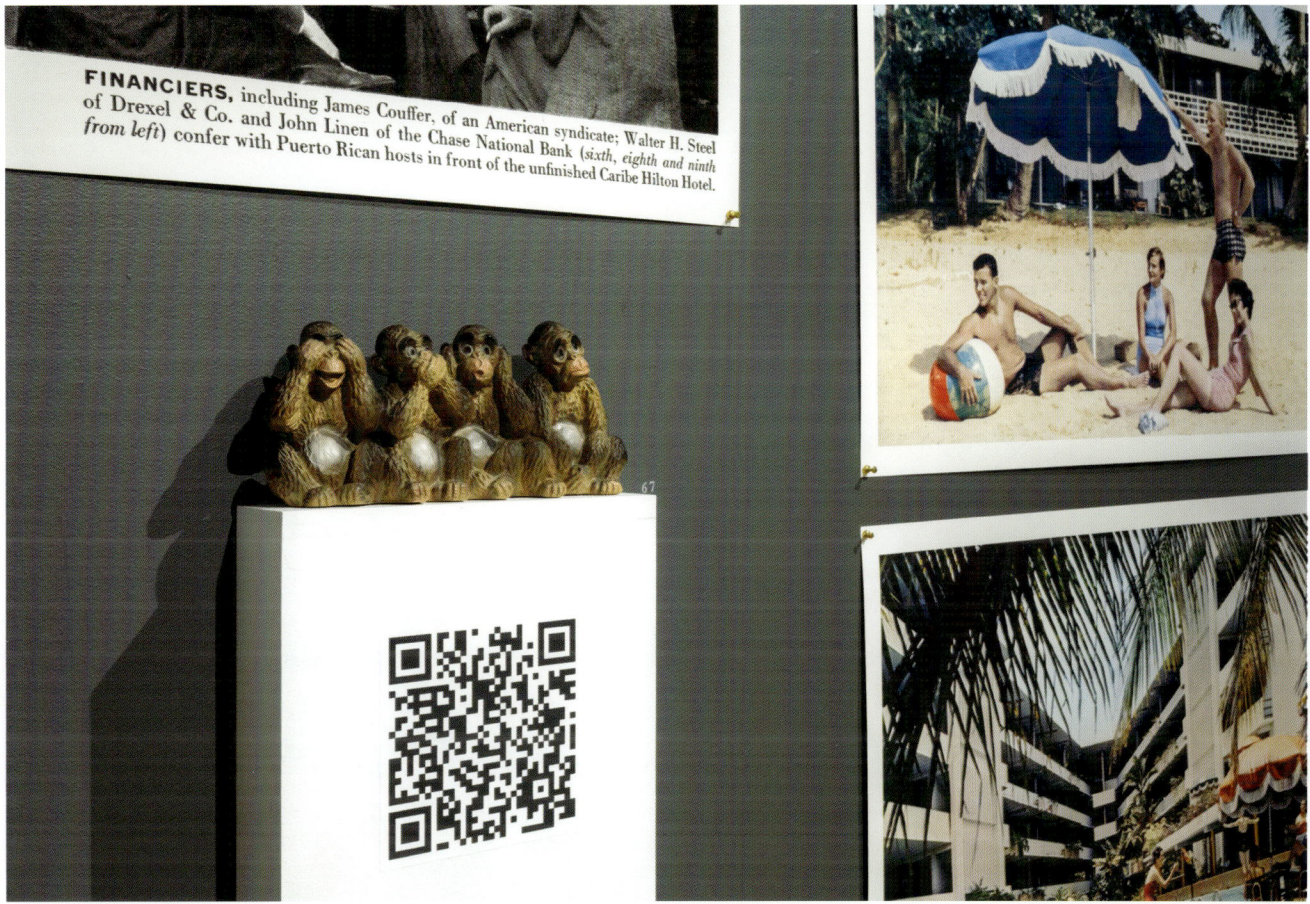

Plate 49. Installation view. *Platos y Cocos* (foreground) and tourism and coconut-related photographs, objects, and captions. *The Museum of the Old Colony*, 2022. Checklist Nos. 63–79.

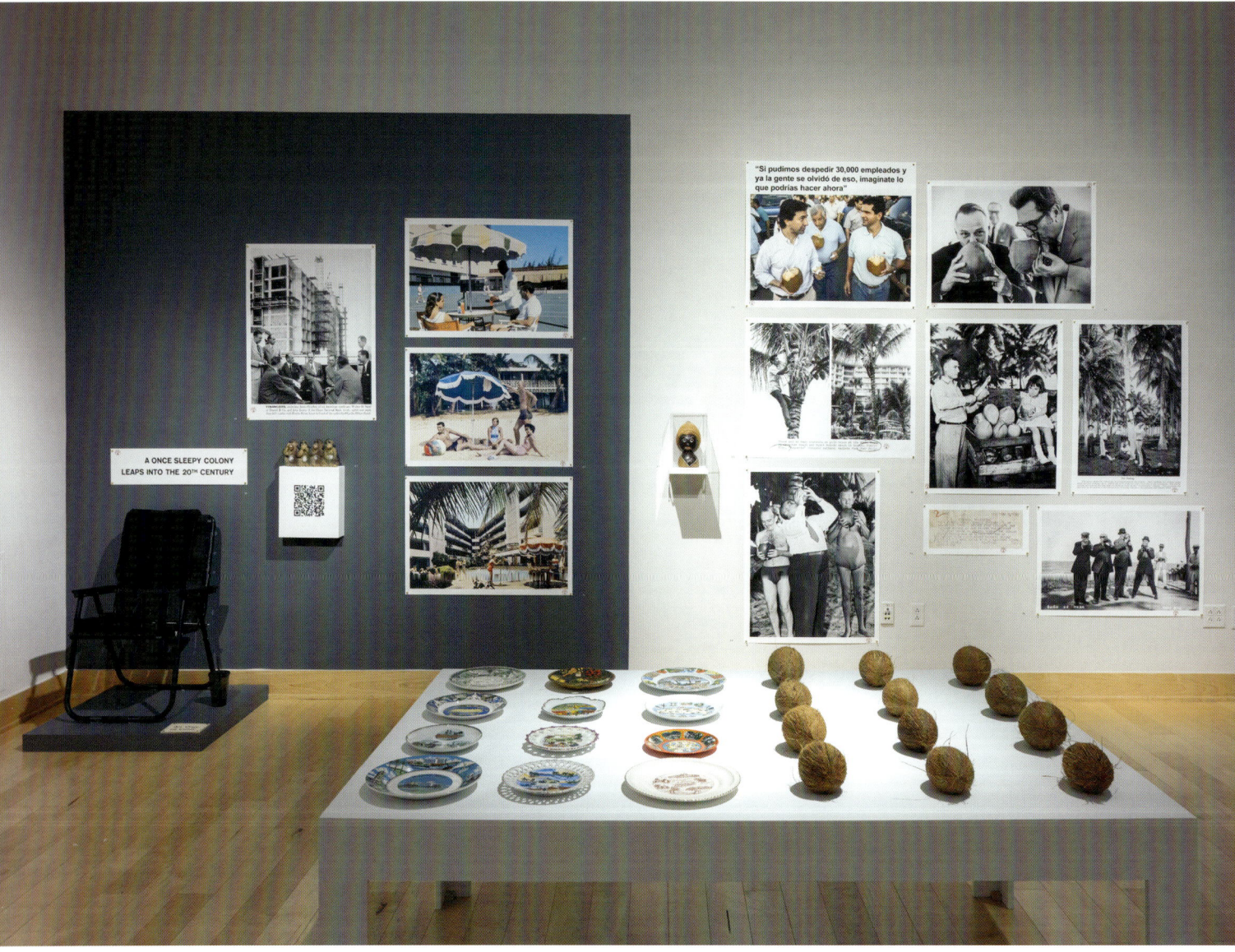

Plate 50. Installation view. *Coco-man Souvenir* and coconut-related photographs and captions. *The Museum of the Old Colony*, 2022. Checklist Nos. 71, 73–74, 76–79.

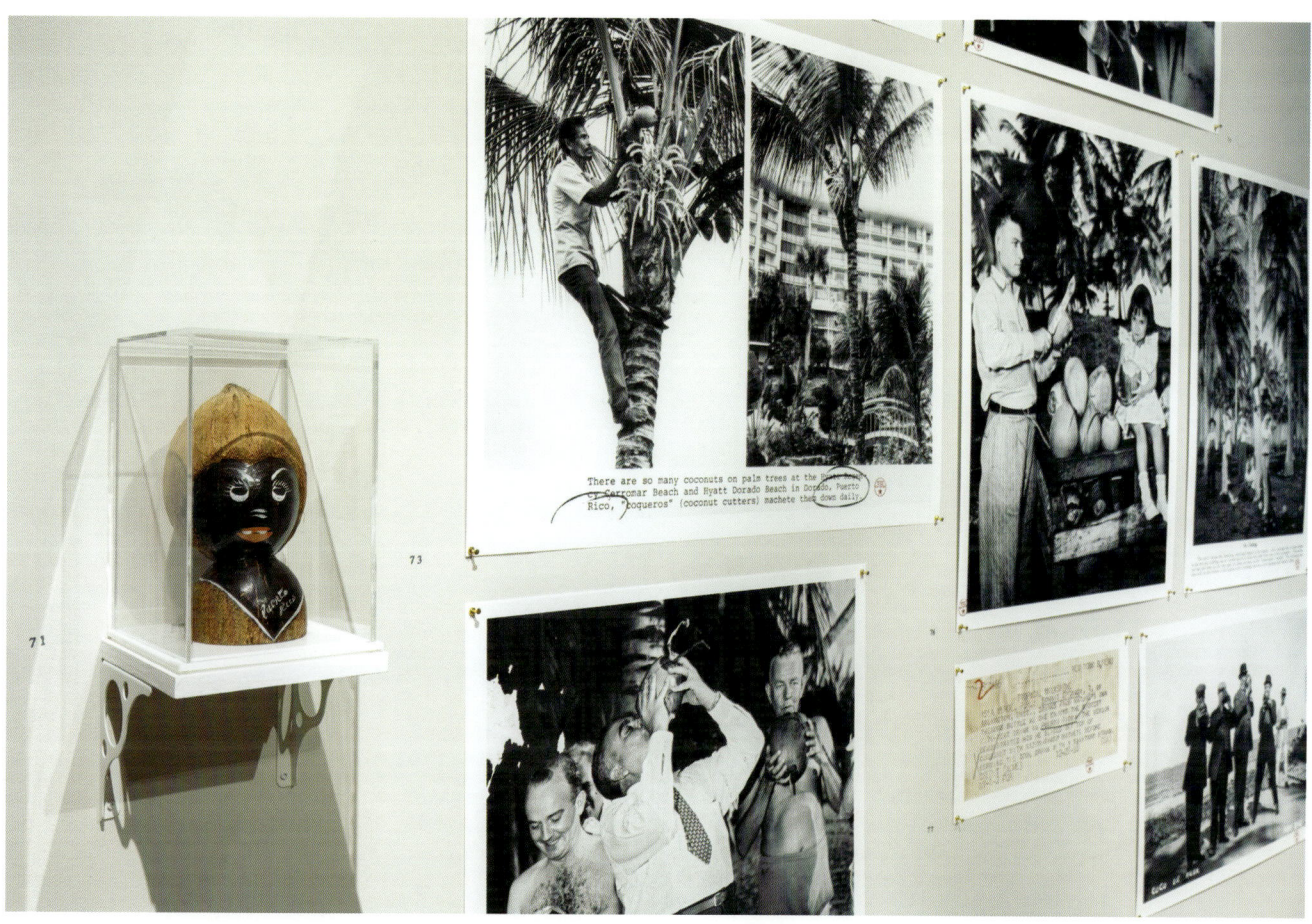

Plates 51–52. Installation views. Military parade
photographs and *Military Police Helmet* (including detail).
The Museum of the Old Colony, 2022. Checklist Nos. 80–86.

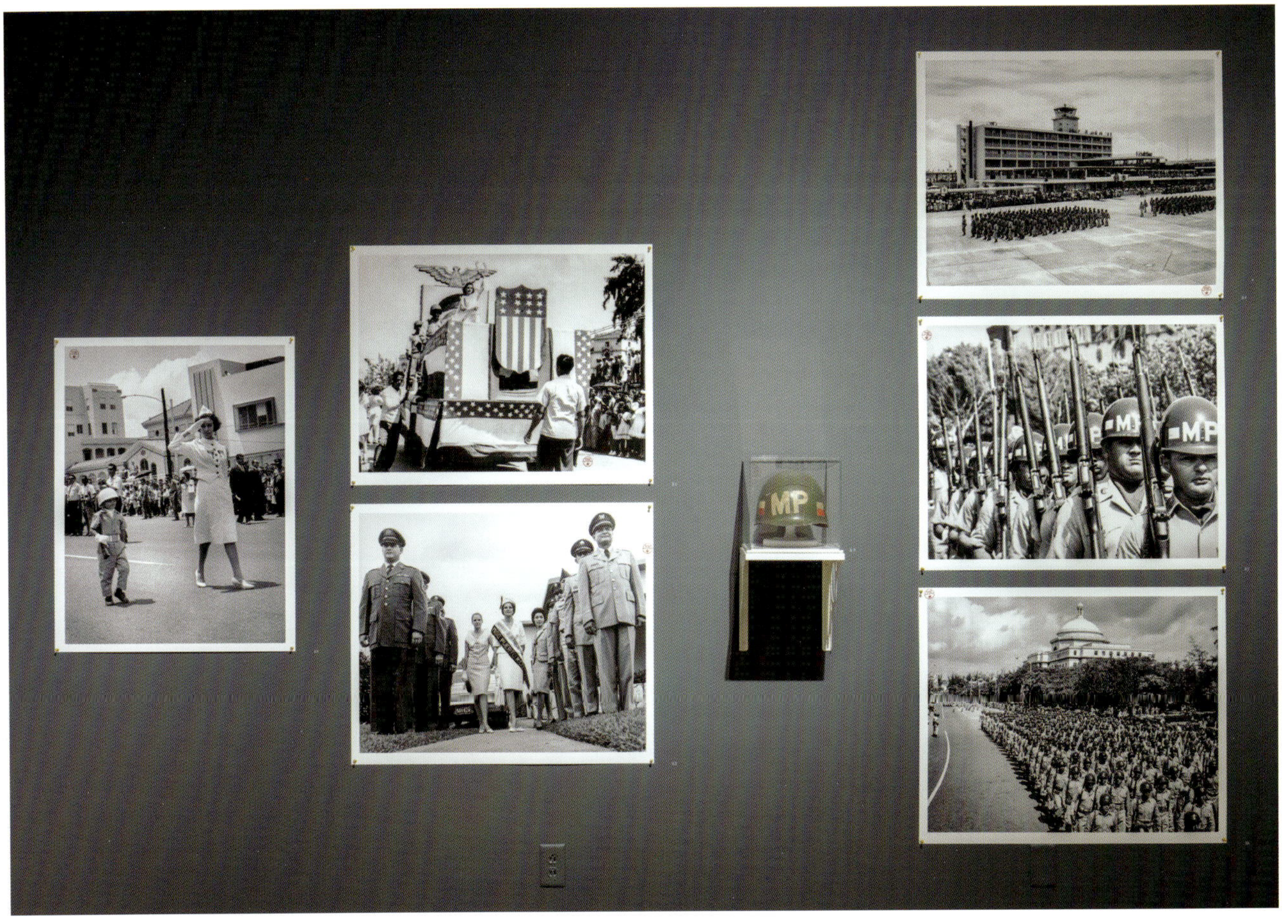

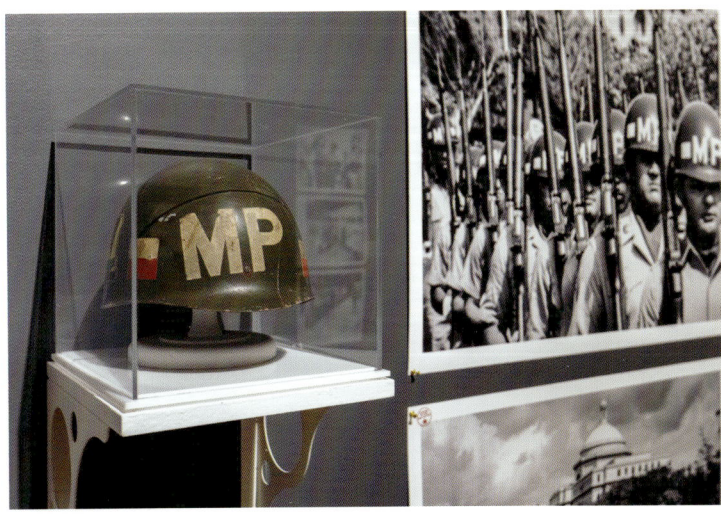

Plate **53**. Installation view. *A Splendid Little War*
(foreground) and *Souvenir handkerchief* and military-
related photographs. *The Museum of the Old Colony*, 2022.
Checklist Nos. 88, 90–92.

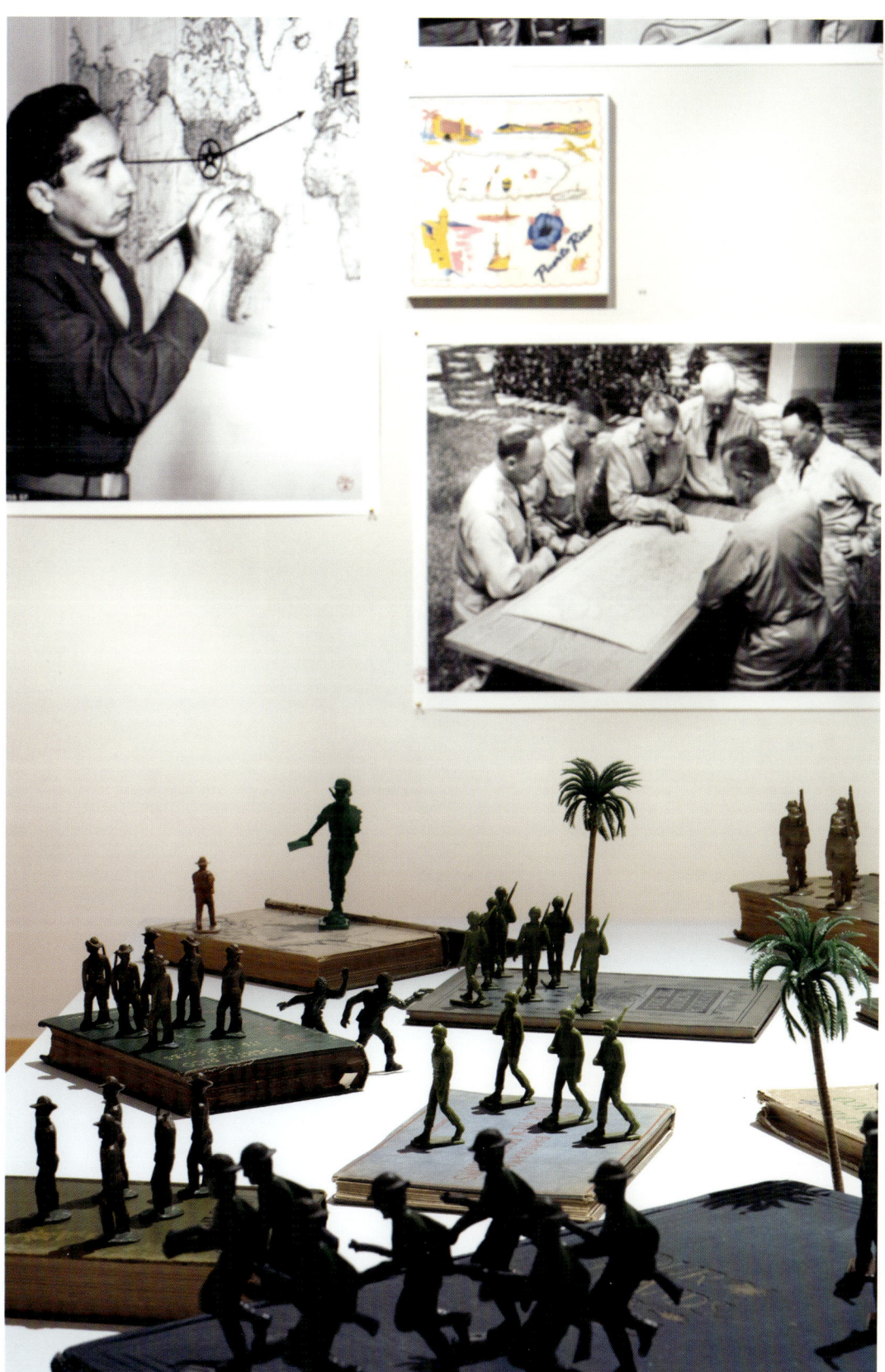

Plate 54. Installation view. *A Splendid Little War* (foreground) and military and flag-related photographs. *The Museum of the Old Colony*, 2022. Checklist Nos. 88–100.

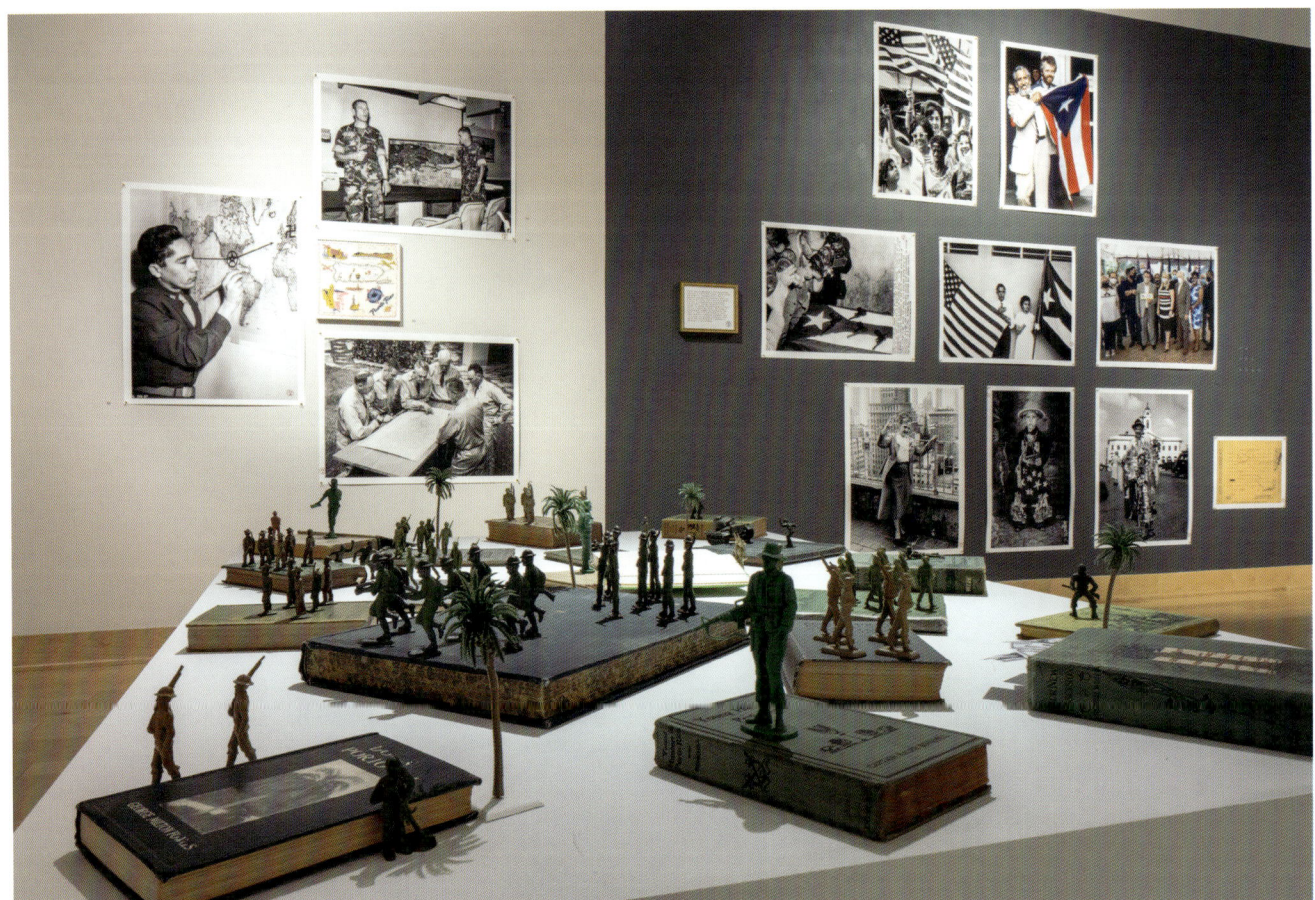

Plate 55. Installation view. *Alcaldesa de San Juan; Boy with Cowboy Costume;* and *Real Yankee Doodle Dandy. The Museum of the Old Colony,* 2022. Checklist Nos. 98–100.

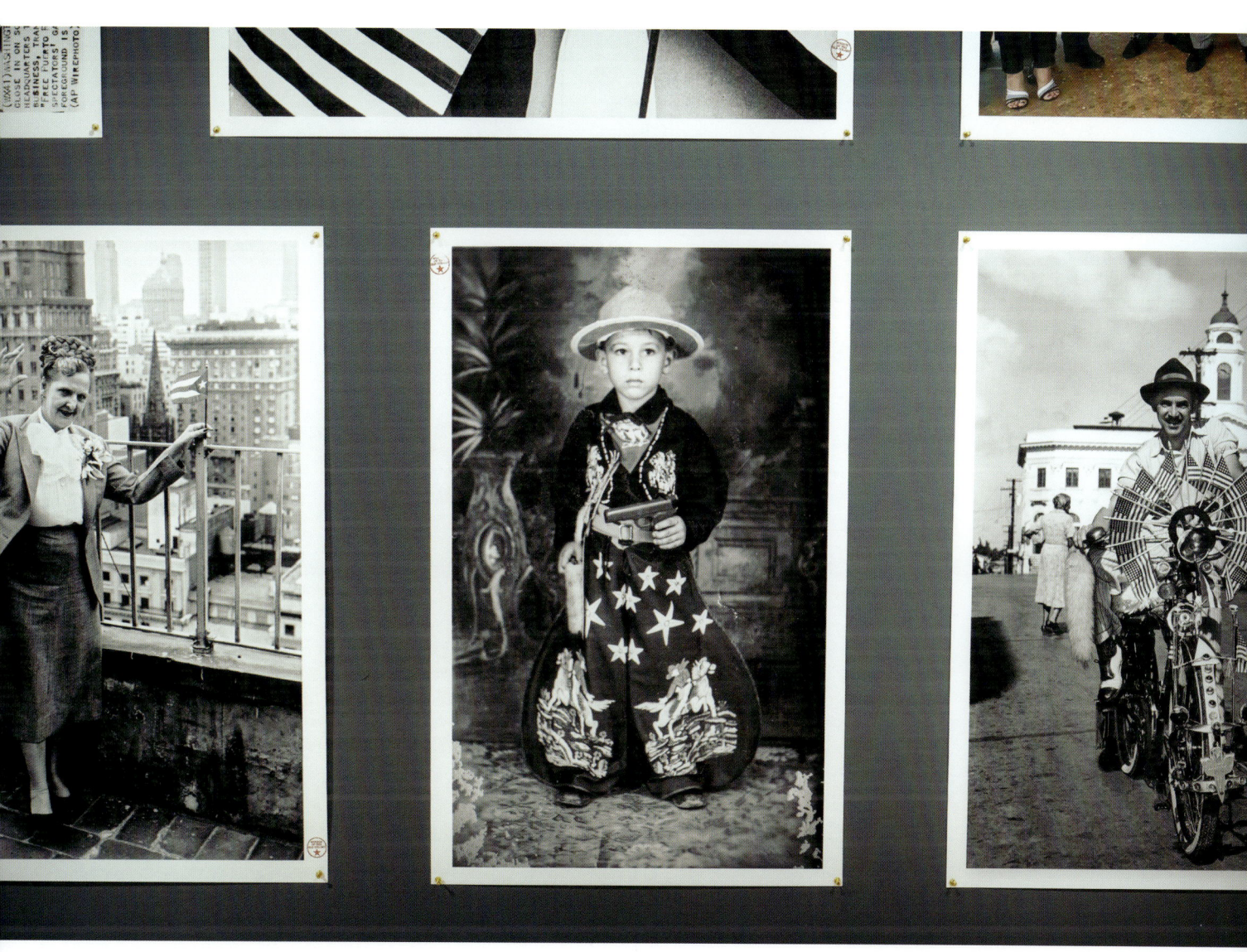

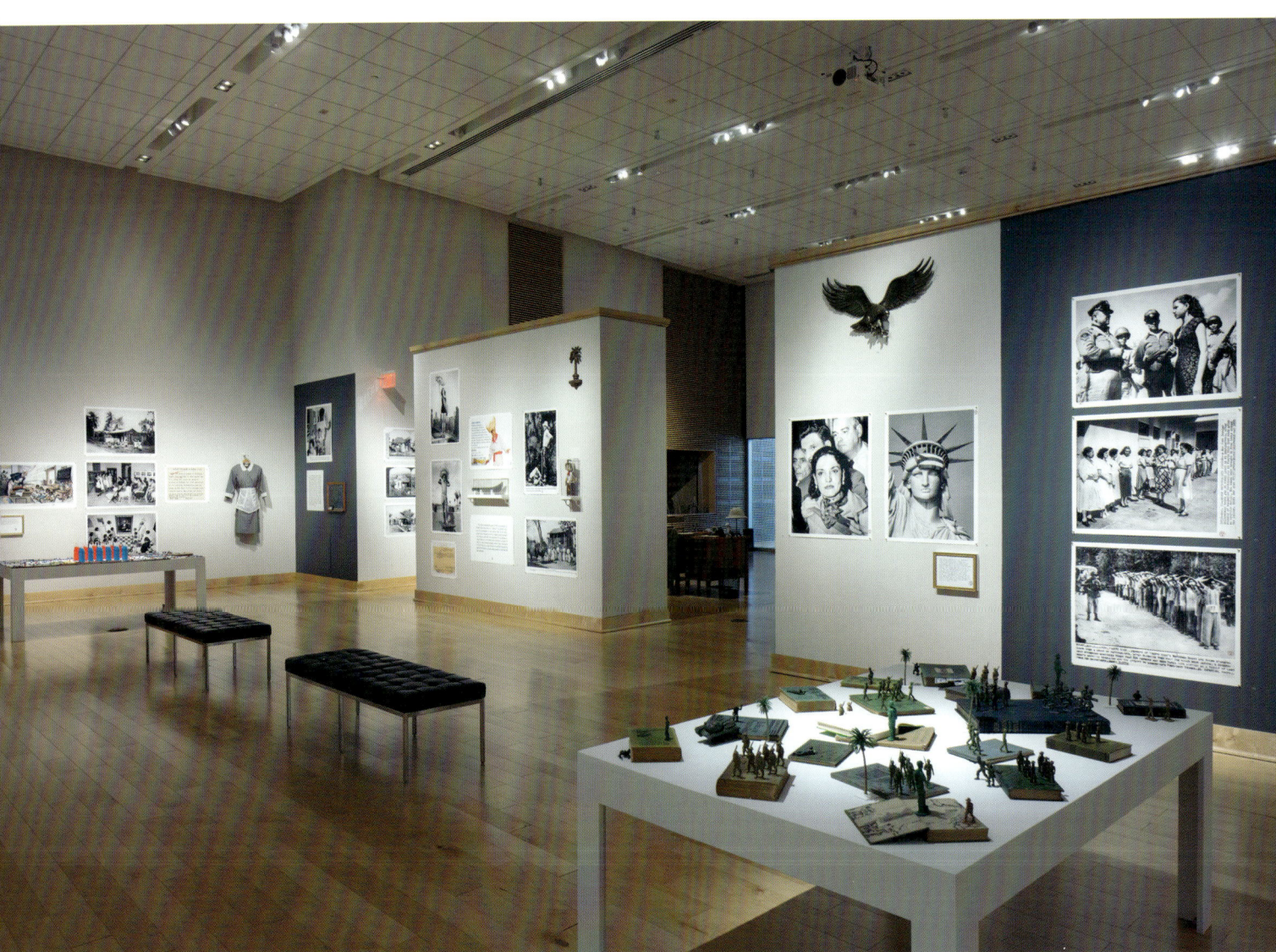

Plate 57. Installation view. *Watchful Eagle* and Puerto Rican Nationalist-related photographs. *The Museum of the Old Colony*, 2022. Checklist Nos. 53–58.

105

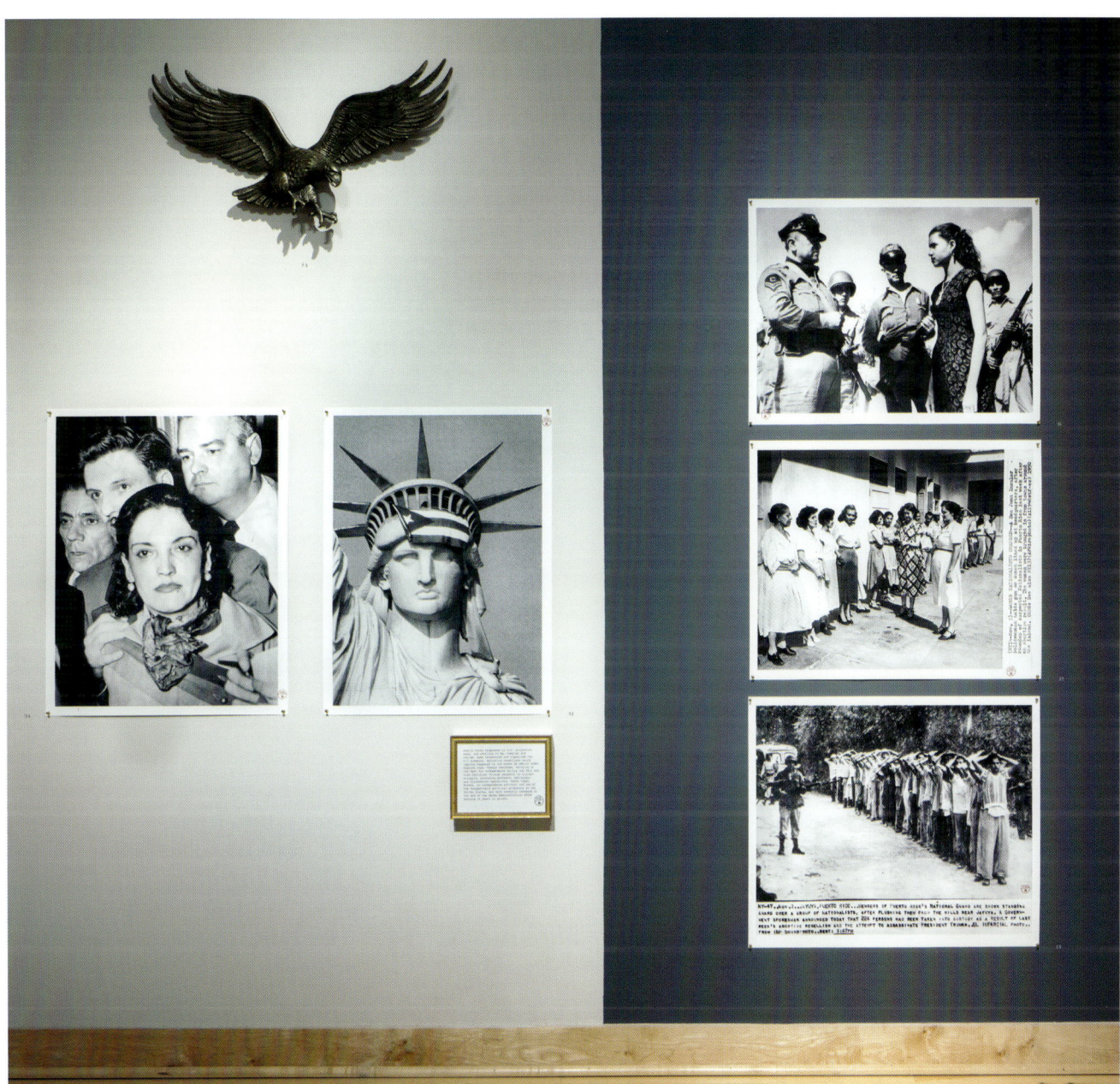

Plate 58. Installation views. *Jibaro*-related photographs, objects, and captions. *The Museum of the Old Colony*, 2022. Checklist Nos. 43–52.

Plate 59. Installation view. *Jibaro Costume; El Machete; He knows poverty and hardship*; and *Jibaritxs*. *The Museum of the Old Colony*, 2022. Checklist Nos. 46–48, 52.

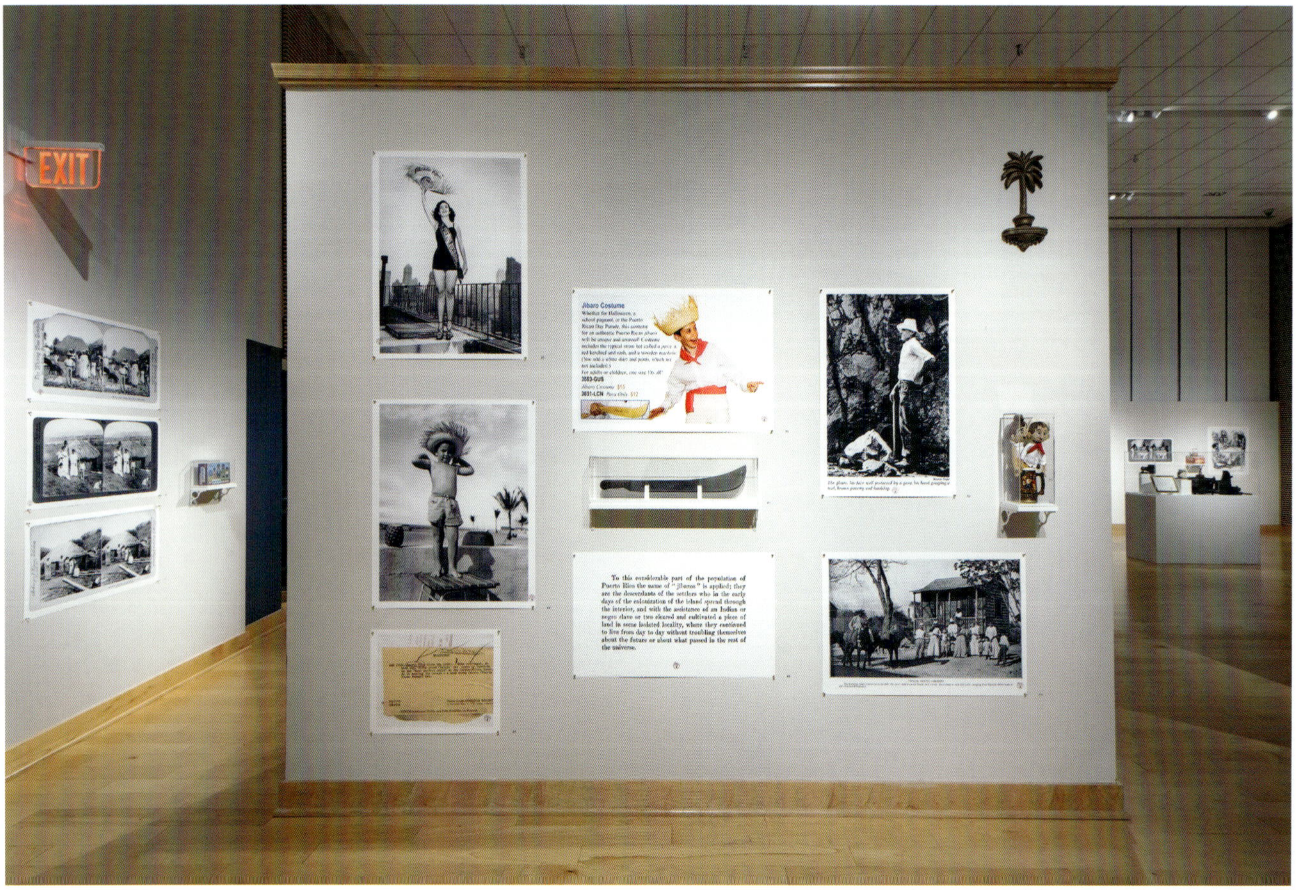

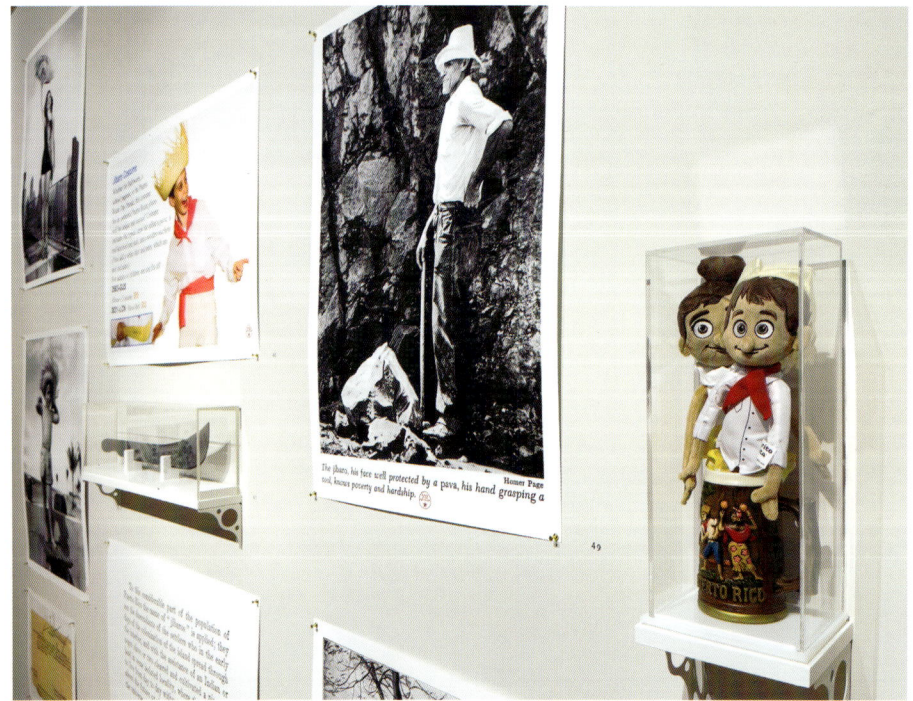

Plate 60. Installation view. Transportation and *jibaro*-related photographs, objects, and caption. *The Museum of the Old Colony*, 2022. Checklist No. 102–106.

107

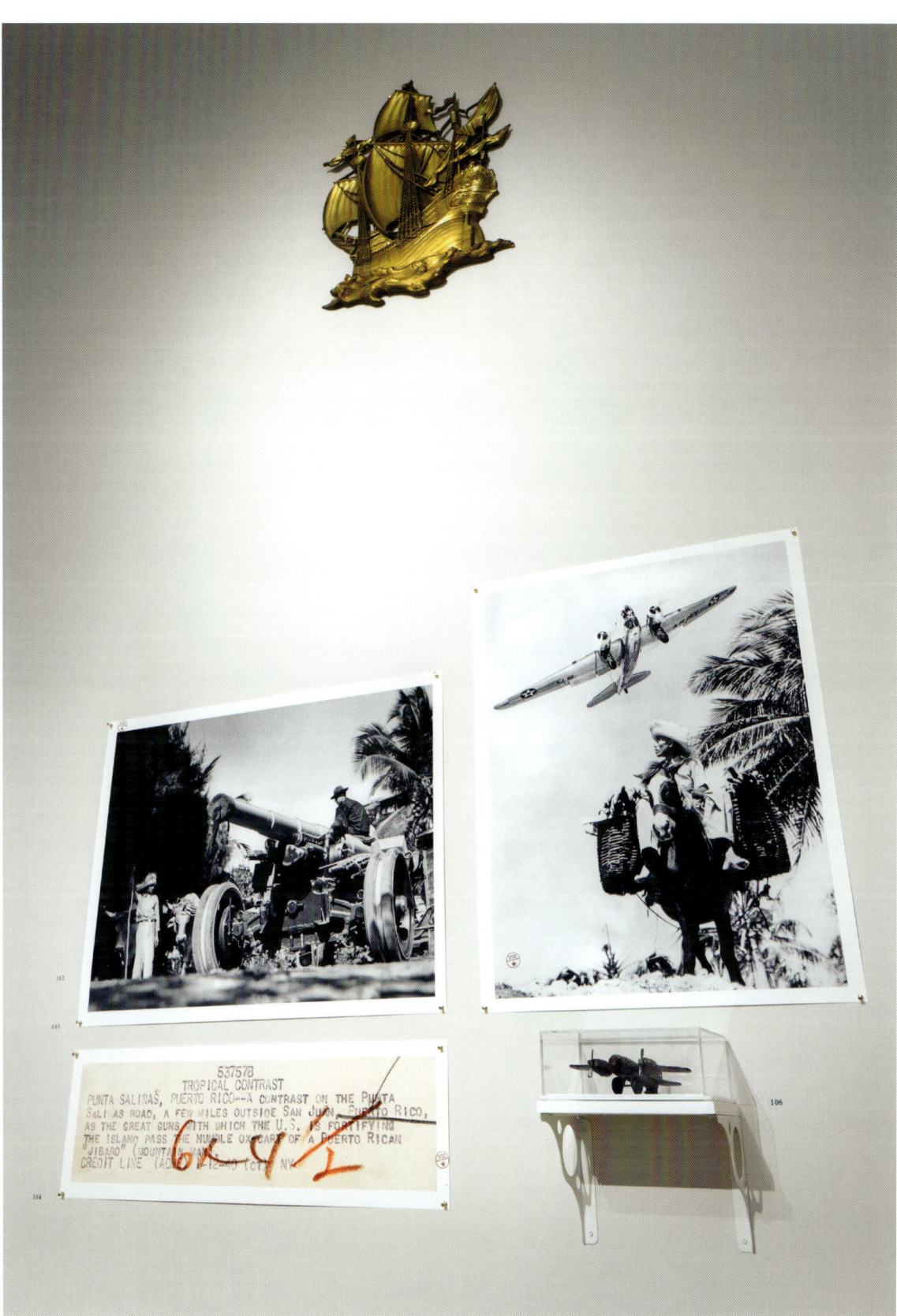

Plates **61–62**. Installation views. *Schoolbooks and Kool-Aid* (and detail); beauty and birth-control industry-related photographs, objects, and captions. *The Museum of the Old Colony*, 2022. Checklist Nos. 107–114.

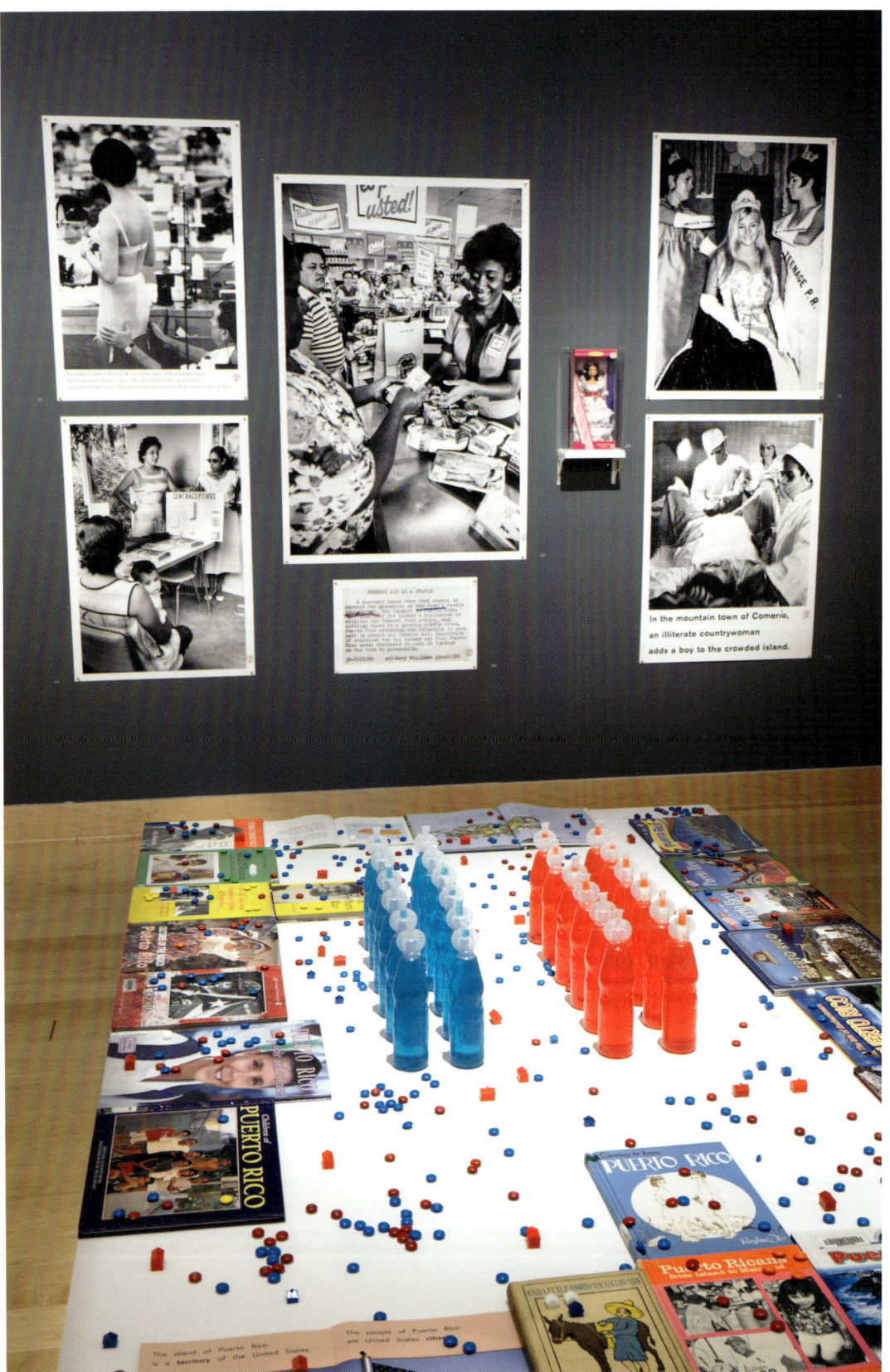

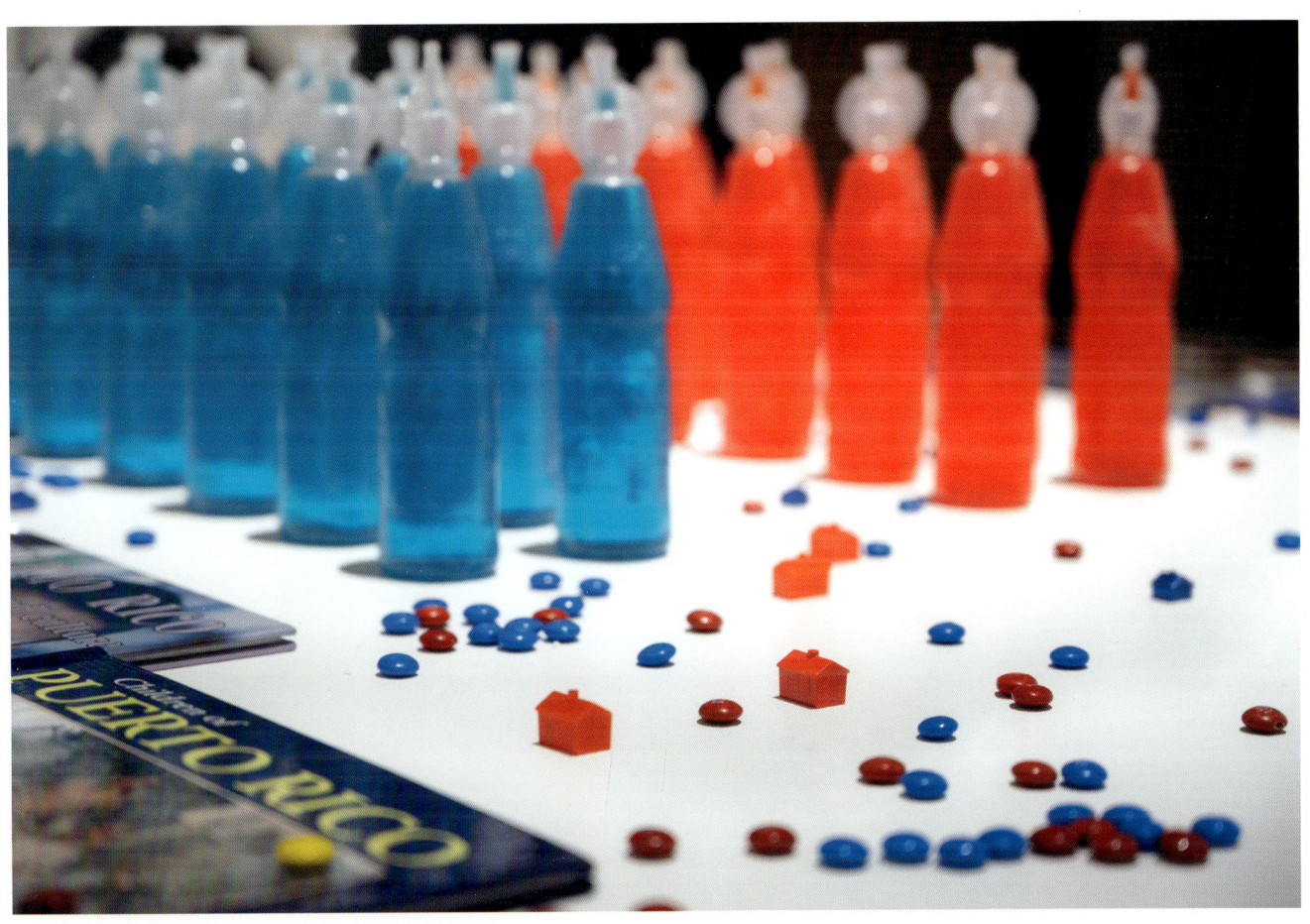

Plate 63. Installation view. Education-related
photographs, objects, and captions. *The Museum of
the Old Colony*, 2022. Checklist Nos. 115–123.

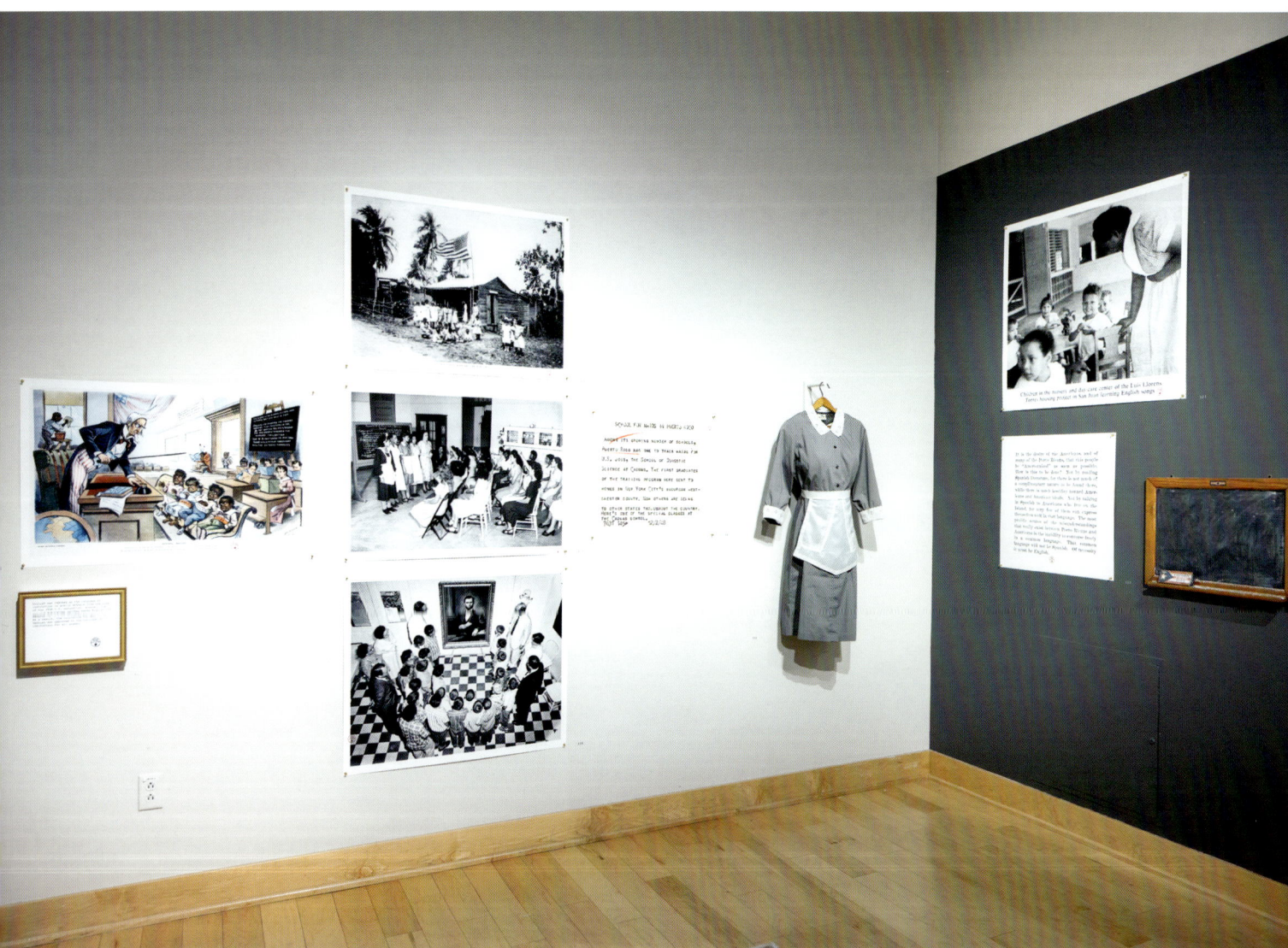

Plate 64. *School Begins*. Louis Dalrymple, *Puck*, January 25, 1899 | 2021. *The Museum of the Old Colony*, 2022. Checklist No. 115.

Plates 65–66. Installation views. *School for Maids in Puerto Rico* and caption (verso). Wide World Photos, Inc., December 2, 1948 | 2019. Checklist Nos. 117, 119.

111

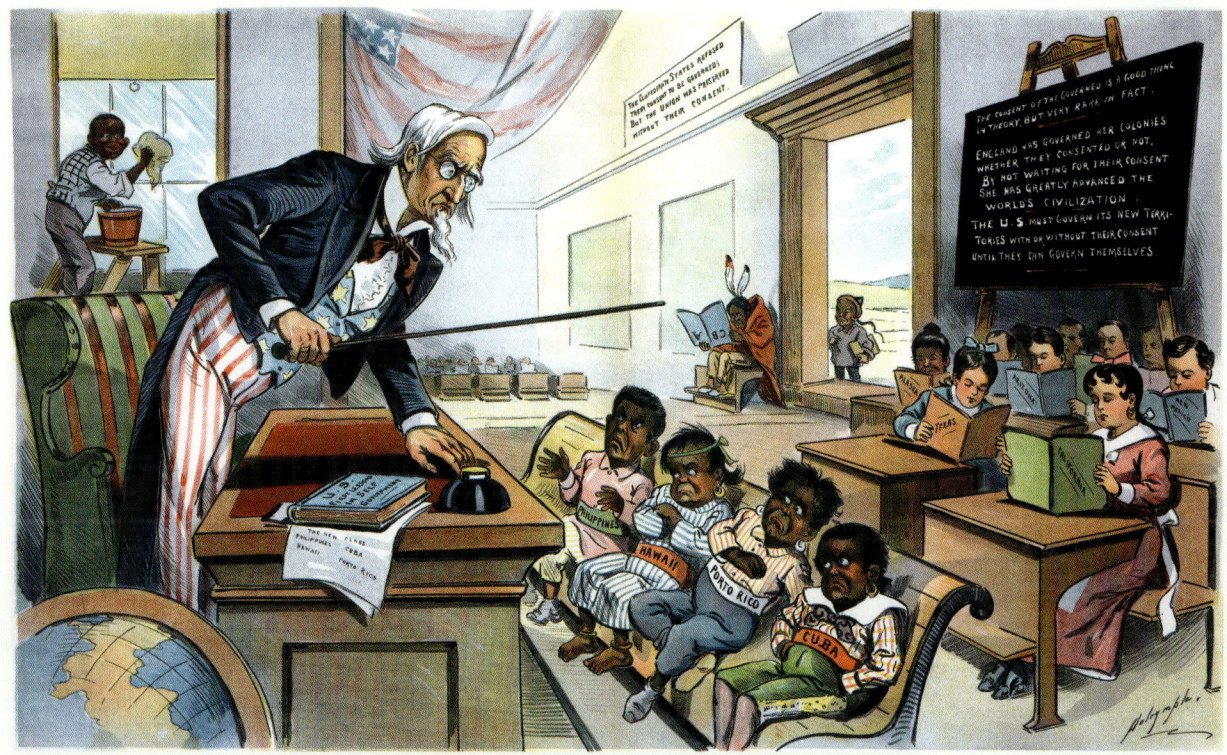

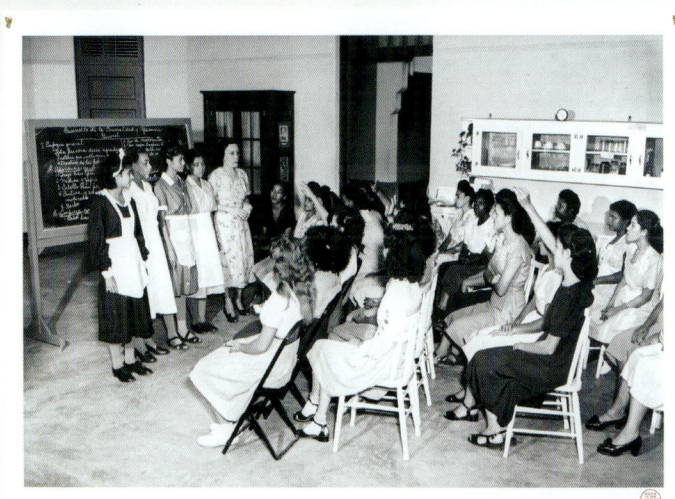

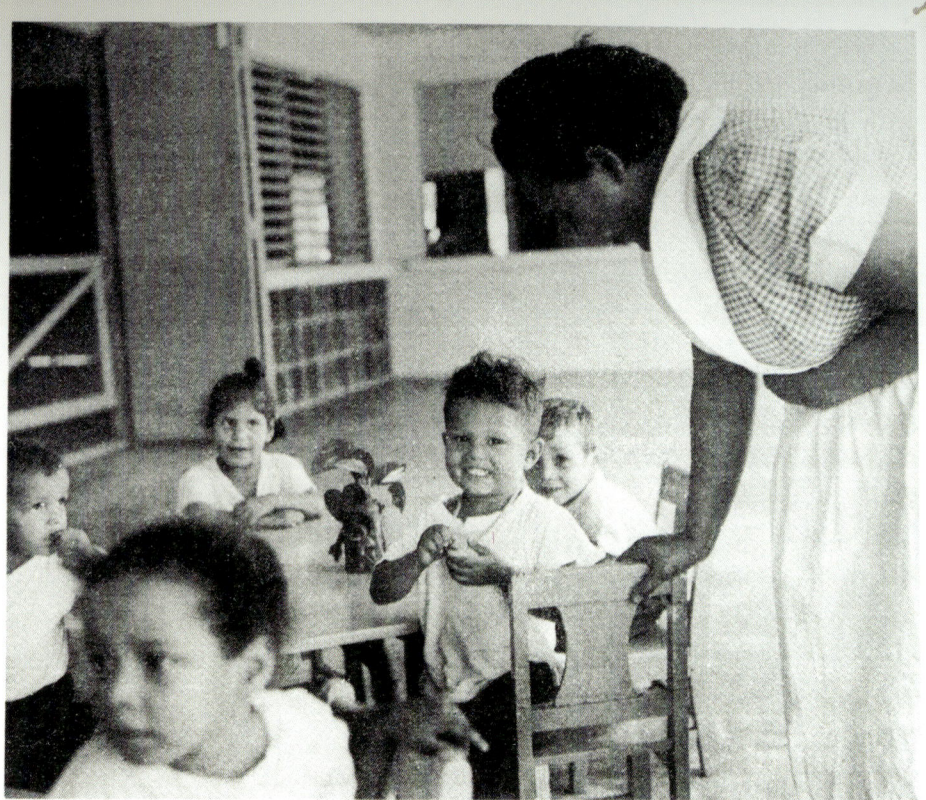

Children in the nursery and day-care center of the Luis Llorens Torres housing project in San Juan learning English songs

It is the desire of the Americans, and of many of the Porto Ricans, that this people be "Americanized" as soon as possible. How is this to be done? Not by reading Spanish literature, for there is not much of a complimentary nature to be found there, while there is much hostility toward Americans and American ideals. Not by talking in Spanish to Americans who live on the Island, for very few of them can express themselves well in that language. The most prolific source of the misunderstandings that really exist between Porto Ricans and Americans is the inability to converse freely in a common language. That common language will not be Spanish. Of necessity it must be English.

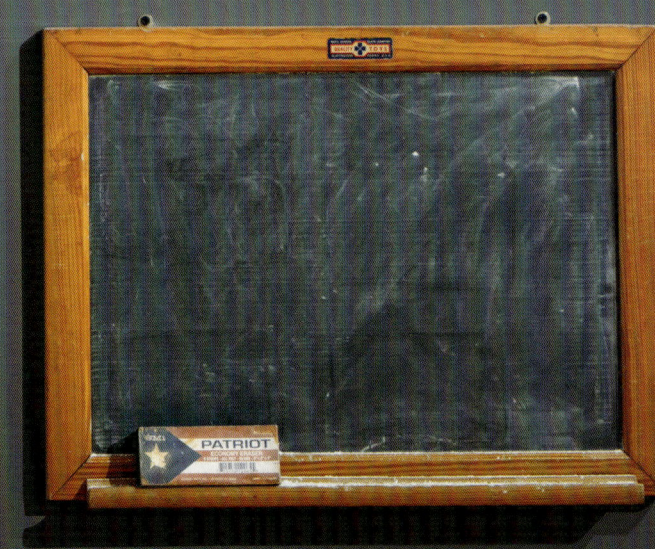

Plate 67. *Installation view. Children Learning English Songs; It is the desire of the Americans*; and *Patriot Economy Erasure. The Museum of the Old Colony*, 2022. Checklist Nos. 121–123.

Plate 68. Installation view. *Patriot Economy Erasure.* Antique chalkboard and eraser | 2017–2021. *The Museum of the Old Colony*, 2022. Checklist No. 123.

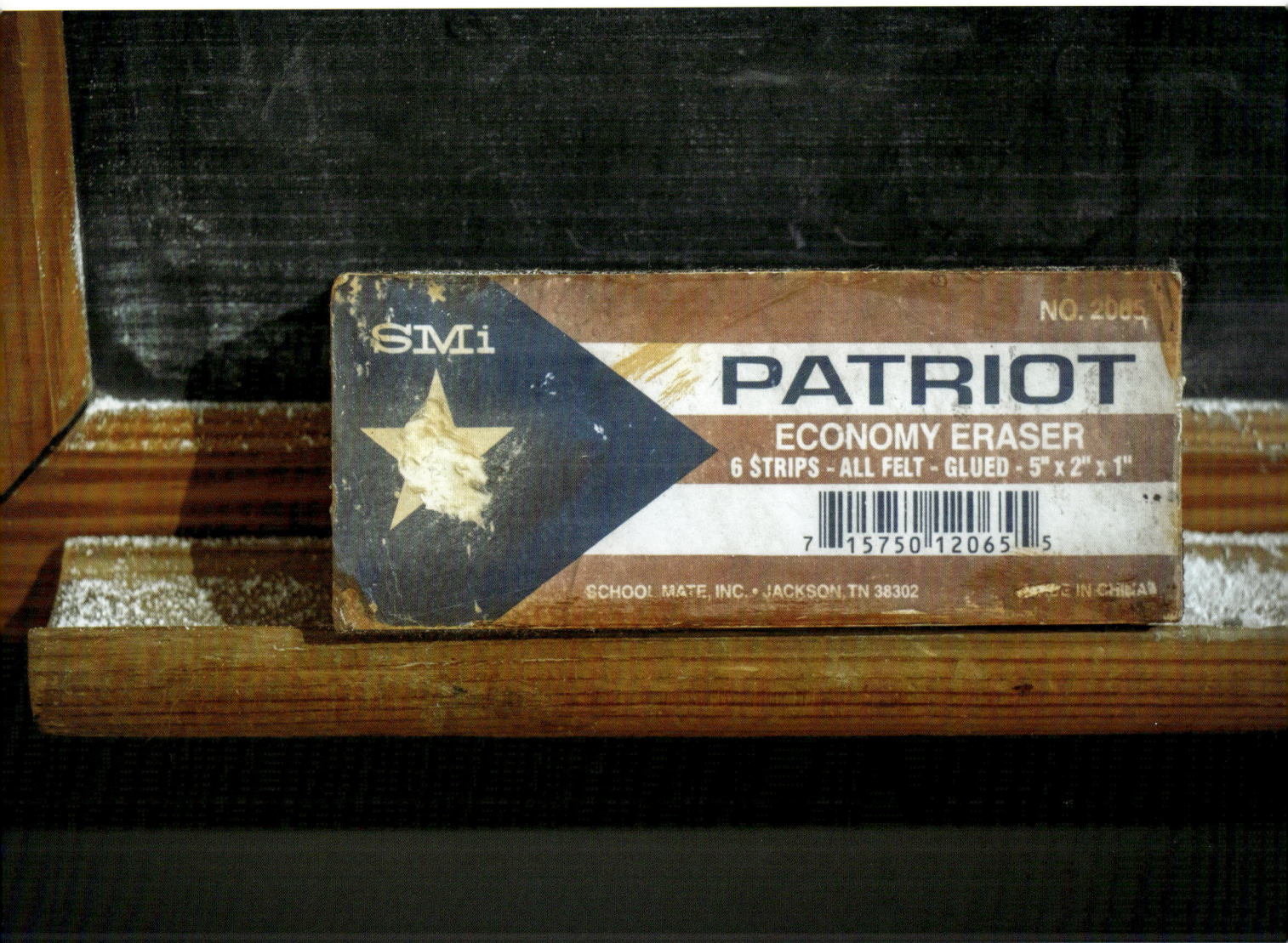

3D Visualization of *The Museum of the Old Colony*

Ángel A. García Jr.

In an exciting collaboration between James Madison University's School of Art, Design, and Art History and the Department of Geology and Environmental Science, we implemented a remote sensing tool for the visualization of *The Museum of the Old Colony: An Art Installation by Pablo Delano*. We constructed a point cloud of 7.5 x 106 points, using a mobile Light Detection and Ranging (LIDAR) scanner with Simultaneous Localization and Mapping (SLAM) technology. To stimulate fruitful exchange between art and science, we adapted scientific tools to accurately document an art exhibition. Our aim has been to make the installation accessible to students and faculty for ongoing engagement and to aid artists and curators in future exhibition design and archiving processes. Technologies used in geological science can offer educators, learners, and makers in the arts rich opportunities to deconstruct exhibition spaces and examine them from perspectives unavailable to the naked eye. Such tools can also help create more engaging and immersive experiences for viewers.

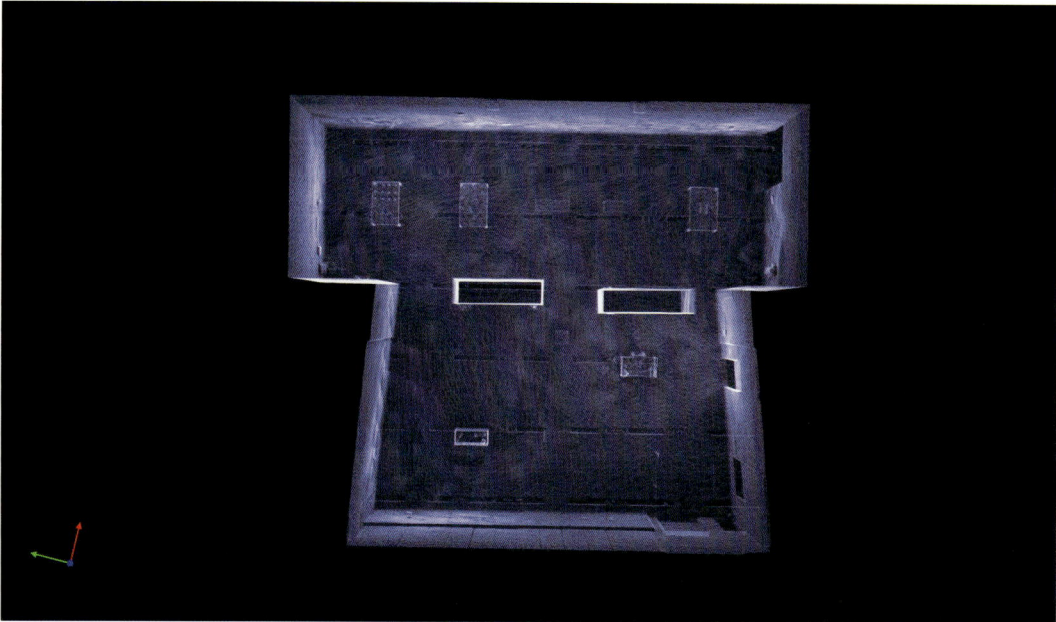

Figure A. (aerial view): General layout of installation in Duke Gallery, showing two moveable walls at center, flanked by artifacts on desk and in free-standing display case in front room, and on three tables in back room.

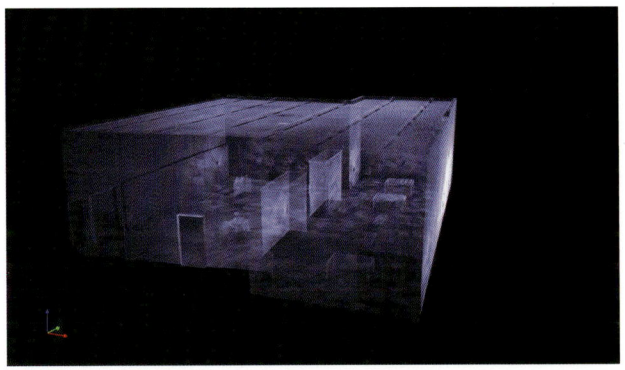

Figure B. (side view): General layout of installation, from back corner (looking west) across Duke Gallery.

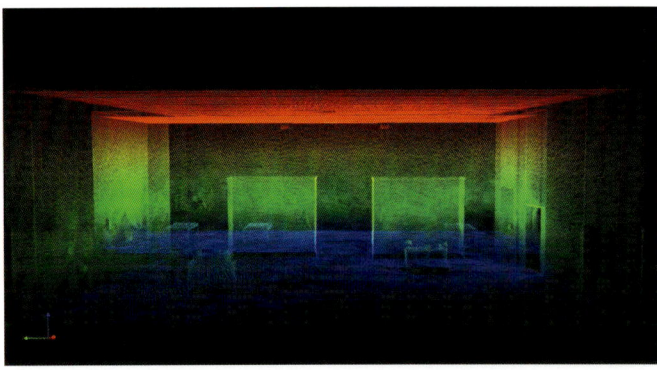

Figure C. General scan of Duke Gallery based on elevation. Hotter colors (moving towards red) show high elevation and colder colors (moving towards blue) denote lower elevation. Blue is thus the floor and red the ceiling.

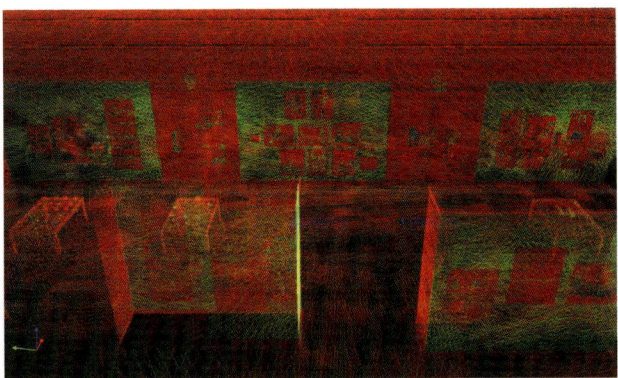

Figure D1. General scan of room based on intensity (return strength of emitted laser pulse, looking north.). Purpose of intensity is to differentiate materials using laser pulse emitted by scanner. Different colors show diversity of materials used and their layout and pattern in the installation. Figure D1 shows view looking west.

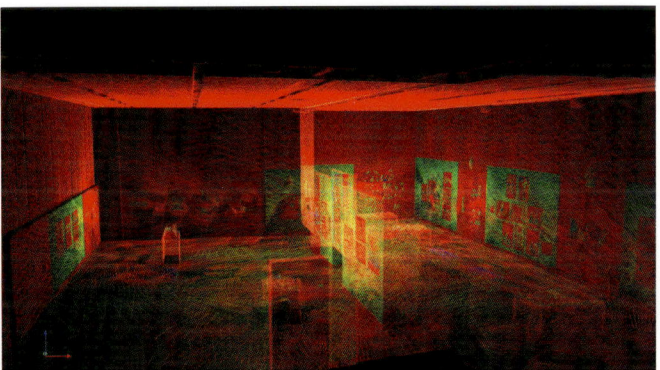

Figure D2. General scan of room based on intensity (return strength of emitted laser pulse, looking north). Purpose of intensity is to differentiate materials using laser pulse emitted by scanner. Different colors show diversity of materials used and their layout and pattern in the installation. Figure D2 shows view looking north.

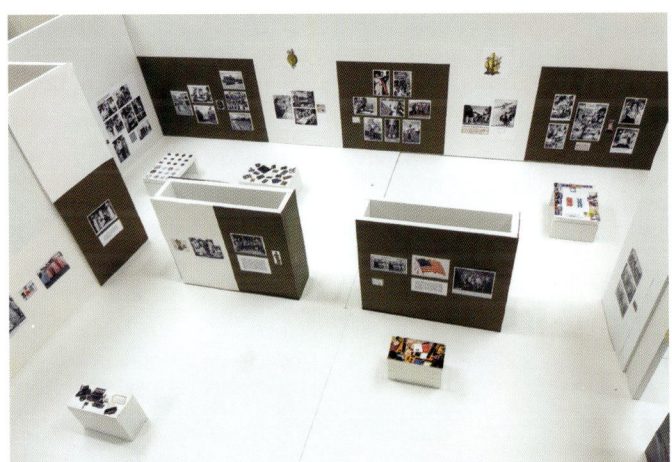

Figure 12. Three-dimensional scale model of *The Museum of the Old Colony*, Duke Hall Gallery of Fine Art, 2022. Model and photograph by Pablo Delano, the artist's studio, Hartford, Connecticut, September 2021.

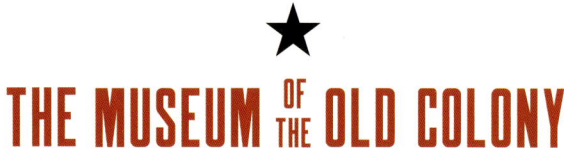

THE MUSEUM OF THE OLD COLONY

AN ART INSTALLATION BY PABLO DELANO

February 1 to March 26, 2022
Duke Hall Gallery of Fine Art

Artwork titles are based on original captions, with some notable exceptions and deliberate deviations. Dates of original sources are listed, when known, followed by artwork date.

1. *Old Colony Timeline.* Found objects: vintage Old Colony brand bottles and cans, circa 1940s–2017 | 2018.

2. *They Don't Need Any Passport.* Video | 2020–2022. See endnote.

3. *At the Crossroads.* Assemblage of found objects | 2021.

4. *The Museum Desk.* Sculptural assemblage of found objects | 2020–2022.

5. *A Group of newly made Americans at Ponce, Porto Rico.* M. H. Zahner Publisher, Niagara Falls, NY, sold by Griffith & Griffith, Philadelphia, 1898 | 2019.

6. *The Star Spangled Banner-Puerto Rico's Flag. A Little Journey to Puerto Rico,* Marian M. George, A. Flanagan Company, Chicago, 1900 | 2019.

7. *Call it Imperialism if You Will....The American Magazine* 47, 1899 | 2019.

8. *Commissioners of Puerto Rico.* Photograph by M.W. Tennant, *Our Nation's Heroes—Army Operations in Porto Rico and the Philippines Concluding the Shortest and Most Successful War in History,* Historical Publishing Company, Philadelphia, 1898 | 2020.

9. *"Plantation Joe," Ponce, P.R.* B.W. Kilburn, Littleton, NH, 1899 | 2021.

10. *White Jesus with the Orishas.* Found object, resin | 2021.

11. *At Work in the Cane Field. Tying Bundles of Fallen Stalks, Porto Rico.* Keystone View Company, Meadville, PA, circa 1898 | 2021.

12. *Cupid.* Found object, 20th century (set of two) | 2020.

13. *"No One Loves Me"—Native Porto Ricans.* Photograph by B.L. Singley, Keystone View Company, Meadville, PA, 1900 | 2021.

14. *Porto Rican Boys in their Sunday Dress, Near Aibonita [sic].* Strohmeyer & Wyman, Underwood & Underwood Publishers, New York, 1900 | 2019.

15. *Waiting for Uncle Sam—On the Beach at Porto Rico* (recto). Photograph by B.L. Singley, Keystone View Company, Meadville, PA, 1900 | 2019.

16. *Waiting for Uncle Sam—On the Beach at Porto Rico* (verso). Keystone View Company, Meadville, PA, 1900 | 2019.

17. *Music Hath Charms—In a Porto Rican Park.* Photograph by B.L. Singley, Keystone View Company, Meadville, PA, 1900 | 2021.

18. *Story Without Words, Porto Rico.* Photograph by B.L. Singley, Keystone View Company, Meadville, PA, 1900 | 2021.

19. *A Porto Rican Family.* Keystone View Company, Meadville, PA, 1905 | 2021.

20. *Plum Pudding.* Assemblage of found objects: Libby's Corned Beef, Nabisco National Sodas, and miniature flags | 2021.

21. *Plenty of Room at the Table.* Illustration by Emil Flohri, *Judge* 50, no. 1268, February 3, 1906 | 2020.

22. *Tools of the Trade.* Assemblage of found and fabricated objects | 2021.

23. *Porto Rico. Women washing clothes, Ponce.* M. H. Zahner Publisher, Niagara Falls, NY, sold by Griffith & Griffith, Philadelphia, circa 1898 | 2021.

24. *Brooks Laundry, Ponce, Porto Rico.* Strohmeyer & Wyman Publishers, New York, sold by Underwood & Underwood, New York, 1899 | 2019.

25. *Washerwomen along the river on the outskirts of Ponce, Porto Rico.* Underwood & Underwood Publishers, New York, 1900 | 2021.

26. *Danaide*. Reproduction of 4th c. B.C. Greek sculpture, Vatican Museum, contemporary | 2019.

27. *Porto Rican Laundries*. Photograph by Margherita Arlina Hamm, *Neely's Panorama of Our New Possessions*, F. Tennyson Neely Publisher, New York & London, 1898 | 2019.

28. *A Colored Belle of Porto Rico. Our New Possessions*, Trumbull White, American Book and Bible House, Philadelphia, 1898 | 2019.

29. *Madamas*. Assemblage of found objects | 2021.

30. *Mamá Inés lookalike contest sponsored by Café Yaucono*. Found photograph, circa 1970s | 2021.

31. *Remnant of the 20th Century*. Found object: wall decor plaque, plastic, mid-20th century | 2021.

32. *Cuadro Plástico de la "Estrella de Oriente"—A Living Picture of the Eastern Star. El Libro de Puerto Rico*, Eugenio Fernández y García, El Libro Azul Publishing Co., San Juan, 1923 | 2019.

33. *The whites, therefore, of Porto Rico….Down in Porto Rico*, George Milton Fowles, Eaton & Mains, New York, 1906 | 2019.

34. *Artifacts of the Aborigines*. Assemblage of found objects | 2021.

35. *Descendants of the Aborigines. Our Islands and Their People as Seen with Camera and Pencil*, José de Olivares et al., N.D. Thompson Publishing Co., St. Louis, 1899 | 2019.

36. *Hombres representando a soldados españoles de la época colonial*. Biblioteca Digital Puertorriqueña, Colección de fotos del Periódico *El Mundo*, 1968 | 2019.

37. *The history of Porto Rico is….United States Colonies and Dependencies, Illustrated*, W. D. Boyce, Rand, McNally & Company, Chicago, 1914 | 2019.

38. *The Golden Conquistador*. Found ceramic object manufactured by Fres-o-lone, wood base, mid-20th century | 2019.

39. *A Peon Cabin, San Turce [sic], Porto Rico*. The Whiting View Co., Cincinnati, 1900 | 2021.

40. *"Be it ever so humble, there's no place like Home"—Cayey, Porto Rico*. Strohmeyer & Wyman, Underwood & Underwood Publishers, New York, 1899 | 2021.

41. *A mountain home near Aibonita [sic] Pass, Porto Rico*. Strohmeyer & Wyman Publishers, New York, sold by Underwood & Underwood, New York, 1899 | 2021.

42. *Soft and Safe Hispanic Family*. Found object (educational toy), plastic, in original box | 2022.

43. *Lovely Helga Monroig, "Miss Puerto Rico of 1952," sees New York and gets the sun from the top of the Hotel Taft. In addition to her exceptional architecture, Helga is reported to have high talent as a dancer, specializing in the mambo*. International News Photos, 1952 | 2022.

44. *Healthiest, San Juan, Puerto Rico* (recto). Hamilton Wright Org., Inc., New York, 1960 | 2019.

45. *Healthiest, San Juan, Puerto Rico* (verso). Hamilton Wright Org., Inc., New York, 1960 | 2019.

46. *Jibaro Costume*. "Isla" mail order catalog, circa 2000 | 2021.

47. *El Machete*. Found object: used machete, wood | 2021.

48. *He knows poverty and hardship*. Photograph by Homer Page, *Puerto Rico, Bridge to Freedom*, Edna McGuire, The Macmillan Company, New York, 1963 | 2021.

49. *This considerable part of the population. The History of Puerto Rico: From the Spanish Discovery to the American Occupation*, R. A. Van Middeldyk, D. Appleton and Co., New York, 1903 | 2021.

50. *Typical Native Farmers*. Photograph by Margherita Arlina Hamm, *Neely's Panorama of Our New Possessions*, F. Tennyson Neely Publisher, New York & London, 1898 | 2019.

51. *The Golden Palm*. Found object: wall decor plaque, plastic, mid-20th century | 2021.

52. *Jibaritxs Inside the Box*. Assemblage of found objects: dolls and souvenir mug | 2021.

53. *Watchful Eagle*. Found object, cast aluminum, contemporary | 2019.

54. *Lolita Lebrón Arrested*. Associated Press Photo, March 1, 1954 | 2019.

55. *Statue of Liberty with Puerto Rican Flag in 1977.* UPI/ Bettmann Archive, *The Puerto Ricans*, Jerome J. Aliotta, Chelsea House Publishers, New York, 1991 | 2019.

56. *Young Puerto Rican woman interrogated by Insular Police.* Keystone Photo, 1950 | 2021.

57. *Women Nationalists Guarded.* Associated Press Wirephoto, November 5, 1950 | 2019.

58. *Members of Puerto Rico's National Guard are shown standing guard over a group of Nationalists, Jayuya, Puerto Rico.* INP Soundphoto, *El Imparcial*, November 3, 1950 | 2021.

59. *La Llave.* Found object, mid-20th century | 2021.

60. *The Closed Door.* Illustration by Edward W. Kemble, *Life* 35, no. 909, April 12, 1900 | 2020.

61. *Cash on the line is acknowledged by a teller in the mobile bank. The depositor is Señora Teresa González Rivera whose 100-year-old mother is also one of the banking unit's customers.* International News Photos, 1952 | 2021.

62. *Better Living Through Better Banking.* Assemblage of found objects | 2021.

63. *Platos y Cocos.* Assemblage of souvenir plates and coconuts | 2022.

64. *A Once Sleepy Colony.* "Puerto Rico: Island at a Crossroads," *Look* 28, no. 6, March 24, 1964 | 2019.

65. *Financiers.* Photograph by Gordon Parks, "A New Puerto Rico Shows Off," *Life* 26, no. 4, January 24, 1949 | 2019.

66. *An Orgy of Color.* Assemblage of contemporary black objects | 2020. Title from "Porto Rico Under the American Flag," *The Outlook* 92, no. 9, June 26, 1909.

67. *See No Evil, Hear No Evil....* Found object and video | 2021. See endnote.

68. *Beach life provides year-round fun at Dorado Beach where summer and winter are indistinguishable.* Photograph by Sam Falk, Mirro-Krome Card, H.S. Crocker Co., Inc., San Francisco, postcard, mid-20th century | 2019.

69. *The Hotel with a Country Club Atmosphere, Hotel Racquet Club, San Juan, Puerto Rico.* Hannau-Robinson Color Productions, Inc., New York, postcard, mid-20th century | 2019.

70. *La Rada Hotel, San Juan, Puerto Rico. Most distinguished of San Juan.* Photograph by Conrad Eiger, Natural Color Publishers, Miami Beach, postcard, mid-20th century | 2019.

71. *Coco-man Souvenir.* Found vintage souvenir from Puerto Rico | 2021.

72. *Imagine...[Luis Fortuño y Pedro Pierluisi, circa 2009].* Social media meme, 2019 | 2021.

73. *So many coconuts.* Found photograph, source not identified, after 1971 | 2021.

74. *Gobernador Jesús T Piñero y otras personas tomando agua de coco.* Biblioteca Digital Puertorriqueña, Colección de fotos del Periódico *El Mundo*, 1946 | 2019.

75. *Luis A Ferré y Roberto Sánchez Vilella.* Biblioteca Digital Puertorriqueña, Colección de fotos del Periódico *El Mundo*, 1969 | 2019.

76. *Tropical Milkshake, Isla Verde, P.R.* (recto). ACME Photos, December 27, 1948 | 2019.

77. *Tropical Milkshake, Isla Verde, P.R.* (verso). ACME Photos, December 27, 1948 | 2019.

78. *An Outing.* Page from unidentified book, circa 1898. Same photograph with caption: *Gathering 'Cocoa de Agua' near San Juan, P.R.,* in *Annual Reports of the War Department for the Fiscal Year ended June 30, 1899: Report of the Major General Commanding the Army, Part I,* Government Printing Office, Washington. D.C., 1899 | 2019.

79. *Coco de agua.* Found real photo postcard, early 20th century | 2019.

80. *Niñito vestido de soldado desfilando junto a una joven en el aniversario del Día de la Independencia de Estados Unidos.* Photograph by Feliciano, Biblioteca Digital Puertorriqueña, Colección de fotos del Periódico *El Mundo*, 1965 | 2021.

81. *Fourth of July parade, San Juan.* Found vernacular photograph, July 4, 1945 | 2021.

82. *Gloria Cobián Díaz escoltada por oficiales de la Guardia Nacional de Puerto Rico.* Photograph by Teodoro Torres, Biblioteca Digital Puertorriqueña, Colección de fotos del Periódico *El Mundo*, 1965 | 2021.

83. *Military Police Helmet from Puerto Rico National Guard.* Gift of Humberto Figueroa | 2021.

84. *Military troops pass in review in front of the terminal building to celebrate the opening of huge international airport here* [Carolina, Puerto Rico]. International News Photos, 1955 | 2021.

85. *Policias militares de la Guardia Nacional desfilando en el 15th aniversario del Estado Libre Asociado.*

Con expresión severa y paso rotundamente marcial, el destacamento marcha a lo largo de la avenida Ponce de León, sus cascos y sus rifles reluciendo al sol. Photograph by Madín Rodríguez, Biblioteca Digital Puertorriqueña, Colección de fotos del Periódico *El Mundo*, 1967 | 2021.

86. *General view of military parade passing the reviewing stand in front of the Capitol in San Juan*. Hamilton Wright Org., Inc., New York, 1952 | 2021.

87. *Defense Strategy*. Found object: wall decor plaque, plastic resin, mid-20th century | 2021.

88. *Flores Colón-Colón of Puerto Rico, U.S. Air Cadet*. N.E.A., 1943 | 2021.

89. *Oficiales de la Marina durante conferencia de prensa sobre maniobras en Vieques*. Photograph by César Silva, Biblioteca Digital Puertorriqueña, Colección de fotos del Periódico *El Mundo*, 1988 | 2019.

90. *Souvenir handkerchief from Puerto Rico*. Found vintage souvenir, mid-20th century | 2019.

91. *U.S. Army heads in Puerto Rico confer*. ACME Photos, 1939 | 2019.

92. *A Splendid Little War*. Assemblage of found objects: books, military toys, toy palm trees | 2021.

93. *Espectadores del desfile del 4 de julio portando banderas americanas*. Biblioteca Digital Puertorriqueña, Colección de fotos del Periódico *El Mundo*, 1969 | 2019.

94. *Filiberto Ojeda Ríos in Hartford*. Photograph by Bob Child, Associated Press Photo, May 20, 1988 | 2021.

95. *Photographers close in on some souvenirs of a busy day in Congress, spread out at Police Headquarters tonight on a flag of Puerto Rico*. Associated Press Wirephoto, March 1, 1954 | 2021.

96. *Puerto Ricans pledge allegiance to two flags*. Photographs by Jack Manning, *Young Puerto Rico*, Jack Manning, Dodd, Mead & Co., New York, 1962 | 2019.

97. *Government Officials* [Wanda Vázquez, Carlos Romero Barceló et al.]. Twitter, 2019 | 2021.

98. *Alcaldesa de San Juan ondea banderita de PR en Nueva York* [Felisa Rincón de Gautier, "doña Fela"] Associated Press Photo/Biblioteca Digital Puertorriqueña, Colección de fotos del Periódico *El Mundo*, not dated | 2019.

99. *Boy with Cowboy Costume, Puerto Rico*. Found vernacular photograph | 2021.

100. *Real Yankee Doodle Dandy, Mayagüez, Puerto Rico* (recto). Official Puerto Rico Government Photo, via Hamilton Wright Org., Inc., New York, April 1948 | 2019.

101. *Real Yankee Doodle Dandy, Mayagüez, Puerto Rico* (verso). Official Puerto Rico Government Photo, via Hamilton Wright Org., Inc., New York, April 1948 | 2019.

102. *Golden Galleon*. Found object: wall decor plaque, plastic resin, mid-20th century | 2021.

103. *Tropical Contrast, Punta Salinas, Puerto Rico* (recto). ACME Photo, January 12, 1940 | 2019.

104. *Tropical Contrast, Punta Salinas, Puerto Rico* (verso). ACME Photo, January 12, 1940 | 2019.

105. *Warbird and Banana Man, Punto [sic] Borinquen, Puerto Rico*. International News Photo, 1940 | 2021–2022.

106. *Toy airplane*. Found vintage toy, cast iron | 2021.

107. *"We moved down here to get more labor into the garment."* Photograph by Douglas Jones, "Puerto Rico: Island at a Crossroads," *Look* 28, no. 6, March 24, 1964 | 2019.

108. *Teaching Birth Control Methods, Puerto Rico*. Photograph by Hank Walker, *LIFE* Magazine Photo Collection, Time, Inc., circa 1960 | 2019.

109. *Federal Aid is a Staple* (recto). Photograph by Gary Williams, Associated Press Newsfeatures Photo, July 22, 1980 | 2019.

110. *Federal Aid is a Staple* (verso). Associated Press Newsfeatures Photo, July 22, 1980 | 2019.

111. *Puerto Rican Barbie*. Found object: Dolls of the World Collection, Mattel, Inc., circa 1996 | 2020.

112. *Coronación de Pamela Hatley como Miss Teenage Puerto Rico*. Photograph by Eddie Vélez, Biblioteca Digital Puertorriqueña, Colección de fotos del Periódico *El Mundo*, 1968 | 2019.

113. *In the mountain town of Comerio….*Photograph by Frank Bauman, "Surprising Puerto Rico," *Look* 25, no. 2, January 17, 1961 | 2019.

114. *Schoolbooks and Kool-Aid*. Assemblage of found objects: schoolbooks, Kool-Aid bottles, M&M's, and Monopoly pieces | 2021.

115. *School Begins*. Illustration by Louis Dalrymple, *Puck* 44, no. 1142, January 25, 1899, Keppler & Schwarzmann Publishers, 1899 | 2021.

116. *Village School near San Juan, Porto Rico.* "A Trip to Porto Rico—Three R's in Porto Rico: American Teachers Training the Young Idea," *The Mentor* 8, no. 19, January 1921 | 2019.

117. *School for Maids in Puerto Rico* (recto). Wide World Photos, Inc., December 2, 1948 | 2019.

118. *Niños del refugio Manuel Fernández Juncos observando pintura de Abraham Lincoln donada a la institución.* Photograph by Jacinto González Trías, Biblioteca Digital Puertorriqueña, Colección de fotos del Periódico *El Mundo*, 1960 | 2019.

119. *School for Maids in Puerto Rico* (verso). Wide World Photos, Inc., December 2, 1948 | 2019.

120. *Uniform for Maids.* Found vintage dress on fabricated armature and hanger | 2021.

121. *Children Learning English Songs.* Photograph by Ruth Gruber, *Puerto Rico: Island of Promise*, Ruth Gruber, Hill and Wang, New York, 1960 | 2019.

122. *It is the desire of the Americans....Down in Porto Rico*, George Milton Fowles, Eaton & Mains, New York, 1906 | 2019.

123. *Patriot Economy Erasure.* Found antique chalkboard and eraser | 2017–2021.

ENDNOTES: MEDIA SOURCES

2. *They Don't Need Any Passport.* Video | 2020–2022.
Video Sources: U.S. Army: *Fort Buchanan, Sentinel of the Caribbean*, undated, circa mid-1980s / U.S. Navy, circa mid-1950s / Puerto Rican Government Film: *Ceremonias de la Fundación del Estado Libre Asociado de Puerto Rico*, 1952 / Michael Rogge: *U.S. Army in Puerto Rico*, 1949 / Hamilton Wright Org,. Inc.: *Puerto Rico, Fiesta Island*, 1953 / British Pathé: *Five Shot in U.S. Congress*, 1954 / Drew Pearson: *Washington Merry Go Round*, 1954 / Unidentified amateur film: *U.S. Soldiers in Puerto Rico* / Encyclopedia Britannica Films: *Puerto Rico's Past, Present and Promise*, 1965 / Paramount Films: *Sabrina*, 1954 / Ben Gradus (producer), *Crowded Paradise*, 1956.

67. *See No Evil, Hear No Evil....*Found object and video | 2021.
Video Sources: Insider: Nine Things to Add to your Puerto Rico Bucket List / Seepuertorico.com / CNN / AP Archives / Peter Schiff on Relocating to Puerto Rico / Peter Schiff on How to Beat Taxes by Moving to Puerto Rico / World Class Destination Tips / 10 Things not to do in Puerto Rico / MSNBC.com / Discover Puerto Rico with Lin Manuel Miranda / WAPA-TV / Whitehouse.gov / Fstoppers.com / New York Times / Daily Caller / Bloomberg: Market Makers / ENDI.com.

EXHIBITION SOUND

Rafael Muñoz y su Orquesta, WKAQ radio, recorded live in 1939 | 2022. Courtesy of *Fundación Luis Muñoz Marín*, San Juan, Puerto Rico.

Plate 69. Installation view. *The Museum Desk* (detail: MotOC rubber stamps). *The Museum of the Old Colony*, Duke Hall Gallery of Fine Art. 2022. Checklist No. 4.

121

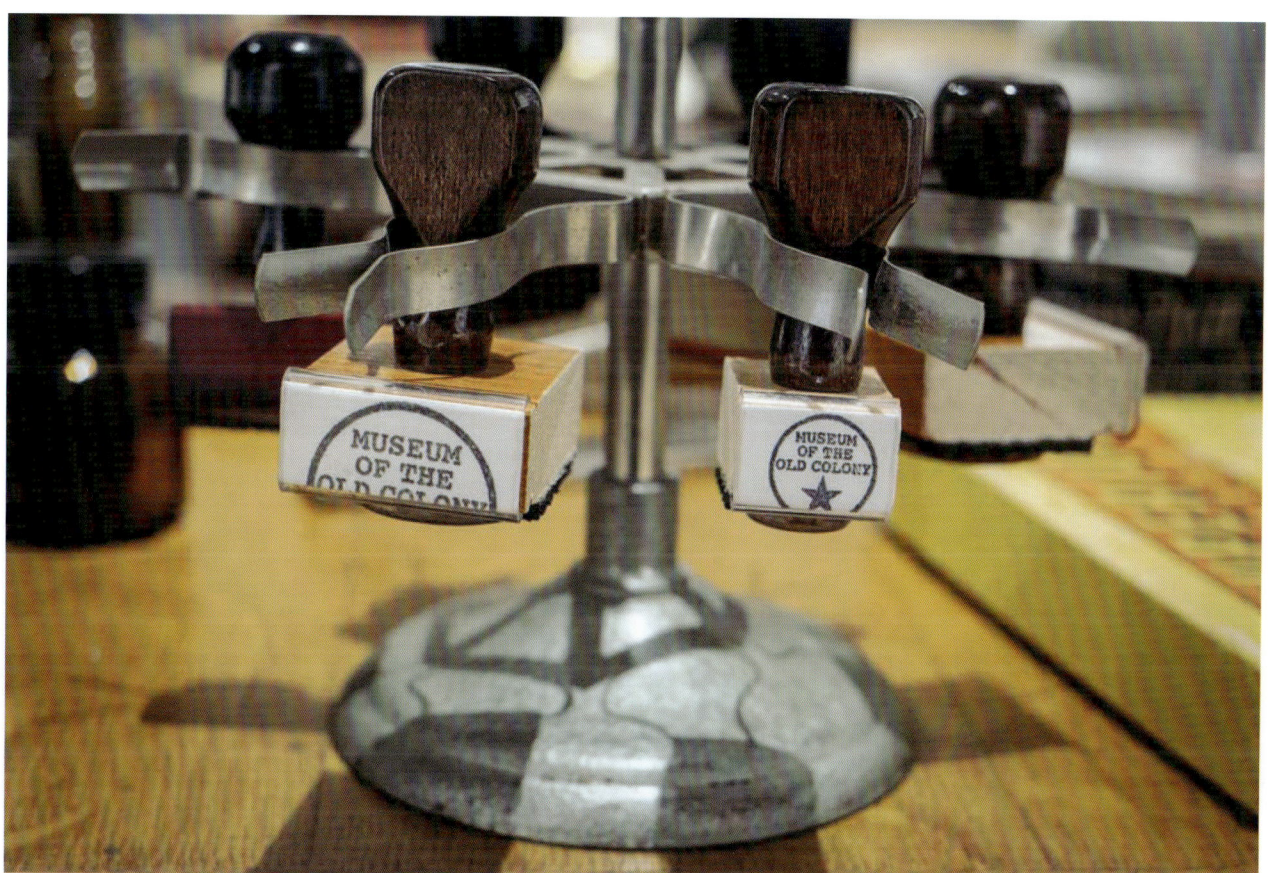

Bibliography
Compiled by Laura Katzman and Lydia Davis

Artist Websites

Artist: www.pablodelano.com
MotOC: www.museumoftheoldcolony.org
Videos: www.museumoftheoldcolony.org/media/video

The Museum of the Old Colony

Berger, Maurice. *The Museum of the Old Colony: An Art Installation by Pablo Delano*. Baltimore: Center for Art, Design and Visual Culture, University of Maryland, Baltimore County, 2020.

Courtmanche, John. "Exhibition Questions History of U.S. Relationship with Puerto Rico through Ironic 'Museum' of Empire." *Hampshire College website*, September, 10, 2018. Accessed August 25, 2022. https://www.hampshire.edu/news/2018/09/10/exhibition-questions-history-of-us-relationship-with-puerto-rico-through-ironic-.

Dávila, Arlene. *Latinx Art: Artist, Markets, and Politics*. Durham and London: Duke University Press, 2020.

Delano, Pablo. "*Museum of the Old Colony*." In *Turning Tides: Caribbean Intersections in the Americas and Beyond*, edited by Heather Cateau and Milla Cozart Riggio, 247-251. Kingston, Jamaica and Miami: Ian Randle Publishers, 2019.

Delgado, José A. "El fotógrafo puertorriqueño Pablo Delano lleva su instalación *The Museum of the Old Colony* a la Universidad James Madison de Virginia." *El Nuevo Día*, February 23, 2022. https://epaper.elnuevodia.com/article/281689733254646.

"Digital: Pablo Delano." *National Gallery of Jamaica Blog*, April 21, 2016. https://nationalgalleryofjamaica.wordpress.com/2016/04/21/digital-pablo-delano/.

Ferrer, Elizabeth. "The Archive." In *Latinx Photography in the United States: A Visual History*, 121-131. Seattle: University of Washington Press, 2020.

Franco, Marina Reyes. "Atlas San Juan: Tropical Depression." *Art in America* (October 2018): 45-49. https://www.artnews.com/art-in-america/features/atlas-san-juan-tropical-depression-63555/.

Gonzalez, David. "The New Museum for an Old Colony, Puerto Rico." *New York Times Lens*, November 15, 2017. https://lens.blogs.nytimes.com/2017/11/15/a-new-museum-for-an-old-colony-puerto-rico/.

Kaufman, Jill. "At Hampshire College, A Mock Museum of Appropriated Puerto Rican Identity." *New England Public Media*, October 11, 2018. https://www.nepm.org/post/hampshire-college-mock-museum-appropriated-puerto-rican-identity#stream/0.

Laughlin, Nicholas. "Pablo Delano: *The Museum of the Old Colony*." *Alice Yard Blogspot*, February 16, 2016. http://aliceyard.blogspot.com/2016/02/.

Lavansera, Maria Jose. "Identity Politics Ring True at KJCC." *Washington Square News*, February 6, 2017. https://nyunews.com/2017/02/06/identity-politics-ring-true-at-kjcc/.

Mirabal, Elizabeth. "*The Museum of the Old Colony*." *SECAC Online Exhibition Reviews*, May 2022. https://secacart.org/page/OldColony.

Mitchell, Frank. *Art from Archive: Works by Lewis Watts and Pablo Delano*. Hartford: Widener Gallery, Austin Arts Center, Trinity College, 2017.

Mitter, Siddhartha. "Photoville, With a Wider Lens." *New York Times*, September 22, 2020 (Cover photo of Arts Section). https://www.nytimes.com/2020/09/21/arts/design/photoville-new-york-photography-festival.html.

Nuthals, Hailey. "Looming Large, Imperially Taking Charge." *Washington Square News*, February 22, 2017. https://nyunews.com/2017/02/22/looming-large-imperially-taking-charge/.

Olson, Christa. "Cruel Looking: From Puerto Rico and Beyond." *Reading the Pictures Blog*, December 17, 2017. https://www.readingthepictures.org/2017/12/cruel-looking/.

"Puerto Rico & The United States: Historical Perspectives Through Conceptual Art." *Centro Voices e-Magazine*, February 2017. https://centropr.hunter.cuny.edu/centrovoices/arts-culture/puerto-rico-united-states-historical-perspectives-through-conceptual-art.

Ramírez-Aponte, Marianne. "The Importance of Politically Engaged Artistic and Curatorial Practices in the Aftermath of Hurricane María." In *Aftershocks of Disaster: Puerto Rico Before and After the Storm*, edited by Yarimar Bonilla and Marisol LeBrón, 161-177. Chicago: Haymarket Books, 2019.

Rivera, Nelson. "Pequeños nativos y bellezas renegridas." *80grados*, March 10, 2017. https://www.80grados.net/pequenos-nativos-y-bellezas-renegridasthe-museum-of-the-old-colony-de-pablo-delano/.

_____. "Pequeños nativos y bellezas renegridas: *The Museum of the Old Colony* de Pablo Delano." *Esferas* 13 (Spring 2022): 228-241. https://issuu.com/nyu_esferas/docs/esferas13_issu_corrected_v2.

Rivera, Nelson and Amy Halliday. *The Museum of the Old Colony: An Installation by Pablo Delano*. Amherst: Hampshire College Gallery of Art, Hampshire College, 2018.

Romero, Ivette. "Pablo Delano: A Brief Interview with *Repeating Islands*." *Repeating Islands*, February 9, 2017. https://repeatingislands.com/2017/02/09/pablo-delano-a-brief-interview-with-repeating-islands/.

Books by the Artist

Faces of America: Photographs by Pablo Delano. Washington, D.C.: Smithsonian Institution Press, 1992. Introduction by Robert Coles.

Hartford Seen: Photographs by Pablo Delano. Middletown: Wesleyan University Press, 2020. Introduction by Laura Wexler. Essay by Guillermo B. Irizarry.

In Trinidad: Photographs by Pablo Delano. Kingston, Jamaica and Miami: Ian Randle Publishers, 2008. Introduction by Peter Minshall. Essays by Milla Cozart Riggio and Gordon Rohlehr.

Selected Essays and Photo Essays by the Artist

Delano, Pablo. "Foreword." In *The Railroad Photography of Jack Delano*, by Tony Reevy, viii-x. Bloomington and Indianapolis: Indiana University Press, 2015.

_____. "Reflections on My Father's Railroad Photographs." In *Railroaders: Jack Delano's Homefront Photography*, edited by John Gruber, 12-19. Madison: Center for Railroad Photography & Art, 2014. Photographs by Jack Delano and new photographs by Pablo Delano.

_____. "Teaching Tiple Fever: Pedagogy, Heritage, and Activism" [on Puerto Rican luthier William Cumpiano]. *Centro Voices e-Magazine*, March 10, 2016. https://centropr-archive. hunter.cuny.edu/centrovoices/barrios/teaching-tiple-fever-pedagogy-heritage-and-activism.

_____. "Visual Beauty and History in Hartford." *New York Times Lens*. January 9, 2015. https://lens.blogs.nytimes. com/2015/01/09/visual-beauty-and-history-in-hartford/.

_____. "Visually Breathtaking Hartford Explored." *Connecticut Explored*, August 22, 2021. https://ctbythenumbers.news/ctnews/ visually-breathtaking-hartford-explored.

Euraque, Darío A. y Yesenia Martínez. *La diáspora africana en programas educativos de Centroamerica*. Tegucigalpa, Honduras: Editorial Guaymuras with the Harriet Tubman Institute, York University, Toronto. 2013. Fotografías por Pablo Delano.

_____. *African Diaspora in the Educational Programs of Central America*. Trenton: Africa World Press, Inc., 2016. Photographs by Pablo Delano.

Vidal, Teodoro. *San Blas en la tradición puertorriqueña*. San Juan: Ediciones Alba, 1986. Fotografías por Pablo Delano et al.

_____. *Los milagros en metal y en cera de Puerto Rico*. San Juan: Ediciones Alba, 1974. Fotografías por Pablo Delano et al.

Selected Essays on the Artist [since 1992]

Boryga, Andrew. "Carnival's Essence in Black and White" [Pablo Delano in Trinidad]. *New York Times Lens,* March 4, 2014. https:// lens.blogs.nytimes.com/2014/03/04/carnivals-essence-in-black-and-white/.

Coles, Robert. "An American Identity." *In Faces of America: Photographs by Pablo Delano*, by Pablo Delano, 1–8. Washington, D.C.: Smithsonian Institution Press, 1992.

Dunne, Susan. "Pablo Delano's Photos of Puerto Rico's Street Art at Mattatuck." *Hartford Courant*, November 21, 2016. https://www.courant.com/ctnow/arts-theater/hc-mattatuck-waterbury-1122-20161121-story.html.

_____. "Trinity College Professor Pablo Delano Seeks to Show the Real Hartford, with New Photography Book, *Hartford Seen*." *Hartford Courant*, July 17, 2020. https://www.courant.com/ctnow/arts-theater/hc-ctnow-arts-hartford-photography-book-20200717-d25y7oatobdm3kv5pgvmfqdb54-story.html.

Goldman, Francisco. *Inside Honduras: Photographs by Pablo Delano*. Hartford: Charter Oak Cultural Center, 2009. http:// www.pablodelano.com/honduras/essay/.

Gonzalez, David. "Showcase: Cultural Tapestry, Under Wraps" [Pablo Delano in Honduras]. *New York Times Lens*, January 26, 2010. https://lens.blogs.nytimes.com/2010/01/26/ showcase-115/.

_____. "A Biscuit Tin of Memories on Film" [Pablo Delano in Barcelona]. *New York Times Lens*, April 24, 2012. https://lens. blogs.nytimes.com/2012/04/24/a-biscuit-tin-of-memories-on-film/.

Irizarry, Guillermo B. "Hartford Unseen." In *Hartford Seen: Photographs by Pablo Delano*, by Pablo Delano, 1–7. Middletown: Wesleyan University Press, 2020.

_____. "A Specific Beauty: Pablo Delano's Photography in New York City, Hartford, and Santurce." *Centro Journal*, 31, no. 1 (Spring 2019): 4–25.

Martinez-San Miguel, Yolanda. "Visualizaciones de la identidad nacional desde la migración: Las fotografías de Jack y Pablo Delano." In *Caribe Two Ways: Cultura de la migración en el Caribe insular hispánico*, 51-102. San Juan: Ediciones Callejón, 2003.

Minshall, Peter. "Introduction." In *In Trinidad: Photographs by Pablo Delano*, by Pablo Delano, viii-xi, 151. Kingston, Jamaica and Miami: Ian Randle Publishers, 2008.

Ollman, Arthur. *Pablo Delano Photographs: Public and Private*. Hanover: Jaffe-Friede & Strauss Galleries, Hopkins Center, Dartmouth College, 1997.

Pennybacker, Susan D. *Hartford Seen: Photographs by Pablo Delano*. Hartford: Connecticut Historical Society, 2014.

Riggio, Milla Cozart. "In Trinidad." In *In Trinidad: Photographs by Pablo Delano*, by Pablo Delano, xiii–xviii, 151. Kingston, Jamaica and Miami: Ian Randle Publishers, 2008.

Rohlehr, Gordon. "Imaging Trinidad." In *In Trinidad: Photographs by Pablo Delano,* by Pablo Delano, xix–xxii, 151. Kingston, Jamaica and Miami: Ian Randle Publishers, 2008.

Wexler, Laura. "Split City." In *Hartford Seen: Photographs by Pablo Delano*, by Pablo Delano, x–xi. Middletown: Wesleyan University Press, 2020.

Artist's Work in Permanent Collections

Archives of American Art
Smithsonian Institution, Washington, D.C.

El Museo del Barrio
New York, NY

Hood Museum of Art
Dartmouth College, Hanover, New Hampshire

Hostos Community College Library
City University of New York, Bronx

Instituto de Cultura Puertorriqueña
San Juan, Puerto Rico

Museo de Arte Contemporáneo de Puerto Rico
San Juan, Puerto Rico

Museum of the City of New York
New York, NY

National Park Service
U.S. Department of the Interior, New York, NY

New York City Board of Education
New York, NY

New York City Health and Hospitals Corporation
New York, NY

The Duke Ellington School
New York, NY

The William Benton Museum of Art
University of Connecticut, Storrs

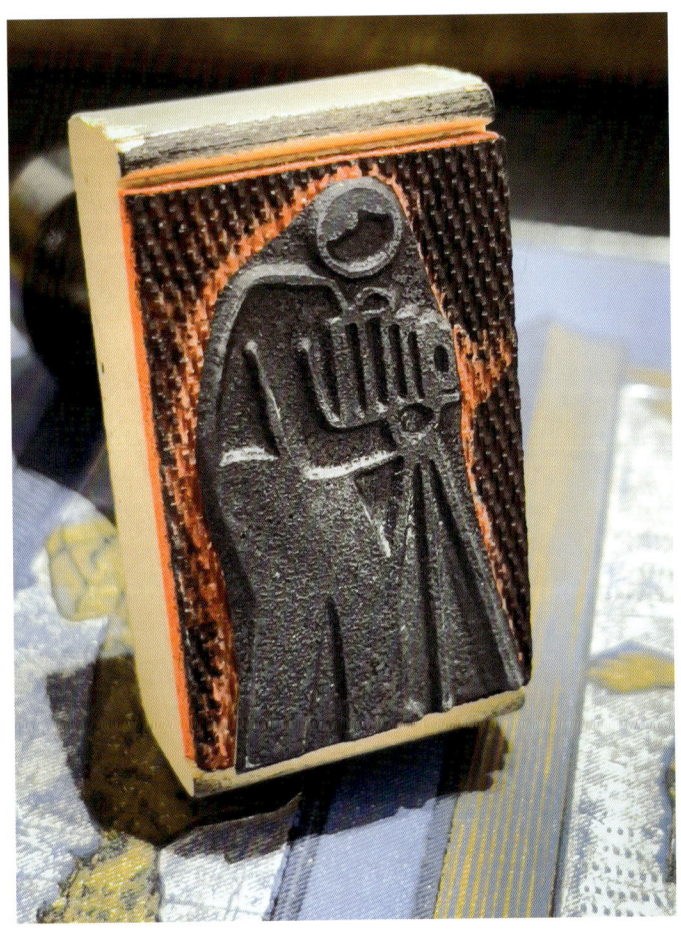

Plate 71. Installation view. *Jibaritxs Inside the Box*.
Assemblage of found objects: dolls and souvenir mug |
2021. *The Museum of the Old Colony*, Duke Hall Gallery of
Fine Art, 2022. Checklist No. 52.

125

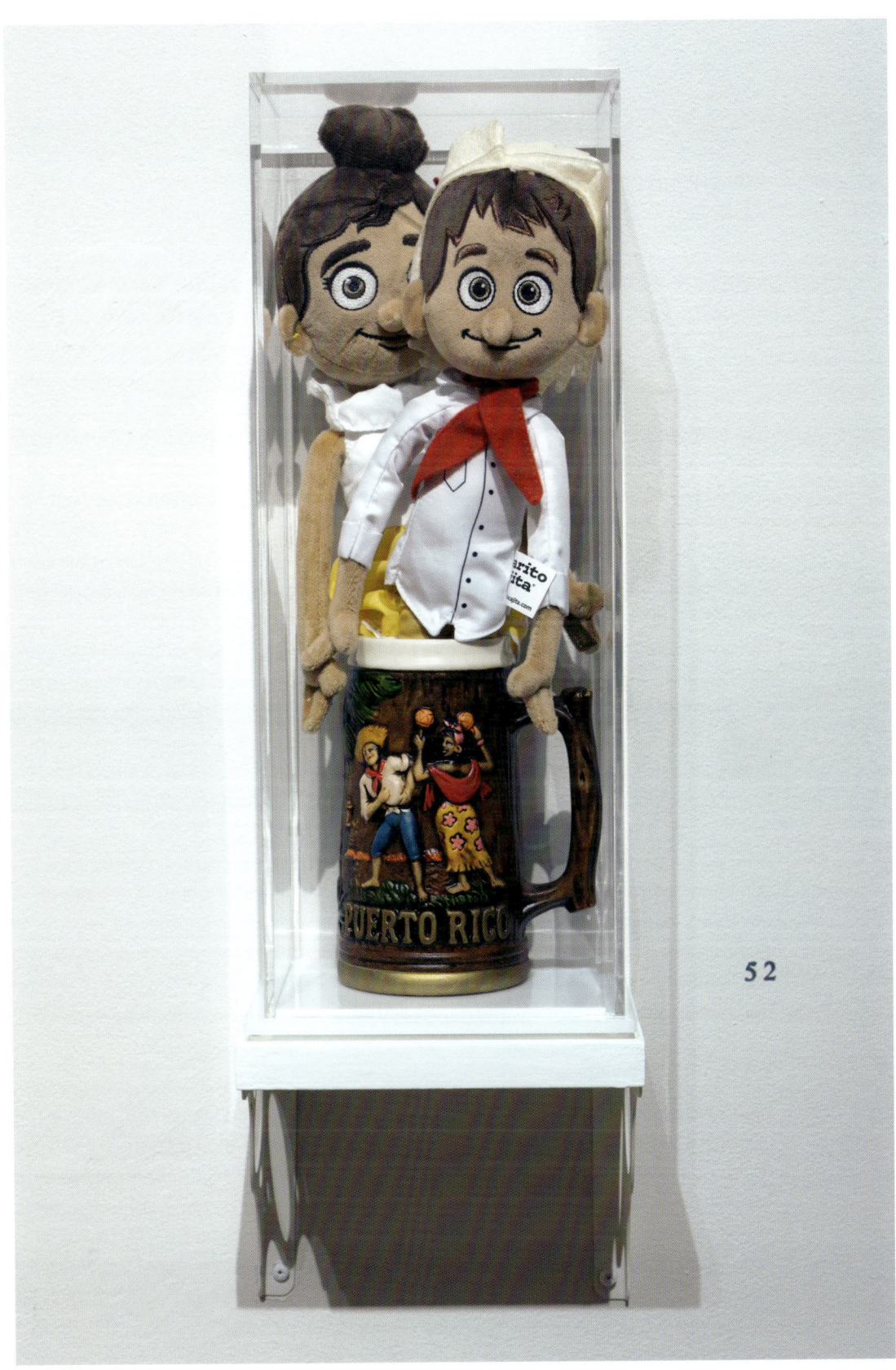

52

Contributors

Artist Biography

Pablo Delano was born in 1954 in San Juan, Puerto Rico. He and his younger sister were raised on a hillside just outside the capital city, near the town of Trujillo Alto. As a child, he enjoyed climbing a huge *flamboyán* tree and savoring a spectrum of fresh fruits including delicious mangos, acerolas, and pink guavas. After completing high school, he relocated to the U.S. East Coast to study art. He holds a BFA from Tyler School of Art/Temple University and an MFA from Yale University, both in painting. In 1979 he moved to New York City, where he initially pursued a career as a painter, but quickly turned to photography, a skill that he had learned from his father, the photographer Jack Delano, and that offered him a more interactive connection to the world. Substantial projects grew out of his work on the Lower East Side, including commissions from the New York City Department of Cultural Affairs and the Ellis Island National Immigration Museum. One unifying thread was a consistent interest in the lives and traditions of Latin American and Caribbean communities, both in their homelands and in the diaspora. In 1996, Delano accepted a teaching position at Trinity College, in Hartford, Connecticut, where a colleague offered him the opportunity to travel to Trinidad and Tobago, in the Southern Caribbean. Fascinated by that nation's process of post-colonial nation-building, he returned countless times over the next 10 years, ultimately producing a book of black-and-white photographs titled *In Trinidad* (2008). During his first years at Trinity College, Delano also began collecting archival images from Puerto Rico, and conceptualizing the project that would eventually grow into his art installation, *The Museum of the Old Colony*. In 2019, Delano was appointed Trinity College's Charles A. Dana Professor of Fine Arts. A year later he published the book, *Hartford Seen* (2020), which has been praised as "the first modern-day art photography book to focus on Connecticut's capital." While continuing to expand *The Museum of the Old Colony*, Delano is at work on *Cuestiones Caribeñas/Caribbean Matters*. In this new project, with his characteristic wit and irony, the artist creates increasingly aggressive juxtapositions of found objects and appropriated photographs, taking his examination of the complexities of the Caribbean condition into ever more transgressive territory. For more on the artist see: www.pablodelano.com/.[1]

Editor and Essayists

Laura Katzman is professor of art history at James Madison University and a scholar of documentary photography on the U.S. continent and in Puerto Rico from the New Deal to the early Cold War eras. She served as guest curator for *Picturing Puerto Rico Under the American Flag: The Photographs of Louise Rosskam, 1937–1948*, at the Hunter East Harlem Gallery, sponsored by the Center for Puerto Rican Studies, City University of New York. She is co-author of *Ben Shahn's New York: The Photography of Modern Times* (2000) and principal author of *Re-viewing Documentary: The Photographic Life of Louise Rosskam* (2014), which accompanied an exhibition she curated for the American University Museum. Her current book project examines Puerto Rico's Office of Information photography archive

Figure 13. Pablo Delano photographing *Tools of the Trade. The Museum of the Old Colony*, Duke Hall Gallery of Fine Art, 2022. Photograph by Laura Katzman, January 31, 2022.

127

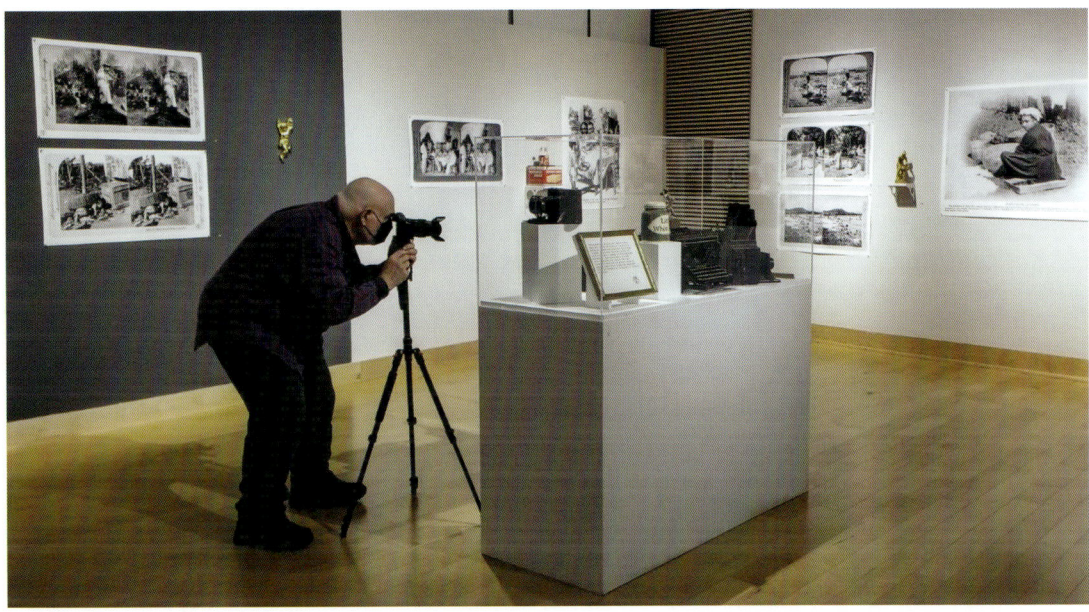

in the early *muñocista* period. Her essay on Lorenzo Homar and North American artists in Puerto Rico is forthcoming in José Orlando Sued and René Rodríguez-Ramírez, eds., *La mirada en construcción; ensayos sobre cultura visual.* A noted Ben Shahn scholar, Katzman was invited by the *Museo Nacional Centro de Arte Reina Sofía* in Madrid, Spain to organize the retrospective, *Painting for the People: Ben Shahn and the Art of Social Justice*, scheduled for late 2023 through early 2024.

Ángel A. García Jr. is assistant professor of geology and environmental science at James Madison University and holds a PhD in geological sciences (with a focus on ethnogeology) from Arizona State University in Tempe. He has examined the culturally influenced geological interpretations among long-term residents of the Dominican and Puerto Rican karst. As a self-identified *Boricua* (Puerto Rican) geologist, García specializes in cave and karst science, ethnogeology, plant-based education, community-based research, and the promotion of diversification and multiculturalism within geosciences. He leads study tours through caves in the Shenandoah Valley, Dominican Republic, and Puerto Rico, and has published in the journals *Cultural Studies of Science Education; AlterNative: An International Journal of Indigenous People*; and *Geoheritage*.

Amanda J. Guzmán is assistant professor of anthropology at Trinity College in Hartford, Connecticut, and holds a PhD in anthropology from the University of California, Berkeley. She specializes in the field of museum anthropology, focusing on the history of collecting and exhibiting Puerto Rican material culture at the intersection of intercultural representation and national identity formation. Her writing has been featured in *Museum Anthropology* and *Sapiens* as well as in blogs sponsored by the Digital Library Federation and the University of the West Indies Museum. Her research has been supported by Smithsonian Fellowships from the National Museum of American History, the Smithsonian American Art Museum, the National Museum of the American Indian, and the National Museum of Natural History. Guzmán serves on the Board of Directors of the Pre-Columbian Society of New York, as an

Innovative Cultural Advocacy Fellowship Mentor for the Caribbean Cultural Center African Diaspora Institute, and as a Grant Panelist on the Bronx Council on the Arts.

Beth Hinderliter is the director of the Duke Hall Gallery of Fine Art and associate professor of art history at James Madison University. As a curator, she works inclusively to organize contemporary art exhibitions engaged in the care of new possible worlds and social relations. Her recent exhibitions include *Colonial Wounds/Postcolonial Repair*; *Skeena Reece: Honey and Sweetgrass*; and *Exuberance: Dialogues in African American Abstract Painting*. A scholar of race and gender studies within contemporary culture, she is the co-editor of *More Than Our Pain: Affect and Emotion in the Era of Black Lives Matter* (2021); *Antagonizing White Feminism: Intersectionality's Critique of Women's Studies and the Academy* (2019); and *Communities of Sense: Rethinking Aesthetics and Politics* (2008). Hinderliter's essays have appeared in *Nka: Journal of Contemporary African Art*; *Journal of Postcolonial Writing*; *TDR/ The Drama Review*; *African and Black Diaspora: An International Journal*; and *October*.

Marianne Ramírez Aponte is executive director and chief curator of the *Museo de Arte Contemporáneo de Puerto Rico* (MACPR). Her curatorial projects include *With Ruler and Compass: The Harmony of Geometry*; *Arnaldo Roche-Rabell: Blue*; *Poetic Science: Artistic-Scientific Approximations to El Yunque Wilderness*; *In Question*; and *(Re)knowing the Future*. Under her directorship, MACPR was granted the 2014 Wilderness Legacy Award by the United States Forest Service and the 2017 Solidarity Prize in Education by the Miranda Foundation. In 2018, MACPR was awarded the Tina Hills Prize by the Ángel Ramos Foundation for its exemplary leadership and outreach work in the aftermath of Hurricanes Irma and Maria. Ramírez Aponte is co-founder and member of the board of directors of *Alianza de Museos de Puerto Rico, Centro de Conservación y Restauración de Puerto Rico,* and *Movimiento Una Sola Voz*. As creator and curator of the program *MAC en el Barrio*, she joins contemporary artists and underrepresented communities to give voice to marginalized populations, demonstrating the power of art to promote the processes of cultural equity and social justice.

Laura Roulet is an independent curator and writer, specializing in contemporary, Latinx, and Latin American art. She was one of five international curators chosen for the first *5x5*, a major public art initiative in Washington D.C. Roulet has organized exhibitions at the American University Museum, Washington Project for the Arts, the Mexican Cultural Institute, and the OAS Art Museum of the Americas, as well as for venues in Mexico City and San Juan. She is the author of *Contemporary Puerto Rican Installation Art: The Guagua Aerea, the Trojan Horse and the Termite* (2000). Roulet's writings have appeared in *American Art, Art Journal*, and *Art Nexus*, and she is a regular contributor to *Sculpture* magazine. Her essay on Puerto Rico is included in *Relational Undercurrents*, the catalogue that accompanied the *Pacific Standard Time: LA/LA* exhibitions in 2017. She contributed to the Ana Mendieta retrospective at the Hirshhorn Museum and Sculpture Garden (2004–2005) and to its related catalogue.

César A. Salgado is associate professor of Spanish and Portuguese and graduate adviser in comparative literature at the University of Texas at Austin. As a critic, scholar, and theorist, he situates Puerto Rican, Cuban, Latinx, and Caribbean literary and visual culture in Global South geopolitical currents and contexts. Salgado is author of *From Modernism to Neobaroque: Joyce and Lezama Lima* (2001) and co-editor of *TransLatin Joyce: Global*

Transmissions in Ibero-American Literature (2014) and *La futuridad del naufragio: orígenes, estelas y derivas* (2019). He co-edited two reference works, *Latino and Latina Writers* (2004) and *Cuba* (2011). He also edited and wrote the prologue for *La tumba de Buenaventura Roig* (2008), a bilingual anthology of poems by Martín Espada, winner of the 2021 National Book Award for Poetry. In 2016, Salgado was awarded the José Lezama Lima Prize by Cuba's Union of Artists and Writers for his contributions to Cuban Studies. His current book project addresses archival survival and custodial sustainability in colonial Puerto Rico.

Designer

Carissa Henriques is associate professor of graphic design at James Madison University. She teaches courses in typography; professional practice and portfolio development; design for social impact; and experience graphic design. Her design and research focus on social/democratic design practice, multidisciplinary and collaborative research, social entrepreneurship, branded environments, exhibition design, experience design, cognitive mapping, placemaking, and collective memory. Other areas of her professional interest include expressive/experimental typography, publication design, participatory and co-design methods, wayfinding, and signage. Henriques is the exhibition designer for the permanent installation on the history of James Madison University in the campus' Wilson Hall (2019–), and the graphic designer for the Duke Gallery exhibition catalogues *Drawing on the Left: Ben Shahn and the Art of Human Rights* (2018) and *Colonial Wounds/Colonial Repair* (2019).

---

1 Delano's biography was adapted and expanded from Maurice Berger, *The Museum of the Old Colony: An Art Installation by Pablo Delano* (Baltimore: Center for Art, Design and Visual Culture, University of Maryland, Baltimore County, 2020), 10.

Plate 72. Installation view. *Tools of the Trade* (detail). *The Museum of the Old Colony,* Duke Hall Gallery of Fine Art, 2022. Checklist No. 22.

The Museum of the Old Colony resides in the permanent collection of the *Museo de Arte Contemporáneo de Puerto Rico* / The Museum of Contemporary Art of Puerto Rico

June 26, 2022–April 16, 2023
Museo de Arte Contemporáneo de Puerto Rico
San Juan, Puerto Rico
(part of group exhibition *(Re)conocer el futuro*)

February 1–March 26, 2022
Duke Hall Gallery of Fine Art
James Madison University
Harrisonburg, Virginia

June–August 2021 | August–October 2021
Pope Park and Colt Park
Hartford, Connecticut

September 17–November 29, 2020
Photoville Festival
Brooklyn Bridge Park
New York, NY

January 30–March 14, 2020
Center for Art, Design and Visual Culture
University of Maryland
Baltimore County, Maryland

June 2–November 11, 2018
Hampshire College Art Gallery
Hampshire College
Amherst, Massachusetts

December 15, 2017–August 11, 2018
Museo de Arte Contemporáneo de Puerto Rico
San Juan, Puerto Rico
(part of group exhibition *Entredichos*)

October 12–December 9, 2017
Widener Gallery/Austin Arts Center
Trinity College
Hartford, Connecticut
(part of two-person exhibition *Art from Archive*)

February 2–June 21, 2017
King Juan Carlos I of Spain Center
New York University
New York, NY

October 7–30, 2016
7th Argentine Biennial of Documentary Photography
Tucumán, Argentina

April 2–July 4, 2016
National Gallery of Jamaica
Kingston, Jamaica
(part of group exhibition *Digital*)

February 19–26, 2016
Alice Yard
Port of Spain, Trinidad and Tobago

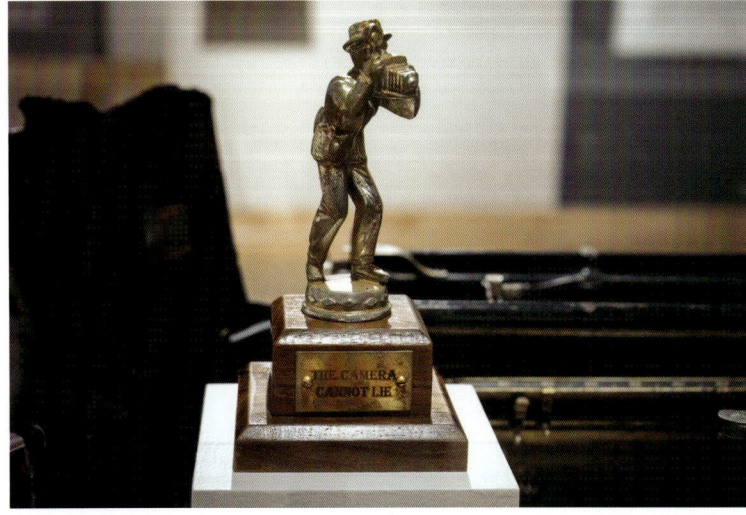

See videos of *The Museum of the Old Colony* at the Duke Gallery of Fine Art at www.museumoftheoldcolony.org/media/video/

Follow *The Museum of the Old Colony* trajectory at www.museumoftheoldcolony.org

Plate 73. Installation view, *Tools of the Trade* (detail). *The Museum of the Old Colony*, Duke Hall Gallery of Fine Art, 2022. Checklist No. 22.

131

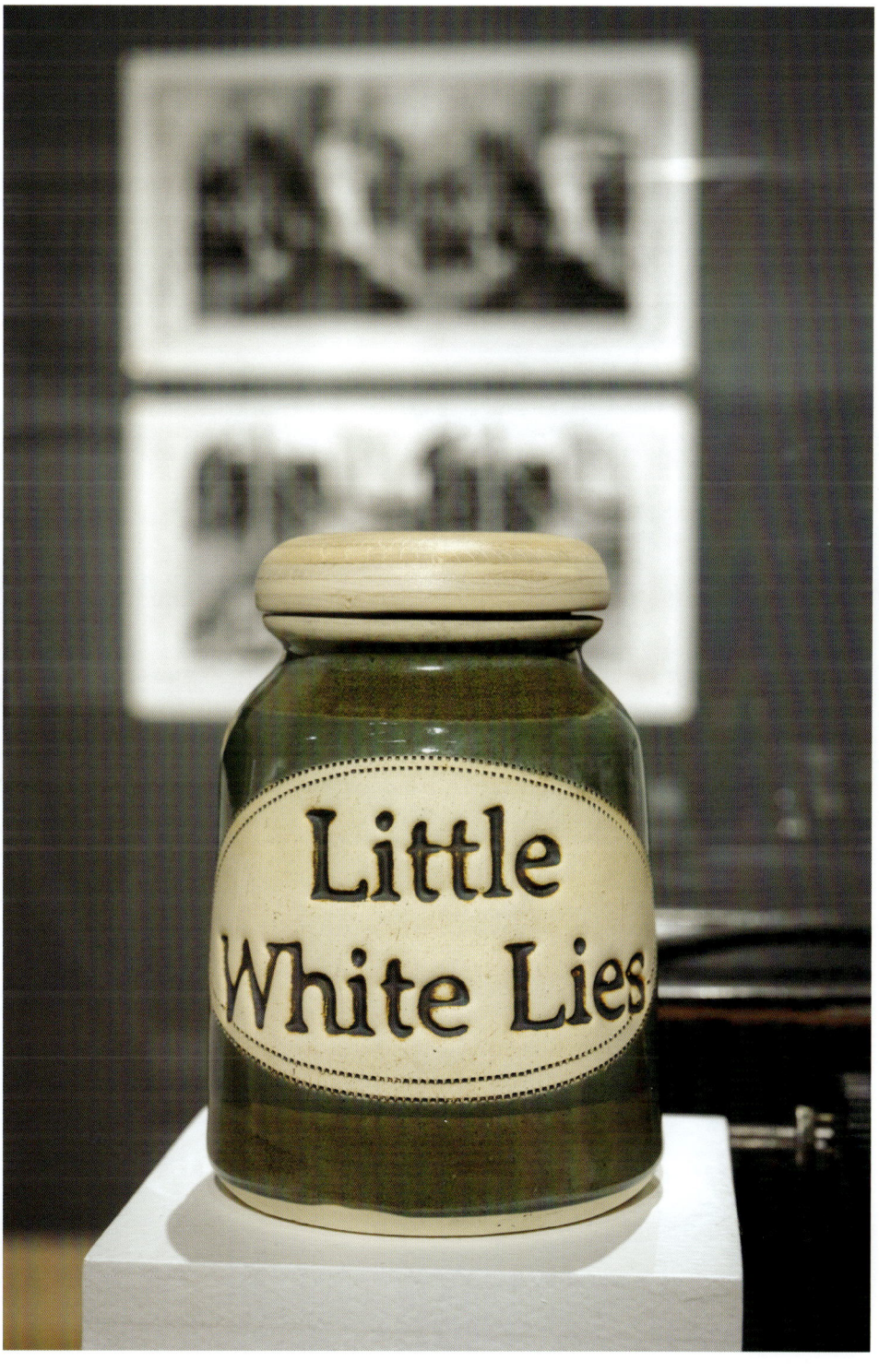

Figure 14. *Oldest Colony Piña, Avenida Las Palmas, Santurce, San Juan, Puerto Rico.* Mural by unidentified artist. Photograph by Pablo Delano, 2015.

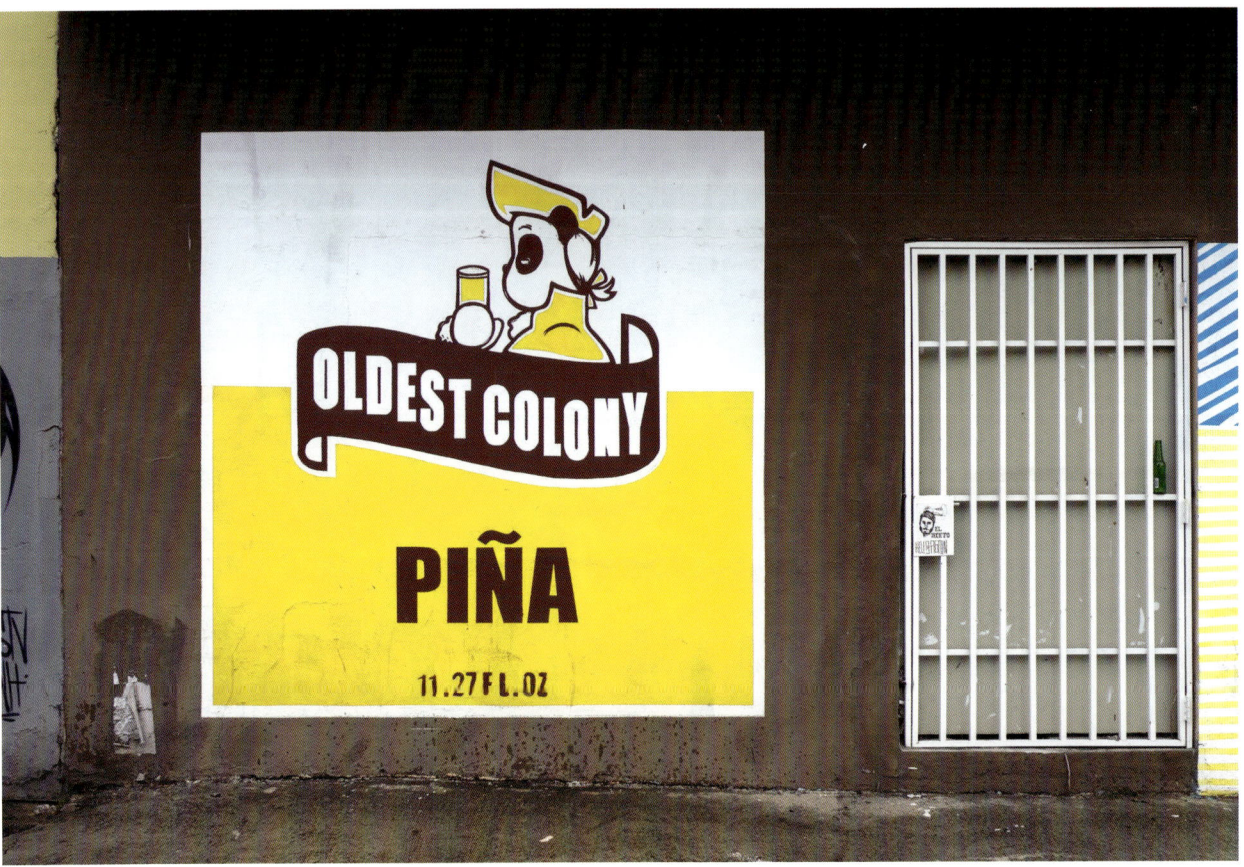